MESSAGE
and
MISSION

The Communication of
the Christian Faith

Eugene A. Nida

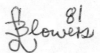

William Carey Library

533 HERMOSA STREET • SOUTH PASADENA, CALIF. 91030

First edition in 1960 by Harper & Row, Publishers
Reprinted 1972, 1975, and 1979
by the William Carey Library

Library of Congress Catalog Card Number 60-11785
International Standard Book Number 0-87808-711-7

Published by the William Carey Library
1705 N. Sierra Bonita Avenue
Pasadena, California 91104
Telephone (213) 798-0819

PRINTED IN THE UNITED STATES OF AMERICA

CONTENTS

Contents v

PREFACE

ONE highly significant fact in the present world is the recent converging of interest and effort in several fields of study and research on problems of communication. Linguistics, which would seem obviously related to the problems of meaning and communication, remained preoccupied for many years with the formal structures of languages. Within the last few years, however, keen concern has been shown for the relation of language to culture and of formal structure to the problems of meaning. Linguists have rendered important service to the theory and techniques of communication, first by separating the formal elements of language from the entangling alliances of meaning. They have also shown clearly that there is no such thing as a "primitive language," but only languages (with all imaginable degrees of complexity) spoken by so-called "primitive peoples." Moreover, they have also demonstrated that anything said in any language can be communicated in another, though often with greatly altered ways of speaking. Furthermore, language has been recognized not only as an integral element in the functioning of any society, but also in a sense as a kind of "model" of the way of which people view their world and a "grid" by which the experiences of people are perceived and then classified, stored, and manipulated.

Anthropologists have recently become increasingly absorbed in the problem of symbols and their relation to human behavior. They have for many years studied the use of magic formulas, the forms of curses, and the esthetic symbols of design and ritual. Now, however, the almost innumerable ways of communicating are being studied in terms of their dynamic effect on behavior and culture change, thus providing significant insights for the whole field of intercultural communication.

Psychologists have always been keenly aware of the problems of perception and have struggled with the seemingly ever elusive meanings of words. Of late, especially under the influence of Gestalt psychologists, meaning has taken on an even greater significance, for it has been recognized that people do not merely perceive the "outside world," but that they select, organize, and interpret all that they perceive. These findings have been an additional source of clues as to how communication actually takes place.

Information theory (also known as the science of cybernetics), which has constituted one of the important scientific breakthroughs of our generation, has likewise contributed appreciably to our understanding of communication. Even though such concepts as encoding, decoding, feedback, redundancy, noise, and transitional probabilities may seem too remote from our everyday experience to be of practical relevance, they have nevertheless provided, as we shall see in subsequent chapters, some of the most important insights into the process of communication. By means of the analytical tools made available by information theory we have ways of judging more precisely such matters as "How difficult will this translation of Romans 1:1–7 be in Guajibo, an Indian language of Venezuela?" and "Why is Basic English, which should be so easy, really so hard?"

The philosophers of our day have increasingly turned their attention to the problem of symbols and their meaning. Of course, from the earliest times philosophers have been concerned with meaning as expressed in symbols, especially verbal ones. For the philosophers who preceded Socrates, language and reality were more or less two sides of a single coin, and meaning was largely taken for granted and meaningful relationships were assumed, though not with naïve oversimplification. Socrates and Plato were not satisfied with the seemingly "too easy" answers of their predecessors or with the popular tendency to find hidden truth and logic in etymologies. For them, words became useful labels, means of communicating truth, but not the embodiment of truth. With Aristotle language became a more refined tool with which to view reality, even though he continued to regard it as basically a good reflection of what was real. The Epicureans, however, argued that language is wholly and completely arbitrary.

With these different views of language and reality philosophers have been concerned in varying degrees down to recent times. Of late, however, a new dimension has come into prominence, namely, the construction of whole symbolic systems, where the symbols have nothing to do with concepts outside the system but only with those within it. For this development mathematics has proved to be not only the delight of philosophers, but also the practical key by which to unlock many secrets of the universe. As a result, the perspective has shifted, and philosophers are not too concerned with the problems of linking thought with reality or of relating perception to truth. Rather, they are engaged in the study of the functioning of symbols and systems of symbols as means of communication.

In our study of communication we shall be concerned primarily with the ways in which the message of the Bible has been communicated—whether in the boroughs of New York or the villages of Ubangi, Congo. However, choosing this basis for our study does not limit its range. In a certain sense this background makes possible a wider analysis of the problems of communication than would be the case with any other field of inquiry, for in the dimensions of cultural diversity no other type of communication equals that of the Christian gospel. At least some parts of the Bible have been translated into 1,151 languages, with entire Bibles in 219 tongues and New Testaments in 271 others. These translations reflect the cultures of more than 95 per cent of the world's population and represent every cultural area on the globe. Furthermore, the message of the Bible deals with every aspect of life, and thus the problems of communication are fully representative of all types of difficulties.

In addition, the communication of the Christian faith involves not only some highly abstract and abstruse symbolism; because of its essentially religious character it is related as well to the most symbolic area of human behavior. Moreover, the communication of the gospel by its nature requires acceptance or rejection on the basis of a people's most keenly felt values. The New Testament cannot be equated with Homer's *Iliad* or Virgil's *Aeneid*, which are fascinating documents with many religious features. The New Testament comes, rather, as the communication of a new way of life. Thus the impact of its dissemination is highly significant in any thoughtful study of the principles and procedures of communication.

While the particular approach being followed in this volume is being explained, it is perhaps equally important to state what this book does not purport to be. In the first place, it is not a treatment of the history of the expansion of Christianity or of the missionary enterprise during the last two hundred years. References are, of course, made to certain historical developments, but there is no systematic treatment in this book of the historical perspective of communication of the Christian faith. It is omitted not because it is unimportant, but simply because Kenneth Scott Latourette and others have already done it so well. For the purposes of this volume, which deals primarily with methodology, not with historical precedent, such an account seems unnecessary.

In the second place, this is not a study of comparative religions, for in the analysis of techniques of communication we are concerned, not with the classification and comparison of religions, but with the principles of communication as they apply to a wide cross section of religions. Moreover, the book does not attempt to focus attention on the so-called higher religions, as volumes on comparative religions usually do. Rather, it is concerned with all types of religious phenomena, largely as classes of religious practice, beliefs, and resultant behavior, and not as systems to be compared. The orientation is thus cross-cultural, rather than "comparative" in the traditional sense of the word.

In the third place, this volume is not a "theology of missions" or a "comparative theology of religions." For the student there are a number of excellent treatments of these problems. Ernst Troeltsch, in *The Absolute Validity of Christianity* (1909) and *The Social Teaching of the Christian Churches* (1912), was one of the first highly creative thinkers to tackle this problem, and though his point of view was liberal (he spoke of Christianity as "a point of culmination up to now"), nevertheless, his insights are challenging and his learning impressive. Rudolf Otto, in *The Idea of the Holy* (1923), undertook a strictly scientific study which had broad implications for the comparative study of religion. William Ernest Hocking, as the leading figure in the controversial *Re-Thinking Missions* (1932) and in his book *Living Religions and a World Faith* (1940), proposed a strongly syncretistic view (though rejecting the term), but not without remarkable insight on many issues. His classification of missionary methodology in terms of "radical displacement" (the traditional attitude toward non-Christian religions), "synthesis" (a kind of syncretism), and "reconception" (in which he proposes for Christianity a constantly widening horizon of incorporated truth), may seem unrealistic, but it nevertheless demands serious consideration.

A number of persons have made important contributions to the entire field of the theology of missions and the relation of Christian theology to that of non-Christian religions. Among these are Archbishop Nathan Söderblom (*The Living God,* 1933), G. van der Leeuw (*Religion in Essence and Manifestation,* 1938), Archbishop William Temple (*Nature, Man and God,* 1951), H. H. Farmer (*Revelation and Religion,* 1954), J. E. Leslie Newbigin (*The Household of God,* 1954), Max A. C. Warren (*The Christian Imperative,* 1955), and Daniel T. Niles (*The Preacher's Task and the Stone of Stumbling,* 1958).

Certain persons of late have made an unusually significant contribution to this whole area, not primarily as scholars in this specialized field, but as the result of their wide theological interests. Emil Brunner, in *Revelation and Reason* (1947), contrasts Christianity with non-Christian religions and comes to an emphatic declaration of the uniqueness of Christianity. In other words, he concludes, only at one place and only in one event has God revealed Himself truly and completely. Karl Barth, in his customarily incisive manner, lumps all "religion" (in contrast with faith as an answer to pure grace) as "unbelief"; thus in his view all religion in its customary formal aspects becomes either "idolatry or justification by works."

Rudolf Bultmann has had great influence, especially in the field of the communication of symbols, for his concept of demythologizing has opened up a new field for the interpretation of the New Testament message in other categories. Paul Tillich's emphasis on the *Logos* doctrine (a tradition going back to Justin Martyr, Clement of Alexandria, and Origen), as a point of contact with contemporary philosophical developments, and A. C. Bouquet's more recent detailed exposition of the *Logos* theory as a means of effective missionary communication (*The Christian Faith and Non-Christian Religions,* 1958) have provided some thought-provoking observations which cannot be ignored, even though most leading exegetes have concluded that the use of the Greek *logos,* "Word," in the prologue of the Gospel of John reflects predominantly an Old Testament background, not the world of Stoic, Neoplatonic, or Gnostic philosophy. Nevertheless, it must be recognized that Tillich's influence on the field of symbolic interpretation is very great and in varying degrees will have considerable influence in the future.

Martin Buber has made very significant contributions to certain philosophical and theological aspects of communication through his brilliant insistence upon the focal importance of the "dialogue" in the comprehension as well as the communication of truth.

Arnold Toynbee has entered the field, not as a theologian, but as a historian, and has recommended a grand synthesis of certain higher religious beliefs in a way that seems to reflect a failure to appreciate fully the essential differences between religious systems and the historical processes by which religious changes take place.

Undoubtedly the leading conservative protagonist in the field of the theology of missions is Hendrik Kraemer. His earlier book, *The Christian Message in a Non-Christian World* (1938), became a focal point of controversy in the international missionary conference held in Tambaran in South India and it has had an immense influence on missionary thinking ever since. His more recent work, *Religion and the Christian Faith* (1956), and a smaller volume, *The Communication of the Christian Faith* (1956), reflect the same general point of view, which emphasizes the radical distinctiveness of Christianity in comparison with other religious systems. Kraemer's long missionary experience in Indonesia (he therefore speaks the missionary's language) and his basically conservative orientation as to the uniqueness of Jesus Christ and the authority of the Scriptures, while not repudiating the results of contemporary scholarship, have made him an able and effective exponent of certain aspects of the modern missionary movement, which in many respects is more conservative than many elements of the churches represented.

While Chapters 1 through 9 do not deal with essentially theological problems, there are certain obvious theological presuppositions, which will be evident to all. These concepts are presented particularly in the final chapter, and some persons may prefer to read this chapter before proceeding with the others. This chapter on the theological implications of communication is purposely left to the end, where it logically belongs in this type of treatment, employing, as it does, a descriptive scientific procedure, which draws primarily on the disciplines of anthropology and linguistics, with important help from psychology, sociology, information theory, and certain restricted aspects of symbolic logic and semantics.

The purpose of this book is not, however, to prove any point or thesis, but to introduce the reader to principles and procedures of communication and to focus attention on the outworking of such factors in the communication of the Christian faith. One must not presume, however, that the application of such techniques as are described here will automatically guarantee results or that the operation of God's Spirit can be regulated or predicted by such communicative procedures. In this volume we are only attempting to describe important features of divine-human communication, not to prescribe formulas for success.

I trust that the limitation of this volume in terms of its methodology and goals will not be felt to imply an inexcusable failure to re-examine known ground or a lack of appreciation for the significant contributions of the many scholars in the field. It is only that its emphasis and approach seem to call for the breaking of new ground with some new tools. It will be up to the specialists to say whether the soil looks propitious for the planting and reaping of a good crop.

In the preparation of this book I have drawn constantly on the stimulating suggestions and human-interest accounts of many missionaries and Christian workers whom it has been my privilege to know in different countries. I have also had the advantage of important critical analyses by Paul Verghese and by my colleagues in the American Bible Society: William L. Wonderly, William A. Smalley, William D. Reyburn, and Robert P. Markham. In many matters of editorial detail Charles S. Ridgway and Anna-Lisa Madeira have provided important help, while for professional editorial assistance I am indebted to Dorothy L. Tyler.

EUGENE A. NIDA

New York
March, 1960

PREFACE TO THE SECOND EDITION

Since this volume was first published in 1960 several important developments have occurred in missions and the communication of the Christian message. First, there has been a growing spirit of nationalism among the leaders of mission-sponsored churches. These local leaders have increasingly demanded that every aspect of authority and control be passed completely to the national churches. In general such churches have been happy to continue to receive financial aid from abroad, but the leaders have often been suspicious and resentful of any and all strings attached. In a sense the political slogans of "White Man Go Home" have also invaded the church, and sometimes with unexpected virulence. As a result, some missionaries have understandably begun to seriously doubt whether their continued presence on the field is really justified. Would the national church be better off without them? Would national leadership mature more rapidly if left completely on its own?

Second, there has been a broad-based rethinking of the priorities in the home base. A number of Christian leaders, both laymen and ministers, have begun to wonder whether they have the right to tell the world what they should believe and do, when seemingly both the church and society at home have made such a bad job of effectively living out the implications of the Good News of Jesus Christ. Is it possible that the problems at home ultimately deserve higher priority? Must one rethink the goals and purposes of the church? What message does the church have for the world? This reflective attitude is not essentially isolationist, but it is certainly introspective and may represent some of the guilt complex which the Western World has felt as the result of reassessing its colonial and imperialist past. Some of the more thoughtful young people are afraid that institutional missions implies a subtle religious and cultural paternalism. There is no lack of qualified young people to volunteer for overseas service in the name of Christ, but they are very suspicious of the traditional methods of organized religion, since the "establishment" has become more or less synonymous with "imposition."

Third, there has been a serious retrenchment in the mission programs of a number of major denominations. For the most part these churches have not suffered any significant reduction in overall giving — in fact, most of these churches have experienced an increase. But the local churches are insisting that the money be spent to meet local needs, not necessarily because their immediate problems seem more important than the larger issues of the world as a whole, but largely because the lay leadership of these local churches has lost confidence in the administrative leadership of the denominations and mission boards. There has been a serious communication gap in several denominations. In some cases leaders in the local churches are not at all convinced that their denominational leadership is really interested in missions — or even in evangelism. When everything becomes "mission," then in essence nothing is distinctively mission; and when everything is reputedly "evangelism" then nothing is decisively "evangelism." As a result the church has seemed to many persons to have lost its prophetic message and evangelistic motivation. And since it appears to be content to send out persons whose primary goal is to provide technological services rather than to proclaim a redemptive message, the inevitable questions are: Then what is so imperative about technological services? Why cannot governments or social service agencies provide the same services, and perhaps even better?

At the same time, however, there has not been any appreciable decline in the overall rate of expansion of the church in the so-called mission countries. Though in a number of instances the rate of growth in the mission-sponsored churches has levelled off or even declined, there has been a phenomenal growth in many of the completely indigenous churches. These are not churches which have been turned over by missions to national leadership (those might be better called "indigenized churches"), but these truly indigenous churches have grown up entirely under local leadership. In a number of instances this leadership is only one "spiritual generation" separated from some mission program, but the entire history of such a church is strictly national. Such churches are especially strong in Mexico, Chile, Argentina, Brazil, Ghana, Nigeria, Congo (Zaire), Indonesia, Taiwan, and the Philippines. A number of these churches are doubling in membership every ten years, largely because their leadership speaks with prophetic conviction. It is true that their beliefs and practices often seem quite unorthodox, and some even appear heretical, but it is equally important to recognize that most of these groups do use the Bible, even more than many of the more traditional churches. The people in these new churches simply do not feel at home in Western institutions, but they are able to identify relevantly with "the people of God" in the Bible. One may accuse some of these new churches of misusing the Bible to defend polygamy, but it was not many years ago that many churchmen in the Western World were defending slavery by quoting Holy Writ.

While communication in missions has been moving more and more in the direction of the mass media, largely with an impersonal-

ized message designed to satisfy intellectual needs, the communication within these new churches is intensely personal, highly
emotional, and employs essentially a one-to-one approach. These
features of communication are also the essential elements in the
recent youth movements in America and Europe.

Certain failures of modern missions may be said to be due in
large measure to three serious faults in communication. First, the
truly prophetic message of God's redemptive love as expressed in
the death and resurrection of Jesus Christ and the victory which
the believer may experience through the power of the Holy Spirit
has been increasingly set aside for other important, but basically
peripheral messages. Not having a truly prophetic message from
God, mission structures have found it difficult to recognize local
prophets in their midst and to give them the proper stimulus and
guidance. More often than not such prophets have been forced
by circumstances and personal predeliction to work outside the
framework of the traditional churches.

Second, the preoccupation of missions with statistical growth of
their own constituency has resulted at least in part in depersonaliz-
ing the message so as to reach the masses, with the result that the
masses simply have not been reached. Missions have sometimes
purchased planes so as to facilitate travel, only to discover some
years later that the really important growth in the churches had
occurred as missionaries travelled more slowly from place to place,
with time to meet people out where they were, rather than in
centers which seemed strategic but which were largely "foreign
settings" for the local inhabitants. The focus upon transplanting
churches, rather than upon sowing the seed has also been a source
of real difficulty, for it has meant transporting bag and baggage all
the institutional forms which are often so poorly suited to the needs
and backgrounds of the local constituency.

Third, the concentration upon sending out primarily technicians
with specialized information and skills has often resulted in everyone thinking that the primary role of such individuals was to
perform their highly specialized function, rather than to serve as a
personal representative of the lowly Galilean. The compartmentali-
zation of activities and the highly specific roles which resulted
from institutional elaboration have meant that more often than not
there was little or no time or opportunity for a medical man to be a

doctor of souls, for a nurse to heal a broken heart or for a builder to help a man rebuild his life. In a sense, the specialized roles of missionaries resulted in a secularization of their activities, with the result that many missionaries quite unwittingly became spiritually dehydrated.

Any really significant change in institutional missions will inevitably call for radical rethinking of goals and commitment and will require important changes in both structure and methodology. A number of these are touched upon in this volume and a number of others are dealt with in successive numbers of *Practical Anthropology*, a journal dedicated to bringing to missions the results of important studies in the fields of communication and cultural anthropology.

At the present time, however, there is emerging a very significant new type of missionary work, being carried out by a few small, but far-seeing mission boards. The leaders of these missions have established important personal and institutional links with some of the new independent churches and are seeking to supply such churches with the types of helpers which they can use, for example, teachers, doctors, builders, and nurses. In such situations there is a surprising lack of the customary fear and jealousy which so often occurs in traditional, mission-sponsored churches, in which national leaders are apprehensive of missionary domination and basically insecure about their own ability to "run the show." In the indigenous churches there are no such fears, for the leadership has been able to run things without the missionaries in the past and they are confident they can do so in the future. Furthermore, the missionaries come by invitation and because they are needed and wanted. As a result, interpersonal relations can be built upon quite a different foundation from what is often the case in traditional settings.

From the standpoint of communication this linkage between the serving mission and the leading church is excellent, for the prophetic role rests with the leadership. This means that the prophet is in administrative control. He is the focus of concern and communication. In the traditional mission structure, the administrative control has rested with the technicians and the phophetic function has been left to the local preachers, or as they are too often called "the preacher boys."

This new pattern of missionary work should be watched with great interest, since it may provide one of the most important means by which an increasing number of persons from the sending countries may serve meaningfully outside the framework of the established structures.

If the radical and extensive changes in missions during the last ten years have seemed almost overwhelming to those with traditional orientations, it is difficult to predict how such persons will react to what will inevitably happen during the next ten years. Undoubtedly the rate of change will increase in geometric proportion, and within ten years it will be difficult to recognize the old ways. The institutional churches in the sending countries are themselves undergoing rapid changes, but these are by no means as rapid or as radical as what is happening in the new world. Such changes may be frightening to some, but they will be thrilling opportunities for others, for changes always supply the openings for new and dynamic movements of the Spirit of God, provided there are Spirit-filled men and women willing to walk with confidence in the Lord and Savior of all mankind.

Greenwich, Connecticut   Eugene A. Nida
December, 1971

CHAPTER 1

An Introduction to Communication

Thy word is a lamp to my feet
and a light to my path . . .
The unfolding of thy words gives light;
it imparts understanding to the simple.
—Psalm 119:105, 130

THE major difficulties in communication result largely from the fact that we take communication for granted. Whenever we hear someone speak, we tend to assume that what is meant is precisely what we understand by these words. But words do not always mean what we think they mean, even in our native tongue, and our seemingly most transparent idioms are rarely translatable into other languages. In a number of languages of Central Africa the phrase "beat his breast" (used in speaking of the Publican who went into the temple to pray and in great contrition of heart "beat his breast," Luke 18:13) can be grossly misunderstood if translated literally and without explanation. To these people it would mean "to congratulate oneself," equivalent to our "patting oneself on the back." In that part of the world a person who is truly repentant will "beat his head," not "beat his breast." One of the special problems of communication in our contemporary cold war is that words have utterly different meanings to different people. "Peace" for the West means "the absence of strife and conflict," but in Communist ideology "peace" defines a state of being propitious for the outworking of dialectical materialism. Such a state is generally anything but peaceful, since it requires not only violent class conflict but also the subverting of other nations and military encouragement to revolutionary movements.

These problems of communication arise largely because essentially the same symbols may have radically different meanings. For Amer-

1

icans the wheel is usually regarded as a perfectly logical and appropriate symbol of progress. For the Buddhist world, however, the eight-spoke wheel symbolizes "reversion of type"—the cyclical view of the world which ultimately denies any real progress. We find it entirely polite to offer a gift to a person with one hand, but in many parts of Africa to do so is a serious insult. There one offers food to a dog with one hand while anything for a person must be presented with two. If, after a long, arduous journey, we should arrive, tired and hungry, in a Kaka village of the Cameroun, we would probably not think it improper to ask a woman for food; but she would not interpret the request as merely a desire for something to eat, for asking a Kaka woman for food is the generally accepted way of suggesting that she become one's mistress.

On the other hand, not only do similar objects and actions have quite different meanings for different peoples, but very different symbols may convey essentially similar meanings. We speak of "a hard-hearted man," but the Shipibos of the jungles in Peru describe such a person as "without holes in his ears." We normally motion to a person to come by extending the arm and moving the fingers with the palm of the hand turned up, but in Latin America, as well as in many parts of the Orient, such a gesture seems ridiculous. As a man once exclaimed, "What do you want me to do, fly?" In many regions Americans must learn to turn the palm of the hand down while motioning with the fingers.

To make matters even worse, there are some types of symbols which we rarely use—at least not in the highly elaborate ways that other people use them. The New Caledonians in the South Pacific make a great deal of the condition of the skin, and by "decoding" its various conditions—flushed, dry, perspiring, pallid, etc.—they describe and communicate subtle meanings about psychological states of being. In the Sudan some of the Nilotic tribes have a complex set of symbols in their dance forms, and in the Southwest of the United States the intricate geometric forms employed by various Indian groups express many distinct meanings.

The Mysterious Power of Symbols

Our difficulties with symbols, especially words, which are symbols *par excellence*, would not be so great if it were not for the great power they exercise over people. Not only can words, when properly used, soothe our emotional tantrums; they can also inflame us into rage. Some words delight us with pleasant associations; others deeply embarrass us. With words men sway the multitudes and even try to wring concessions from God. Similarly, they are convinced that by words evil spirits can be placated, if not deceived. Among some Indians of South America one of the standard ways of keeping evil spirits from harming small children is to call the boys and girls by bad names so that the malignant spirits will have no reason to think them attractive.

By means of word symbols we frequently reveal our status in society, betray our upbringing, or reflect our education. Certain words become the badge of membership in our group, and woe to the visiting lecturer who uses the wrong word.

The real power of word symbols results not, however, from these secondary features of social control or class identity (much as we may fear the insidious effects of "the organized lie" in our age), but from the indispensable function of symbols in the processes of conceptualization. Some thinking is possible without word symbols, but it is usually very diffuse and unmanageable and tied to immediate impressions and stimuli. It is only when we have acquired a symbol which can serve as a label or identification tag for our conceptions that we can be said really to think. Only then can we readily manipulate our thoughts, rearrange our perceptions, test our impressions against our remembrance of experience, and satisfactorily recall the infinite variety of phenomena which surround us. Helen Keller's deeply moving account of her first experience with a word symbol "water" is the most striking evidence of the power of words.[1] When as a young girl she sensed that the movement of her teacher's fingers constituted a symbol of the cool liquid pouring over her hand from the pump, there was released within Helen Keller a great reservoir of mental energy. By means of a symbol for water she now had a tool by which to grasp the reality. All of us in lesser ways also experience the need for tools by which to understand the world around us. My wife and I, for example, enjoy our bird feeder, where scores of birds come each day, especially in the early spring. But until we had a bird book by which to identify these beautiful creatures, we felt strangely cut off from our feathered friends. They remained strangers to us until we learned their names, and then in an almost uncanny way we seemed to have established rapport with them. The use of a symbol by which to identify these birds had not in any way changed them or us, but it altered completely our feeling of relationship. Here lies the heart of our problem of symbolism.

The Abundance and Variety of Communication

Whatever else we may say of human communication, one thing is true, "Speech is the greatest interest and most distinctive achievement of man."[2] This distinctly human activity takes more of our time and attention than any other. From the alarm clock in the morning until "lights-out" at night—and even in our dreams—we are producing and responding to symbols, most of which are either words or are readily translatable into words. We find words suitable for all kinds of occasions, from "Soup's on!" to "Here comes the bride!"

But communication is not limited to speech. We receive communication by means of all our senses: hearing (language, music, barking of dogs), seeing (words, pictures, signs), touching (kissing, stroking), tasting (the gourmet's language of good and rare foods), and smelling (pleasure in the rare symbolism of perfumes, the painful response to foul odors). Moreover, communication comes to us through an amazing variety of forms (e.g., speech, gestures, dance, drama, music, plastic art, and painting) and is transmitted to us through many media (e.g., radio, television, books, billboards, and even sky-writers).

Part of the complexity of communication results from its wide range of purposes. Though, in general, we assume that communication is designed to convey information, and by this means to influence or control the behavior or attitudes of others, much that purports to be communication of information is merely self-expression. Many poems, for example, are essentially an expression of an author's emotion; the information content of the "message" is quite secondary. Unfortunately, too many orations and not a few sermons are primarily expressive, rather than informative, for they are too often means of impressing people with the speaker's erudition or of acquiring prestige.

While the range of our purposes in communication may be wide, the variety of objects with which communication is concerned is even greater. Speech, for example, can be used not only to yell at a dog and to curse an enemy, but also to court a lover and to philosophize about the nature of reality. Speech may be employed as an indispensable magical ingredient in successful gardening in the Trobriand Islands, while it is thought to be a prerequisite for worship, even when it is not understood, in the Latin mass of Roman Catholicism. The very same communication may be thought cleverly humorous when addressed to a good friend, but provocative of bloodshed when said to a stranger or an enemy. A Hopi Indian, for example, can make all kinds of joking remarks, some of them highly suggestive, to or about his father's sisters or his father's brother's daughters, who are traditionally supposed to be jealous of a man and to insist, all in fun, that he is their sweetheart. But these same remarks directed to other women would certainly get him into serious trouble.

Added to these difficulties of communication is the fact that an acceptable manner of communication within one society may be inappropriate in another. In some places in the United States one can go in for the old-fashioned "spread-eagle oratory," which though taboo in the North and East, is still popular in some places in the South and West. In general, Americans favor straightforward simplicity and a direct approach, looking one's audience squarely in the face. In Madagascar, on the contrary, in certain types of communication it is important to avert one's gaze; otherwise one will be accused of being brazen and lacking in respect.

Communication of the Christian Faith

No other religion is so thoroughly word-oriented as "Judeo-Christianity." It is true that words play an important part in all religions, whether in the sacred formulas of the mystery rites in ancient Eleusis or in the utterances of the Egyptian creator-god Ptah, "who thought in his heart and spoke with his tongue" in order to bring all things into existence. But only in the Judeo-Christian tradition is there so strong a rejection of visual images and likenesses and such utter dependence upon "Thus saith the Lord." While the Greeks beheld the mysteries, the Jewish prophets heard the voice of God. Jehovah could not be seen, but he could be heard, not in the noise of nature, but in the "still, small voice." Pre-eminently this emphasis upon

verbal communication as an integral element of revelation is symbolized even further by "The Word" as a title of the Second Person of
the Trinity.

The God of the Scriptures is one who entered history. But unlike
the gods of the Australian aborigines who were thought to have left
their traces in sacred pools, streams, and rocky hills, the God of
Abraham, Isaac, and Jacob is remembered in written words, which
not only describe what He did but undertake to interpret these deeds
from His point of view. In the description of God there are seeming
contradictions, for though He is plainly said to be "Spirit" He is also
spoken of as having eyes, a mouth, ears, a right arm, and a throne. A
closer study, however, reveals that these are not really the features of
"an old man upstairs," but refer to God's functions—His knowledge,
revelation of Himself, power, and authority. The exploration of these
problems leads us directly into the heart of the communication
problem.

For the Christian there is the difficulty not only of apprehending
adequately the distinctive form in which the gospel has been communicated, but also of appreciating some of the reasons for the
diverse responses to it of different peoples. How has it happened, for
example, that in Thailand in a population of more than 20,000,000
there are only approximately 20,000 Protestant Christians, despite
intensive missionary work for a century, while in Sumatra among the
previously cannibalistic Bataks, who ate the first two Methodist
missionaries, there are now more than 1,000,000 Christians, with
their own schools, churches, seminaries, and even missionaries? Certainly Adoniram Judson never dreamed in Burma that his seemingly
rather dull Karen servant, Ko Tha Byu, would be the first Christian,
and would witness to a people who would eventually accept the
gospel by tens of thousands (there are now more than 100,000 Pwo
and Sgaw Karen Christians); while the church among the Burmese-
speaking people, for whom Judson was so devotedly translating the
Scriptures, would not be much larger than 5,000. We cannot but ask
ourselves the question: How does it happen that the gospel has had
wide acceptance in Uganda and Ruanda-Urundi (where almost 50
per cent of the population is at least nominally related to the Christian community), while in Japan not one half of 1 per cent are
Christians, in China scarcely 1 per cent, and in India as a whole not
2 per cent? On the other hand, in India, among such groups as the

Uraons, Mundas, Hmars, and among many of the Nagas, nearly whole districts have become Christian. In general, the explanation given is that, because of their credulous nature, the animistic peoples, who do not follow any of the "world religions" (e.g., Buddhism, Hinduism, Confucianism, Taoism, Islam, etc.), are easy victims of "missionary exploitation." But this is not the whole story. There are radically different responses even among the so-called animistic peoples. In southern Mexico the Tzeltals and the Tzotzils are closely related tribes, living in very similar circumstances, but their response to the gospel has been wholly dissimilar.

A people's response to the Good News about Jesus Christ depends on a host of factors. It has been found, for example, that in Latin America people in new communities are much more likely to be interested in the gospel than are those living in old towns, with age-old traditions and strong social pressures. Moreover, people in new suburbs are much more likely to be attracted than are those in more settled areas. Furthermore, the problem of reaching people living in the impersonal atmosphere of a large urban center is quite different from that of approaching people dwelling in the narrow confines of a village or rural town, with its small face-to-face society.

The communication of the gospel sometimes results in a fierce, fanatical reaction, while in other situations, which superficially appear quite similar, the opposition is largely of a token nature. When the gospel is accepted and a large mass movement results, Christianity tends to flourish for a time and then gradually to die back. More often than not the critical stage in the life of a church is reached not in the early years, but when the so-called "second generation" problems arise.

If we are to obtain any satisfactory answers to the evident problems of communication which have confronted the Christian church in the past and which continue to challenge it in the present, we must first analyze the nature of religion as it is related to communication (Chapter 2), and then consider the structures of communication (Chapter 3) and of meaning (Chapter 4). Following this we can most profitably deal with the relationship of communication to the structure of society (Chapter 5), and the dynamic power of communication, especially in terms of the rise and fall of religious movements (Chapter 6). We then take up certain psychological aspects of communication (Chapter 7) and the ways in which communication takes place within the total context of a people's life (Chapter 8). We have next introduced a special phase of communication as it is specifically related to problems of translation and revision of the Scriptures (Chapter 9) before going on to a concluding chapter on the theological bases of communication.

CHAPTER *2*

Religion and Communication

> *Then the king sent, and all the elders of Judah and Jerusalem were gathered to him. And the king went up to the house of the Lord, and with him all the men of Judah and all the inhabitants of Jerusalem, and the priests and the prophets, all the people, both small and great; and he read in their hearing all the words of the book of the covenant which had been found in the house of the Lord. And the king stood by the pillar and made a covenant before the Lord, to walk after the Lord and to keep his commandments and his testimonies and his statutes, with all his heart and all his soul, to perform the words of this covenant that were written in this book; and all the people joined in the covenant.*—2 KINGS 23:1–3

RELIGION involves an almost incredible variety of activities: bloody sacrifices, mumbled curses, painful ordeals, frightening seances, ecstatic tongues, drunken orgies, fantastic visions, and pomp and ceremony. How to find in all these activities some unifying principle or means of meaningful classification is not easy,[1] especially when the motives of many religious activities are so different, or even contradictory. The sorcerer, who seeks to coerce the power of black magic in order to kill his rival, and the mystic, who desires only to be utterly controlled by his God, seem to live in entirely different thought worlds, with nothing to unite them. Nevertheless, despite the utterly different outward forms and the diametrically opposed motives which prompt religious actions, one basic characteristic runs through all these activities: namely, communication to and from the supernatural. In order to understand how closely communication is linked with religion—how, in fact, it is in large measure the very essence of religious practice—religious activities must be investigated in a wide range of cultural expression.

If we are to study these problems fruitfully, we must, however, distinguish three different aspects of religion: (1) the practice of religion (the *cultus*), (2) the beliefs that prompt religious practices, and (3) the results of such practices and beliefs in terms of general behavior. In the past the tendency has been to concentrate primarily upon the beliefs, on the assumption that these are the truly relevant features in religious systems. An analysis of the actual practices of religion indicates, however, that perhaps this view is too limited, and that we can more adequately view the actual nature of the beliefs, once we have carefully studied the accompanying varieties of religious practices, in terms of their specific relationship to the sending and receiving of "messages" and the re-enactment of such religious communication.

The Sending of Messages

Religion may be said to involve first and foremost the sending of messages to the supernatural: but this supernatural may be, and is in many instances, a completely nonpersonal power or force. When a Trobriand Islander gathers selected herbs, then mutters to them his formulas for garden magic before burying them in his newly dug garden, he is communicating—but not to a spirit or god. The words themselves are believed to have power to compel the nonpersonal supernatural powers that control the growth of the garden. The herbs are carriers of the message, but it is the words, in and of themselves, that perform the necessary function. This garden magician (and all Trobriand Islanders regard magic as an essential element in raising a garden) is not a scientist, in our sense of the word, for the results he expects from his magic are entirely out of proportion to the effort he puts into the process of tapping this supernatural power. Moreover, he is not so foolish as to think that his gardening can be made successful by magic alone—he himself must clear the land, dig the soil, mix proper types of dirt, and carefully nurture the plants. But when all this work is done, there are still factors over which his efforts and skills apparently have no control. To ward off disease and blight, magic must be used. For the unknown sources of trouble he must use the supernatural power.

The communication of the magician with impersonal supernatural forces may not seem like communication in the usual sense, for we normally think in terms of one who receives the message and who can consciously evaluate it and determine when, how, and if to answer. The communication of the magician is more like that of the electrical engineer, who may "communicate" with a power site some miles away and may, by pushing the right buttons and manipulating the correct dials, operate the machinery in a distant location. The magician engages in an analogous type of communication, not with a spirit which has the capacity to make a decision as to whether to act or not, but with blind supernatural forces which *must* act, provided that the magic formulas are performed with absolute correctness or that no one else has employed some contrary magic to "jam" or overpower the communication. Such competition from other magicians provides the excuse for instances in which magic does not work; someone else with a more powerful magic is thought to have nullified the effects of the first spell.

This system of control of the supernatural through magic, of whatever form, is essentially amoral, for there is no personal receptor of the message to make moral judgments. Hence this power can be used for good or for evil. It all depends on who is "paying the bill."

Despite many instances of blending and mixing of types, there are only two principal varieties of magic: (1) imitative and (2) contagious. When, for example, the sorcerer makes an effigy of his intended victim and then after ritual slaying buries the "body," this activity is thought to be effective in communicating a deadly force against the victim; for, according to the primitive world view, such symbolic actions, even though separated from real events by space and time, have inexorable power. In contagious magic the "transmission of the passage" is even more obvious, for if the sorcerer can obtain a nail paring, a small lock of hair, a piece of clothing, or some leftover food from the intended victim, these ingredients, which have been in contact with the person, are supposed to retain something of their metaphysical link with their former owner, even when separated from him in space or time. By means of these materials, therefore, the magician can work all sorts of black (harmful) or white (beneficial) magic, for these substances are believed to permit a sure communication of supernatural power.

In some religious systems the impersonal supernatural power that exists in the universe is formally recognized, and in the South Pacific it is known primarily as *mana*. Among other peoples a similar type of supernatural power has been variously represented, e.g., as *wakan* by the Dakotas, *orenda* by the Iroquois, and *manitou* by the Algonquins, but irrespective of name it is essentially this nonpersonal force that dwells in all things that is the secret of their power and distinction. In some respects this power is thought of in terms not too different from the way in which we describe electricity. Thus, it is said to flow from one person to another by personal contact; it may be stored up in greater quantities in certain persons of distinction and in sacred emblems; and it is essential for the realization of one's fullest powers, but extremely dangerous if possessed to an extent beyond one's "storage capacity." Thus a king must and can have great quantities of *mana*, but the poor commoner dare not even touch the king for fear that too much power may surge through him and kill him.

One form of communication may on the surface seem rather removed from the types already described. However, it is nothing other than symbolic communication, even though the intention is not to communicate a verbal or ritual message, but a body itself. When, for example, the Motilones of Colombia place the bones of their dead in the fetal position and wrap them up to carry them off to a mountain cave, there to leave them, they are in essence communicating this "body-soul" to the next world, where it will be reborn from the womb of the cave. Even quite dissimilar practices may have the same ultimate goal. For example, the Egyptians, who tried to preserve the body intact, did so with the purpose of communicating it to the next world. Similarly, certain island peoples of the South Pacific, who put a body in a canoe and let it float off upon the ocean, or those who burn the body in order to transport the essence by means of smoke into the "other world," are all concerned fundamentally with "communication" in this somewhat broader sense.

In the sending of messages in religious activity, even more important than an impersonal power as the target of the communication is a personal supernatural being, whether demon, ancestor, spirit, or god. Communications to the supernatural are primarily prayers. They may be either spontaneous utterances or formalized ritual recitations. Often the names of the supernatural beings must be listed, and not infrequently people believe that such spirits give heed only when the words are uttered with special intonations or under certain circumstances (e.g., after fasting or in a kneeling position). Moreover, there is a tendency to regard a prayer with fixed form as being more powerful than a spontaneous utterance, since it must have proved its worth in the crucible of time and therefore is more likely to excite God's interest or elicit His favorable response.

Many people, however, seem to feel that the spirits (even as human beings) regard words as cheap, and therefore some effort must be made to convince the deity of one's sincerity, thus insuring that he not only understands the message but also recognizes the sincere intent of the source. The ancient Aztecs used to draw blood from their ears and tongues as gifts to the gods, for blood from these two sources was considered as intimately related to the oral-aural process of communication. The ancient prophets of Baal cut their flesh as a kind of symbolic dying. Most peoples tend to reinforce their communications to the supernatural with gifts, even as they believe that they can influence earthly rulers more successfully if their requests are accompanied by valuable favors. There is also a sense in which gifts are considered to communicate power to the spirits of the dead, for food placed on graves is often regarded as able to keep the dead strong. Accordingly, offerings not only inveigle the spirit to help, but provide the spiritual substance which makes him strong to assist. Certainly some aspects of the Ashanti prayer to the ancestors has this implication:

> Today is Adai;
> Come and receive this and eat:
> Let the tribe prosper,
> Let those of childbearing age bear children;
> May all the people get money;
> Long life to us all;
> Long life to the tribe.[2]

In many religious systems special techniques must be employed in communicating any "gift" to the supernatural. If, for example, one wishes to give an animal, it can be sent to the other world only by killing it, for death is the one means of gaining entrance into the unknown realm of the supernatural. Similarly, other objects must be ritually slain: jewels must be smashed, pottery must be broken, and vestments must be torn. Quite obviously these objects are not transported physically into the supernatural realm, but their symbolic values, or spiritual substance, can be said to be communicated. In the case of the holocaust, the rising smoke serves as a medium for carrying this "message" to the spirit world.[3]

Receiving Messages

The sending of messages to the supernatural without the possibility of receiving messages in return is, from the point of view of religion, quite meaningless. And in receiving as in sending, communication may be with either nonpersonal forces or personal beings.

Astrology represents one of the oldest sources of presumed communications from the nonpersonal supernatural world. Probably the present revival of popular interest in astrology reflects a craving to find some meaning and place in the impersonal world. It is not dissimilar to the way in which the people of ancient Rome, after destroying the gods of heaven, became subject to star-worship cults. In Rome the people who had imbibed the idea of the harmony of the universe from the Stoics but who refused to follow their stern discipline, found spiritual support in repopulating their world with supernatural powers, even though they did not give them personalities. Apparently modern man feels likewise lost in his cosmos. Hence his desire to feel that he really belongs, that he is somehow related to all that surrounds him, prompts him to seek word of his destiny in the weird variety of double-sounding horoscopes.

Astrology, however, is only one medium of communication from the supernatural. There are many others: casting lots, reading tea leaves, manipulating the ouija board, examining the cracks in animal shoulder blades roasted over the fire, watching the flight of birds, and looking at the entrails of chickens killed with poison. Certain elaborate communications from the supernatural are to be found in ordeals, where usually there is no thought of the personal intervention of a spirit or god. In these instances the activity itself supernaturally indicates who is guilty. In Central Africa the accused may be required to drink a cup of poison or to take palm nuts from the bottom of a cauldron of boiling oil with bare hands. In some parts of North Africa a man may similarly be required to have the red-hot blade of a knife laid on his tongue. If the result of such ordeals is death, fear, blistering, or injury, it is believed that the supernatural has indicated certain guilt.

The receiving of messages is not limited to impersonal sources. In all religious systems there is belief in the reception of communication from personal beings, including demons, spirits, ancestors, or god. One form of receiving involves ecstatic possession, when, as in voodoo worship, the celebrant is thought to be "ridden" by his god. Such reception of messages may be accomplished by many means, e.g., through mediums, spirit voices, speaking in tongues (including interpreting), visions, dreams, magic writing, oracles (as at ancient Delphi), and even by the bull-roarer, which is claimed by Australian aborigines to be the very voice of the spirits.

Some mystics believe that supernatural revelation is not merely verbal, but that in mystical identification they can receive supernatural communication through all the senses. In such an ecstatic moment the recipient is totally possessed by his deity in timeless communion, or, as we may also say, in complete communication by means of all the senses.

A traditionally recognized means of receiving messages is for men to speak or write as they are prompted by their gods. In this way they have produced a vast amount of literature which purports to record not only the very words of the deity, but also the reasons and motives for his actions. Such productions must likewise be regarded as part of the receiving aspect of religious practice.

Re-enactment of Communication

The sending and receiving of communications are only part of the story of religion. A very important element consists in the re-enactment of earlier communications by means of rites and ceremonies, which in themselves constitute media for the communication of religious concepts to other devotees. In Judaism the celebration of the Passover is the re-enactment of a great event of communication, when the angel of the Lord passed over the Children of Israel in mercy and initiated their deliverance from oppression. The Communion service in Protestant churches is likewise a commemoration of a communicative event, when Christ explained symbolically to his disciples the significance of his coming death. In the Roman Catholic Church the Mass has taken on certain additional features, for it is no longer merely a commemoration. In the re-enactment

Christ is actually slain and the wafer and wine become by "trans-substantiation" the literal elements of Christ's body. It is regarded, therefore, as a kind of "receiving," in this instance, of a literal substance. It is not dissimilar—in communication terms—to the reverse process by which the human sender dispatches a sacrificial substance to the supernatural.

Of the many elements in such ritual re-enactments, only a few can be touched upon. But we need to distinguish often between (1) verbal symbols, with which we are most familiar, and (2) visual symbols, which play so predominant a part in many religions. Through such symbols life may be symbolized by images of sex organs, sheaves of grain, and sprays of flowers, and death may be shown by the sacrificial knife, dripping blood, and broken vessels. In many re-enactments of communication the spirits are thought to participate in the ceremonies. In the Trobriand Islands, for example, a special high platform is built for the spirits of the dead to sit on, in order that they may take in all the dancing and fun. At the end of the ceremonies these ancestral spirits are especially instructed to leave, so that their continued presence may not cause undue risk to normal tribal life.

Despite the widespread sexual symbolism in religion and the religiously sponsored sex orgies in some primitive tribes, which are in substance only re-enactments of supernatural communication of fertility, sex seems to play an amazingly small part in religion.[4] There is no doubt that in some ancient fertility cults contact with the temple prostitutes meant a degree of symbolic identification with the goddess herself. Nevertheless, despite the attendant powerful drives, sexual activity has never become an integral part of most religions because it does not seem to provide a channel of communication with the supernatural. Sex is undoubtedly an important adjunct to many phases of religious expression, but it is usually absorbed into the larger framework of life and death, being and nonbeing. The ultimate question for man is not the expression of his sex drive, but the fulfillment of his desire to be.

Some initiation rites are readily classifiable as re-enactments of communication. In fact, the initiates are sometimes supposed to die and depart for the spirit world during the course of the initiation, only to be recalled by the intense religious activity of all those who remain. Sometimes the initiate must learn a new language (a kind of ritual language with strange words and often purposely archaized forms), receive a new name, and even be symbolically born again. For these rites special sacred ground must be prepared, the initiates must be separated from their mothers (symbol of their childhood), and undergo such operations as circumcision, which may be interpreted in many instances as a ritual or mystical death.[5] This type of initiation means a change in a boy's existential status, for he has received a crucial revelation about life and the world. Thus he emerges a new person—an adult. At the same time, however, there are often in initiation rites factors which are not re-enactments of supernatural communication. For example, the initiate may be taught the secular legends of his people, tested as to his physical prowess, and shown his role in adult social life. These experiences have the sanction of the religion; that is to say, conformity is enforced by the spirits. However, such behavior is not necessarily religious, for at this point religion ceases and social instruction begins.

It must be recognized, of course, that practices predominantly associated with some particular type of religious communication need not be related in one way only. Ordeals, for example, may be regarded as expressing the mind of a god, rather than being merely the result of nonpersonal supernatural force. An elaborate ritual may be part of prayer, rather than a re-enactment; and a sacrifice may actually serve to provide a means of receiving messages from the gods through the inspection of the liver, as was the common practice in ancient Roman times. In the discussion of these matters we have tried to point out only some of the principal uses of certain practices, without attempting a detailed cross-classification or delineation.

As already suggested, communication to and from the supernatural may overlap other phases of life, especially in a society in which people regard religion as intimately related to all areas of their existence. Totemism—by which people assume a common mythological ancestor, usually in the form of some plant or animal, and actively maintain such a relationship by certain taboos concerning their totemic "relatives"—is an instance of significant overlapping. The religious belief whereby the members of a clan think of themselves as descended from a crocodile, elephant, or scorpion, has a definite religious significance in so far as this belief relates them to their ancestors in the other world and in so far as the maintenance of certain taboos reflects their desire to keep on good terms with these spirit powers. When, however, this belief in one's totem is only a symbol of one's clan identity, it is essentially a social factor and not a religious one.

Beliefs that Underlie the Practice of Religion

There can be no communication to and from the supernatural unless some beliefs are held about: (1) the supernatural entities and the human participants in the communicative act, (2) the past and present relationships between the participants, and (3) the means by which communication, of whatever kind, is effected and maintained.[6] For primitive peoples these beliefs are generally preserved or "symbolized" in myths, which may be based on some kernel of truth about natural phenomena (e.g., why lightning strikes a particular mountain or the reasons for the phases of the moon), may reflect some historical event such as the exploits of legendary heroes, or may constitute merely the "day-dreaming of the race." But these myths are essentially distinct from folk tales, which are designed for social amusement, and from legends, which are the recital of presumed historical events, however fancifully reconstructed in the storyteller's mind. Myths have a much deeper significance than either, for they constitute the social and moral rules sanctioned by the activities of the supernatural.

Myths are quite different from theology as well, for they present truth within a special symbolic form.[7] Even though the concepts are communicated by means of words, the fundamental form is more that of a picture or a drama than that of a logical exposition. Moreover, the message of myths is intuitively apprehended, while theology is capable of intellectual analysis.

The relationship between participants in religious communication is one of complete interdependence, similar to what biologists speak of as "symbiotic." The gods live on in power because of the fidelity of their worshipers, and the worshipers prosper because they are cared for by their supernatural guardians. That is to say, there must be constant communication between the participants or, as in any kind of interpersonal relations, the co-operation will soon break down. In order to use the supernatural powers at his disposal, man must keep them informed of his situation, must communicate whatever symbolic sustenance they require, and must maintain forms of behavior which will please rather than infuriate them. The supernatural powers, in turn, are required to watch over the social structure in order to insure order and to protect their protégés from inimical forces or hostile human enemies.

It is possible to regard the mythological and theological beliefs that underlie religious practice as being essentially the grammar of religious communication. An analogy from language may make this somewhat plainer, for language is not grammar. Language is what one speaks, the vehicle of communication, while grammar is a description of the rules which govern the use of this vehicle or instrument. Similarly, the communication that takes place in religious practices and constitutes so dominant an element in religious experience is in a sense religion; while the beliefs (or theology) constitute the grammar of religion—in other words, the rules that govern this communicative relationship with the supernatural. Linguists often speak of language and meta-language. The first is the instrument of communication and the second is the way in which this instrument is described. We could similarly speak of religion and meta-religion, in which religion would constitute primarily the communicative acts and theology would be the description of the ideological bases of such communication. Or, from a different view theology may be said to define the presuppositions of religious communication, in terms of (1) the nature and role of the participants, (2) the historical basis of communication, (3) the techniques of communication, and (4) the validated content of communication.

In speaking of beliefs we must, however, distinguish between real and ideal beliefs. Just as anthropologists distinguish between ideal and real behavior (i.e., between what people say they would or should do and what they actually do), so we must discriminate between what people say they believe and what they actually do believe, as witnessed by their behavior. When a person says that he believes in prayer (i.e., the possibility of verbal communication with the supernatural), he may be expressing merely an "ideal belief." He may simply believe that to claim such a belief is expected of him in certain socioreligious situations. Whether such a belief is ideal or real is to be determined by his behavior. Does he pray or not? If a person claims that he believes in God but regulates his life entirely without regard for Him, his belief is only an "ideal" one, a kind of social mannerism—the thing that is "done." We must not, however, assume that the differences between real and ideal beliefs reflect gross hypocrisy. Hypocrisy—a conscious duplicity of attitude toward real and ideal beliefs—is not the issue at all, for in most people the differences between real and ideal beliefs are never consciously realized. It is so much more comfortable in most societies to hide behind the façade of social acceptance rather than to resolve the differences that exist in any and all systems.

In some religious systems there are numerous grades of belief, from the highly animistic to the quite ethereal. Buddhism is just such a system. Unfortunately, most discussions of Buddhism treat only the upper level of theological formulation, with the implication that all Buddhists think accordingly. Nothing could be farther from the truth, for one can find in Buddhist temples in such places as Djakarta and Bangkok some of the most obvious forms of unenlightened animism and fertility cult practices.

Roman Catholicism, as it is practiced in many parts of Latin America, is likewise a system in which real and ideal beliefs show enormous discrepancies. The type of Christo-paganism which exists in many rural villages, with their noisy parades, drunken festivals, and dramatic dances, aimed more at exorcizing evil spirits than at portraying the passion of Jesus Christ, is a far cry from the formulations of the theologians.

Protestantism is by no means free from such differences between real and ideal beliefs. Despite an official belief in the priesthood of the believer, greater and greater concentration of functions is being forced upon the professional ministry. Moreover, though the relevance of the prophetic word as preached from the Scriptures is said to be central to the life of the church, less and less preaching is Biblically based, while ritualistic practices, which merely create a mood, rather than words, which convey a message, are being incorporated into Protestant services.

The Influence of the Social Context upon Communication with Supernatural Beings

The ways in which people regulate their social intercourse inevitably influence their manner of communication with the supernatural. For one thing, societies almost always emphasize the use of intermediaries. Africans are accustomed to explain the relationship in this way: "If you want a favor from a chief, you don't go to him personally with the request; you start by asking someone near to him to speak on your behalf." This means that you tend to call on the lower deities, or the ancestors, who have already gone on to the next world. Hence, the saints become "natural" emissaries for the living, for not only their attested worthiness but their present position as well make them especially useful as mediators of communication.

When there is a breakdown in communication—in other words, when prayers are not answered—the reasons for the failure are usually given in terms of human analogies. Someone failed to pass on the message, either from hostility or lack of interest; in such a case the intermediary must be placated or propitiated. If, on the other hand, a saint continues to fail, then he may even be whipped in public, as in some rural communities in Ecuador. More sophisticated persons do not take out their spite on the visible representatives of the system, whether images or priests, but look within for some personal human failure or finally feel resentful against God for having "let them down."

Since interpersonal relations in society are normally based on the formula, so neatly summarized in Latin, *do ut des*, "I give so you will give," it is not strange that people generally adopt the same bargaining attitude toward God. Even the ancient Greek term *euchomai*, usually translated "to pray," actually means also "to brag." In the first part of the *Iliad*, Homer describes the old priest Chryses praying to Apollo. First he brags to his god about all he has done—the altars he has built, the temples he has restored, and the sacrifices he has made. Whereupon, on the basis of Chryses' having done so much, Apollo is obligated to respond to his prayer. It is at this point that this kind of pagan prayer and Christian prayer part company. The non-Christian expects his deity to respond because of the worthiness of the worshiper. For the Christian prayers are answered only on the basis of God's grace to the believer, for man has no righteousness except that which God gives to him through Jesus Christ.

Just as in human society the communicative system may get completely out of hand when the total structure of the society is upset by revolution or war, so in religious communication there may be dire upheavals which so shift the balance of power that the very focus of religion changes. In West Africa there is now an alarming increase in witchcraft; in other words, in communication to nonpersonal supernatural powers for socially harmful purposes. This has happened in large measure because the old gods and the restraining powers are considered as dead, disposed of by colonial educational systems, the work of missionaries, and the breakup of the social structure as the people have left rural communities for life in the sprawling urban areas. The gods, however, used to keep the witches under control, but now, with the controls thought to be very much weakened or powerless, people can practice their nefarious business with less danger of supernatural punishment. Moreover, possible victims are more terrified by the possibility of witchcraft, for they have no longer the secure confidence of beneficent gods who can help them. Religious communication is thus shifting in considerable measure from sending to a personal being to sending to a nonpersonal force, from prayer to magic.

An analogous change is taking place in American Christianity. Whereas in the past prayer was regarded as a means of influencing the Almighty to act, many now think of prayer as a means of "taking hold" of a supernatural force, of getting themselves in tune with the *force vitale*, the "life force" of the universe, and of conditioning themselves to receive vaguely defined supernatural influences. Rather than addressing a message to a personal God, they are "tuning in" on a nonpersonal power and even thinking that they can use this power to effect almost automatic and mechanical results at some distance from themselves.

Communication in Christianity

The theological implications of all that has been discussed here are treated primarily in the last chapter. At this point it is essential to mention briefly certain aspects of religious communication as they are related to Christianity. Otherwise our discussion would seem purely theoretical and merely a comparison of all religions, without proper regard for the distinctiveness of communication in the Christian faith.

Uniquely in Christianity, God does not merely communicate concepts about Himself (as in Islam). He communicates Himself, in the person of His Son, in whom the Word becomes flesh. In our faith it is God who takes the initiative in communication, and through the Incarnation, both by word and by life, communicates to men. Man in turn communicates with God, pre-eminently through prayer, but in the relation of a son to a father, who reserves the right to decide what is good for His children. We may even say that in the Incarnation God "encoded" His infinite qualities in the limitations of human language and human form, and showed us what He is like by His acts within history. If we were to understand this communication it had to be adjusted to our finite forms of thought and reinterpreted on the basis of our human patterns of behavior.

In prayer we "encode" messages to the Infinite, but "we do not know how to pray as we ought, but the Spirit himself intercedes for us with sighs too deep for words" (Romans 8:26). That is to say, our prayers encoded within the limitations of our own speech are "decoded" by God in terms of His infinite wisdom, and answered, not on the basis of our limited knowledge or unintentionally selfish motives, but in accordance with His divine grace and continual mercy.[8]

Behavioral Consequences of Religion

Any religious system inevitably impinges upon general behavior, for the communicative relationships between human beings and the supernatural, and the contents of these communications (especially those from the supernatural), are predicated upon certain types of behavior on the part of the human participants. What is of special concern to us, in terms of communication, is that so much of the behavior stipulated or required by religion is of a strictly symbolic nature. That is to say, the very practices themselves serve to communicate still other messages, and hence they become highly important in any analysis of communication.

If, however, we are to understand the significance of this symbolic value of religious practices we must analyze behavior in terms of those features which define its character and in large measure determine its course. From our point of view, in the study of the relation of religion to behavior, we must consider behavior from three perspectives: (1) the extent of its symbolic significance, (2) the manner in which it carries cultural approval or disapproval, and (3) the degree to which it has religious import.

In speaking of the symbolic or nonsymbolic significance of any action, we can most conveniently speak of three levels, which, however, actually represent three points on a scale from the least symbolic to the most symbolic type of actions. At the one extreme we encounter those kinds of behavior which within a particular society seem to have the most immediate and direct kind of purpose. For example, eating may be simply to satisfy hunger and killing an animal may be in response to a need to protect oneself from danger. Such actions, with only these immediate and direct goals, would be largely nonsymbolic, thus representing one extreme of the scale.

At the other extreme of the symbolic scale there are other actions which have practically no immediate or direct significance. In fact, their entire meaning (or purpose) is to point to something else quite distinct from themselves, and it is from this nonimmediate event that the action in question obtains all its real importance. When a Mayan Indian in Mexico sends a black rooster off into the jungle to carry away some polluting sin so that the people of a household may be cured of a critical ailment, there is relatively little immediate or direct significance to be found in the actual process of chasing off the poor chicken. The purpose is primarily not to get rid of the fowl, but to be rid of the sin, and hence of the sickness. Sending the rooster off into the woods is a kind of "substitute" action for driving away the offending misdeed. Similarly, when a sorcerer undertakes to destroy a man by burning some of his clothing over a smoldering fire, while he blows the smoke in the direction of the man's house and mutters powerful curses, his purpose is to kill, but his action is a substitute one, and to this extent it is primarily a symbolic one.

Between these two extremes of behavior, in which on the one hand the significance of an action is both immediate and direct, and on the other is quite indirect and nonimmediate, there is another type of action which partakes of both of these characteristics, for one and the same event may have both a nonsymbolic and a symbolic significance. To eat in order to satisfy immediate hunger may be essentially nonsymbolic, but the eating may at the same time follow certain dietary laws, such as those of the ancient Pharisees. In such a situation the eating also becomes highly symbolic, for it indicates that the person involved is a pious member of a certain religious group and in this manner identifies himself as a "child of God." Similarly, to kill an animal in self-defense may be quite nonsymbolic, but if the hunter is at the same time intent upon slaying the beast in order to harm the totemic animal of an enemy or to devour the "spiritual" substance of the animal's courage, and thus become like the animal, the action is no longer a consequence of mere immediate involvement, but becomes symbolic.

An examination of various types of behavior soon indicates that there is probably no completely unmixed kind of action. Everything that we do tends to carry with it some cultural conditioning. In other words, we learn from our parents and contemporaries how to carry out these actions and in so far as we conform to the norm of the group our own actions symbolize our participation in the group. Nevertheless, despite the fact that all actions are to this extent "mixed," there are certainly very significant differences of degree, and for convenience we are listing these as (1) actions which have an essentially immediate and direct significance, with the least possible symbolic value, (2) actions which have both immediate and direct as well as nonimmediate and indirect meaning, and (3) actions which have essentially nonimmediate and indirect significance.

In order to understand more clearly this distinction between levels of symbolization, it may be useful to compare the corresponding degrees of symbolization in objects, for they reflect the same basic scale. In the first place, in our society a comb, a pitchfork, and a pipe wrench may be said to have practically no functional significance other than for the immediate and direct purposes for which they are used. On the other hand, a wheel may have not only an immediate use, but it may stand for "progress" and a hoe is not only a garden tool but a symbol of the hard-working agricultural laborer, "the man with the hoe." An auto license with an especially low number generally serves not only the immediate purpose of permitting the owner to use the car (a value which this license shares with all other licenses), but it also usually symbolizes something about the prestige status of the owner. A number of objects have a dual set of values, e.g., balances with use in weighing and their meaning of justice; the hammer and sickle, not only as tools but as emblems of Communism; and the dove, both as a bird and as a symbol of peace in certain contexts and of the Holy Spirit in others.

Some objects, however, have no such dual values, but are restricted almost exclusively to a symbolic usage. One of these is the cross. It is no longer an instrument of actual execution, as it was in Roman times, but has become a symbol for Christianity. The image of a saint is supposed to have no meaning in and of itself, but only in so far as it represents something else, namely, the personage for which it acts as a symbol.

It must be recognized that as in the case of actions, there is no type of object which cannot be given symbolic significance and there are few objects which have not been chosen at one time or another by some society as having symbolic value. For us an arrow has primarily a sporting function, but it has no such symbolic value as it had among the Plains Indians of the United States, for whom it served as a symbol for declaring war. Similarly, a praying mantis is just a useful bug to have in our gardens, but for some of the tribes of South Africa the praying mantis is the symbolic representation of deity.

In analyzing different types of human behavior one must reckon not only with the scale of symbolic value, but with the distinctions between approved and disapproved behavior and between religious and nonreligious activity. One would think that such classifications would be entirely parallel, for we tend to assume a close relation between morality and religion, but this is not always the case. In fact, more often than not these two factors are not parallel and for society "here lies the rub." All societies of course recognize certain types of behavior as being approved or disapproved, but the lines which are drawn between marriage and adultery, incest and fornication, murder and killing in war, love and hate, truth and dishonesty, and respect and dishonor are never quite the same in any two socio-religious systems. All men recognize good and bad, but they define these terms quite differently in different parts of the world. The problem in some instances can be helpfully analyzed by determining for whom something is good or bad. Black magic, for example, is obviously good for the man who is paying for it to be done, but bad for the man against whom it is directed. Similarly, what is good for the master is usually not approved for the slaves, and what in some societies the king must do, e.g., marry his sister as in ancient Egypt, is prohibited for the commoner. Moreover, the gods may be guilty, and with apparent impunity, of all sorts of atrocious sins, as in the myths of ancient Greece or India, while the people believed they would be stricken down by the very same gods if they were caught imitating them.

It is significant that in the case of primarily nonsymbolic behavior, approval and disapproval (or judgments as to what is good or bad) seem to parallel quite closely the distinction between benefit and harm which may be done to others. On this level stealing, killing, maiming, protecting, nourishing, and helping are judged from a relatively valid standard of equity—an eye for an eye and a tooth for a tooth. However, as one moves up the scale of symbolic action, the violation of equity becomes more acute, for, even as Jesus found, the Pharisees preferred their symbolic keeping of the Sabbath rather than to allow a desperately needy man to be healed. Similarly, what men would never approve of on a nonsymbolic level, e.g., tortures and murders, they not only defend but glory in, once they can justify such actions on the basis of a "higher" system of approval or disapproval. Hence, religion is used to defend these very crimes in the Crusades and the Inquisition (not to mention such minor uprisings as the Lutherans against the Anabaptists).

The distinction between religious and nonreligious activity also intersects the symbolic scale of behavior. In this instance, however, as one ascends the scale, the behavior becomes increasingly more symbolic, for it is the religious significance of an act which imparts a distinctive symbolic meaning to it. However, symbolic meaning is not equivalent to religious significance, for some symbolic meaning has nothing to do with religion. In Communism, for example, the ultimate symbol is the State, not God, and though the emotional attachment to such ultimate symbols may be in many instances parallel, this does not make them both religion, unless as with some writers we define religion in terms of the ultimate, rather than the supernatural. In such a case we could then equate such attitudes and responses. Nevertheless, there are still other symbolisms which may be distinctly not religious, e.g., the symbols of art, music, and dance.

In any comparison of religious and symbolic systems it is essential to recognize that what is religious in one society may be quite non-religious in another. Among the Kaka of the Cameroun incest, stinginess, and theft are definitely religious concerns, for there are supernatural sanctions against them. That is to say, the spirits will punish violation of such "laws." On the other hand, the sweetheart relationship which Kaka men may have with a married woman (which would be classed as adultery by us, and hence contrary to the religious code) is for the Kakas primarily a matter of ownership rights and the results of being caught are handled only in terms of monetary compensation.[9] In other words in the Kaka system this kind of moral offense is a matter of civil, rather than criminal action.

Tensions on the Scale of Symbolic Behavior

Given a scale of symbolic behavior in which the religious aspects tend to increase as symbolic content increases and the moral values (in terms of basic equity) tend at the same time to diminish, it is little wonder that there are serious and important tensions which constantly beset any society, especially in times of rapid social or ideological change.

In the first place, there is the tension induced by the tendency for the religious interpretation of life to absorb everything into it, for as religious communication continues in any society, more and more objects and events are incorporated into the religious matrix and given corresponding symbolic values. All of this is quite understandable, for man is constantly trying to assign meaning to experience. At the same time men find religion to be a convenient blind for their evil, for it is even easier to hide enormous errors behind some mysterious "unknown" or "ultimate" than it is to do so even under the cloak of tribal or national expediency. The result is to heighten the divorce between morality and religion, between right conduct and ritual practice, and between personal accountability and institutional immunity.

At the same time if people are to feel any security in their religious symbolism, they almost always feel that they must extend it to include every phase of life. This has often happened, as with the Pharisees of New Testament times, the Roman Catholic Church in the Middle Ages, and the Todas of South India, who made a religion of their dairying. However, the result of this tendency is for people to lose touch with reality on the one hand and to construct a false kind of morality on the other, for this procedure tends to give precedence to ritual forms over moral consequences. As a result of these developments an opposite force tends to deny any place to religion. Secularization becomes the keynote of the period and men are relieved to escape from the suffocating effects of their intellectual enslavement to religion. A renaissance of learning and cultural vitality often ensues, but this may level off or degenerate into anarchy, for without religion life loses its higher meaning. Usually, the secular powers simply shift the emphasis from the supernatural to the super-state, whether symbolized by the person of the ruler or in the superiority of the culture.

It is tragic to think that man has never realized by experience that the only satisfactory answer to this continual tension between religion and materialism is to be found in Jesus' declaration that all the Law and Prophets hang on two simple principles: "You shall love the Lord your God with all your heart, and with all your soul, and with all your mind." And "You shall love your neighbor as yourself" (Matthew 22:37, 39). This type of love, as the basis of action, is the only effective guarantee against totalitarian or anarchic religiosity or materialism.

The second tension is the conflict between the standards of morality (or immorality as they often prove to be) in the upper levels of symbolism and those on the lower levels. Sabbath observance has a valid symbolic significance in the ritual remembrance of God's resting on the seventh day and hence people's identification with God and His work. However, when the ritual "rightness" of such a symbolic event is placed in conflict with moral justice, as demonstrated by the protests against Jesus' healing on the Sabbath, it is obvious that people think man was made for the Sabbath, rather than the Sabbath for man. What is even worse is the insistence of some that those who have no belief in such Sabbath observance must nevertheless conform outwardly, on the basis that such ritual observance is morally right, in and of itself.

It is quite easy to see how the presumed transcendent morality of religious symbolism would seem to be very superior to the lowly concepts of equity on a nonsymbolic level of day-to-day behavior of people. However, when it is believed that the gods can kill and commit adultery while men cannot, as in ancient Greece, and when the priests as representatives of the deity may deceive in order to gain a supposedly "higher end," while such a right is denied the laity, one can expect nothing other than violent conflict and the final triumph of the market-place justice of the crowd, rather than the Olympian unrighteousness of the deity.

On the other hand, no law of the market place can carry the moral sanctions it needs to implant itself in the conscience of men and women unless it is exalted above the level of the common majority of mob rule. It must acquire the value of ultimacy to be universal, and unless it is universal it is not fully just. All this means that in the realm of the moral, the good vs. the bad, there is a constant struggle along the scale of symbolic behavior.

The third tension is one which is inherent within the behavioral scale itself, namely, the tendency for substitute symbols to acquire nonsubstitute characteristics and conversely for substitute symbols to be denounced as empty forms.

The Christian rite of Communion as presented in the Bible is essentially a substitute symbol, for it is no end in itself. In fact, it has meaning only in terms of the event which it re-enacts. However, the Mass of the Roman Catholic Church is not a purely substitute symbol, for Christ is repeatedly slain and the elements are no mere symbolic substitutions but by transsubstantiation they are believed to become the actual substance of the body of Christ. Images likewise often lose their strictly substitutional character and acquire definite and personal powers, for one image of the Virgin may be good for those having malaria and another for women in pregnancy. One image manufacturer in Sucre, Bolivia, became so alarmed at the extent to which purchasers insisted that his images were truly *dioses,* "gods," that he stamped a sign on each one of them, *No es un dios, es unicamente una representación de un dios,* "This is not a god, it is only the representation of a god." As a result, he failed to sell a single image in the next few months. When at last he determined to destroy all his images and go out of business, he found that some of his employees were aghast that no living blood was found in the very images they themselves had made. In some areas of West Africa it has been the practice to thrust a knife through the cheeks and tongue of criminals being led off to execution, because it was feared that at their end some men might utter some horrible curse against the king or the chief. The people were afraid that such words would not be a mere substitute symbol (mere threats instead of real action), but would constitute an event with power in and of itself to produce vengeance.

One evidence of this tendency for people to think that substitute behavior possesses real, effective power is the inordinate demand of people for the "easy way out." It is so much more convenient to recite the doctrines correctly in church than to follow them faithfully in life, and much less troublesome to offer the correct sacrifices than to do the right thing. Obtaining an indulgence is usually easier than paying penance, and penance is generally a far lighter sentence than making retribution for one's sins. Such addiction to higher and higher levels of symbolic behavior, while avoiding the moral responsibilities of day-to-day social action, means that so often ritual is substituted for righteousness and ceremonies for service. Against such perversion of the truth the Prophet Isaiah declares: "Give ear unto the law of our God. . . . To what purpose is the multitude of your sacrifices unto me? saith the Lord. I am full of the burnt offerings of rams, and the fat of fed beasts. . . . Bring no more vain oblations; incense is an abomination unto me; . . . your new moons and appointed feasts my soul hateth . . . your hands are full of blood. Wash you, make you clean; put away the evil of your doings from before mine eyes; cease to do evil; learn to do well; seek judgment, relieve the oppressed, judge the fatherless, plead for the widow" (Isaiah 1:10–17, A.V.).

In opposition to this tendency for self-deception under the cloak of religious respectability many great religious teachers and prophets have protested. Buddha denounced the enslaving ritualism and debasing idolatry of Hinduism and called men to recognize their need of enlightenment and control over their evil desires. But Buddhism was soon caught up in its own elaborated ritualism and increasing idolatry. The prophets of the Old Testament inveighed against the corrupting ritual of legalism, and Jesus preached a kind of radical obedience to the will of God which swept away the ritualistic and legalistic conception of man's relationship to God. He insisted not on external behavior but on inner motive, and in so far as the Old Testament consisted of purely ceremonial and ritual ordinances, he abrogated them by his own violation of all kinds of mere ritual practice: eating without ceremonial washing, associating with publicans and sinners (those who were excommunicated from the religious community of Israel), violating the Sabbath, touching lepers, and conversing with a woman, which no rabbi was supposed to do. Though he repudiated the false claims of a perverted ceremonial structure, he did not, either in word or deed, violate any of the moral laws of the Old Testament revelation. Nor did he in any way suggest that symbolic behavior is wrong, for he himself instituted the symbolic meal of the new covenant. Nevertheless, he insisted that this rite was a commemorative event, not a magic medium for imparting mysterious power. It was to be a symbolic reminder of his death until he should come.

In view, therefore, of the importance of behavior as an element of communication, in so far as it is symbolic, and the centrality of communication to any expression of religion, it is necessary to look further into the nature of communication by examining its essential structure, for only in this way can we understand the vital role of communication in the propagation of the Christian faith.

CHAPTER 3

The Structure of Communication

> Then Eliakim the son of Hilkiah, and
> Shebna, and Joah, said to the Rabshakeh,
> "Pray, speak to your servants in the Aramaic
> language, for we understand it; do not speak
> to us in the language of Judah within the
> hearing of the people who are on the wall." But
> the Rabshakeh said to them, "Has my master
> sent me to speak these words to your master
> and to you, and not to the men sitting on the
> wall, who are doomed with you . . . ?" Then
> the Rabshakeh stood and called out in a loud
> voice in the language of Judah: "Hear the
> word of the great king, the king of Assyria!
> . . . 'Do not let Hezekiah make you to rely
> on the Lord. . . . Make your peace with me
> and come out to me. . . .'" But the people
> were silent and answered him not a word.
> —2 KINGS 18:26–27a, 28, 30a, 31b, 36a

IN ORDER to understand the structure of communication we must study it in terms of certain models, which will help us determine how this complex process actually operates. Fundamentally, however, communication is simple, for it involves only three essential factors: (1) the source, (2) the message (the actual form of what is communicated), and (3) the receptor.[1] In fact, we may diagram the essential features of communication as:

$$S—M→R$$

All three of these components are essential, for there can be no message unless there is some source of communication, and there is no communication unless someone receives the message.

In some circumstances people tend to overlook the importance of the receptor, for they assume that in communication the only important elements are the source and the message. As we shall see later, however, the way in which the receptor "decodes" the message has as much effect upon its meaning as the way in which the source "encodes" it. The Sunday School teacher may think that she is communicating something about Pontius Pilate; but if her students think that she is talking about "Pontius the Pilot," the actual content of the communication will bear only a slim resemblance to what was intended. Recently a small child completely misunderstood the behavior of the high priest who "rent" his clothing at the trial of Jesus. "Why did he have to rent his clothing?" the teacher was asked. "Was he so poor, or was it a masquerade party?"

It is, of course, easy enough to dismiss such errors in understanding as due to immaturity of language experience, but what about such words as *sanctification, justification, election,* and *predestination?* Certainly that part of the Biblical content which gets through to the average congregation is more often than not a pitiful caricature of the original message.

Nevertheless, if we are to apprehend the real significance of communication we must not only deal realistically with these three essential factors—the source, the message, and the receptor—we must also presuppose two conditions: (1) that the source has an intent (i.e., that he is not merely babbling, or that, if he is, he is honest enough to indicate this fact), and (2) that there is a response from the receptor, though of course this response may be either practical or ideational, or both.

There are scores of means by which we communicate, and after language gestures are perhaps the most frequently employed. Moreover, gestures are in many respects just as different and subtle as words. In the northern Congo I had the experience of trying to work with an informant in the Ngbaka language. In order to obtain the names of various objects close at hand, I did what any American would do— I pointed with my index finger. Before long, however, I was told that this was a vulgar gesture, and that if I were to be considered polite and cultured among the Ngbaka, I would have to point with my lower lip—and I did.

Music is a kind of language with remarkable means of communicating its distinctive messages. Though the component parts of music cannot be equated with the words and syntax of language, nevertheless, music is a kind of code, and each type of music has its own elements and manner of encoding. For example, the music of India, which generally retains a haunting "drone note" throughout a composition, employs not only the equivalent of our own standard scale, but 12 semitones, 22 microtones, and some 600 "mode-scales," presumably able to interpret all the varying moods and feelings of mankind. Actually, of course, we take music so much for granted that we scarcely realize that it is communicating to us, unless we hear it employed in circumstances in which it does not seem to fit, as when rock-and-roll pours out of a church basement and a jazz band takes a fling with "Nearer, My God, to Thee."

Dance forms may also communicate. Compare the erotic dances of the Shilluks in the Sudan, the totemic dramatic performances of the Australian aborigines, the dignified religious processionals of the Zunis, and the snake dances of the Hopis, as they pray for rain.

Despite the fascinating elements in these nonlinguistic forms of communication, the discussion in this volume is limited primarily to verbal communication, since words are far more complex in structure and much more significant for the functioning of any society than are other means of communication.

Communication within a Setting

Communication occurs always in the setting of a particular time and place, and as such it is essentially part of a larger framework. In fact, people can only communicate among themselves because they share a common culture. In this use of "culture" we do not mean, of course, elegant manners, the fine arts, or good literature, but rather the whole behavior patterns of a particular people. Clyde Kluckhohn describes culture in this anthropological sense as "those selective ways of feeling, thinking, and reacting that distinguish one group from another—ways that are socially transmitted and learned (with, of course, some changes through time) by each new generation."[2] Robert Redfield amplifies this description of culture by defining certain other features, such as ethos, national character, and world view, all of which constitute an integral part of the total cultural outlook of a people. He says, "The culture of a people is then its total equipment of ideas and institutions and conventionalized activities. The ethos of a people is its organized conceptions of the Ought. The national character of a people, or its personality type, is the kind of human being which, generally speaking, occurs in that society. The 'world view' of a people . . . is the way people characteristically look outward upon the universe."[3]

All these elements in the culture of a people are intimately related to the problems of communication. In order to describe this type of relationship we can diagram certain of the essential features as follows:

By means of the triangle we are trying to say that communication takes place within the total cultural context.

A closer look at what actually happens in communication soon reveals the fact that the message (as symbolized by M) reflects in innumerable ways the structure of the culture of which it is a part. In Hebrew, for example, the root *qdš*, which usually means "holy," "sanctify," "consecrate," and "hallow," also means in some contexts "sodomite" and "prostitute," especially when referring to the temple prostitutes of fertility cults. Such a range of meanings is unthinkable in a word reflecting our own culture, but it is entirely feasible for the ancient Semitic world, in which persons who were consecrated wholly to the worship of the deities of fertility served primarily as temple prostitutes. Similarly, the Hebrew root *kbd*, with its meanings of "heavy," "much," "many," "slow," "difficult," "burdensome," "grievous," "wealth," "riches," "glory," "prestige," and "honor" may seem utterly irrational to us, but in the nomadic culture in which this series of meanings developed such a range of significance was entirely logical. Something which was heavy proved difficult and grievous enough if it was worthless but nevertheless had to be transported. On the other hand, wealth, which would likewise be heavy, and even burdensome, was a source of distinction, with accompanying glory, prestige, and honor.

Some meanings of words reflect not the cultural behavior of people but the circumstances in which they live. In Genesis the Hebrew text says literally that God walked in the garden of Eden in "the wind of the day," a phrase which is normally translated in English as "evening," for in many parts of Asia Minor when the sun goes down the evening breezes begin to blow. It is therefore quite natural for people to designate the evening as "the wind of the day."

In order to symbolize this relationship between the total cultural framework and the linguistic form of the message, which reflects this culture, we must modify our diagram as follows:†

Even this representation of relationships is, however, inadequate, for in a very real sense both the source and the receptor are integral parts of this same cultural complex. It is quite understandable, therefore, that since the Jewish people always spoke of a large body of water as a "sea" (Hebrew *yam*, corresponding with Greek *thalassa*), whether it was salty or not, the Gospel of Matthew, which was written by a person of distinctly Jewish orientation and directed to a people of Jewish backgrounds, should use the phrase "sea of Galilee." On the other hand, Luke, who was of Greek background and who was writing his two-volume work on Christianity (the Gospel and Acts) for the Greco-Roman world, would most understandably use "lake of Galilee" (Greek *limnê*). Communication, in this sense, depends not merely upon the message as a part of the culture, but also upon the backgrounds of the participants in the culture.

A more complicated problem is to be found in the phrases "kingdom of heaven" and "kingdom of God." Some persons have contended that these two expressions really refer to different events, namely, the millennial kingdom and the eternal rule of God. Those who object to this type of exegesis point out that these two phrases are used in completely parallel passages. However, the solution to the problem involves considerably more than a mere comparison of similar passages. To comprehend what lies behind the fact that Matthew, as judged by Westcott and Hort Greek text, uses both "kingdom of heaven" (33 times) and "kingdom of God" (4 times) and Luke uses only "kingdom of God" a total of 32 times, we must recognize

†As early as 1954 Ralph Winter employed similar diagrams to highlight the important relations between the form of the message and the cultural context in which the message must be expressed.

the significance of the backgrounds of the participants in the communication.

In the first place, there is no dispute as to the Jewish background of the Gospel of Matthew, either in terms of the writer or of the prospective audience. The treatment of prophecy, constant reference to the Old Testament, and the emphasis upon Messiahship and kingship all point to its Jewish orientation. We also know that sometime prior to the time of Jesus the Hebrew word usually transliterated in technical writings as *Yahweh* (but transliterated traditionally as *Jehovah*, because of the Masoretic pointings which used the vowels of *Adonai*, "Lord") had become taboo. It was no longer uttered by the people, and according to tradition was spoken only once a year by the high priest when he went into the Holy of Holies to make atonement for the people. This reluctance to use this "personal name" of God had evidently been extended in some measure to *Elohim* and apparently to the Greek equivalent, *Theos*. As a result, certain linguistic substitutes were used, namely, "the Almighty," "the Presence," "the power on high," "the Holy One," "the Highest," and "Heaven." It is not strange, therefore, that the Gospel of Matthew, which was directed to the Jewish constituency, should use a substitute type of phrase, and it is equally understandable that Luke, who was intent upon explaining the true character of Christianity to people of Greco-Roman backgrounds, should use the phrase "kingdom of God" if he were to be understood.[4]

If we are to reflect adequately the various significant relationships between the cultural context and the communication event, we must then modify our diagram once more, and place each of the three communication elements within small triangles, for they are all integral elements of the total cultural framework:

When we have finally described the communication in terms of its cultural context, the involvement of the participants, and the meaning for those so involved, we have actually completed the *exegesis* of a message. That is to say, the exegetical analysis of any message consists in reconstructing, in so far as possible, all the significance of the communicative event within the totality of the cultural framework. But as far as the communication of the gospel is concerned, this same message must not only be interpreted, but also communicated to those who speak quite a different language and who live within a very different cultural setting. This second stage, which involves a two-language model of communication, is generally called *exposition.*

A Two-Language Model of Communication

If the message as communicated in the Biblical languages and contexts is to be communicated, it will inevitably involve certain formal adjustments to allow for differences in language and culture. Some of the differences we can diagram by a two-language model of communication:

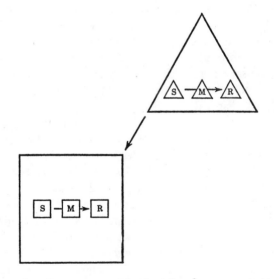

By contrasting the squares with the triangles, we are attempting to symbolize some of the basic differences, and by placing these figures on two levels we are trying to show their temporal sequence. In order, however, to apprehend fully some of the differences which must be introduced into the form of the message in order that the meaning of the communication may be functionally similar, we need to study the formal differences in detail.

One of the most obvious contrasts in any communication involving two languages is that the form of Ⓜ is not the form of ⚠. This difference applies to all levels: words, grammar, style, and symbolic content.

It is quite proper to say in Hebrew, "he is a son of fifty years," but in English this idiom has to be rendered as "he is fifty years old." Similarly, in Hebrew, as well as in the Greek of one New Testament passage, the "kidneys" (translated 14 times into the King James text as *reins*) are spoken of as a center of certain emotional states (cf. Psalm 26:2, Proverbs 23:16, also Revelation 2:23), but in English we use either *reins*, which people do not know and therefore do not understand, or employ some substitute, such as "heart." In Mark 6:34 Jesus is spoken of as literally "intestining" on the multitudes, for that is the literal meaning of *splanchnizomai*, derived from *splanchnon*, "intestines." For us the equivalent expression is, "he had tender compassion." We can use a phrase such as "bowels of mercy," but it is essentially meaningless, if not vulgar, to most people, for though we know the words "bowels" and "mercy," we do not regard the "bowels" as a center of emotion. Thus if we are to communicate an equivalent message in English some formal changes must be made in the choice of corresponding words if the meaning of the message is not to be lost or badly distorted.

What is true of words is equally true of grammar. In the first chapter of Mark, for example, the Nestle Greek text has 31 sentences beginning with *kai*, "and," out of a total of approximately 36 (depending somewhat upon how one decides to punctuate the Greek text and the values assigned to the raised period, or semicolon, in Greek). If one reproduces all of these "and's" we shall have anything but a good English style, for we insist that anyone who begins almost every sentence with "and" is using a childish style. On the other hand, good Greek style required that almost every sentence should begin with a conjunction, and the influence of the Semitic usage of *waw*, "and," in so many sentences undoubtedly accounts for some of Mark's predilection for Greek *kai*. However, one should not do violence to Mark's attempt to use good Greek style by reproducing all of these "and's" in English. Accordingly, most modern translators have seen behind the matter of formal grammatical correspondence and have tried to reproduce an equivalent grammatical style, which calls for drastic reduction in these conjunctions. In translating this passage, J. B. Phillips, for one, uses only two initial "and's," while E. V. Rieu employs only three, but both translators use certain other contextually appropriate equivalents, such as "then," "but," "consequently."

The problems of grammar are not limited, however, to a few conjunctions; they involve all levels of communication, from the length of sentences to the use of nouns instead of pronouns. Here again the differences between language structures require that certain formal distinctions be introduced into any translation. Paul's sentences are not unusually long for Greek (Plato, Thucydides, and Isocrates all wrote longer and more complex sentences), but many of his sentences when translated into English must be broken up into more manageable length (more "manageable," that is, for English sentence structure). As a result, Ephesians 1:3–14, which is only one sentence in Greek, and the longest in the New Testament, is divided up into a number of shorter units in most modern translations: five in Moffatt's translation, six in the Revised Standard Version and in Goodspeed's translation, and eight in J. B. Phillips' rendering.

A combination of the selection of words and grammar gives us the basic elements of style and literary form. Here again we face the problem of equivalent meanings. One woman, who objected violently to what she called Paul's "intolerable conceit" because he began each of his letters with his own name, had to change her mind when she discovered that he was using only a traditional epistolary formula, which was no more a criterion for judging character than the fact that we start our letters with "Dear," whether the person addressed is regarded with affection, utterly detested, or quite unknown.

Not only do words, grammar, and stylistic form have meaning, but the very events described may be symbolic, in the sense that they point to a significance other than the bare fact of the event itself. When the followers of Jesus cast their garments and fronds of trees in his path on the triumphal entry into Jerusalem, they were doing something intended to honor him. In many places of West Africa this same behavior would be interpreted quite differently, for casting a branch or twig in front of a visiting official or chief is a dire insult. Similarly, in the Biblical account, the holy kiss, the wearing of veils, women speaking in church, and wrestling with an angel all have different meanings than in our own culture. As a result we interpret such events in quite different ways. In general, the kiss is forbidden (except in the Middle East where it is culturally appropriate), the veils are reduced to hats (or a handkerchief), women are variously restricted in their religious functions (but rarely forbidden to speak, even if, as in some churches, the pastor must officially dismiss the congregation before a woman is allowed to address the congregation), and wrestling with angels is reinterpreted psychoanalytically or mythologically.

The Lack of Correspondence between Cultures

An obvious reason why the form of the message must be different, if the content of the message is to be equivalent, is that the cultural contexts in which these messages are communicated are so diverse. Even though we, as representatives of the Western cultural tradition, have received so much from the Greco-Roman world, nevertheless there are some significant contrasts which make the communication of the message not so easy as we sometimes tend to imagine. For the ancient world the intellectual atmosphere was dominated by an interest in metaphysics, and Aristotle may be said to symbolize in many regards the scientific outlook of the Hellenistic age. It is true that only a minority understood what the philosophers were saying, but the world view of these Greek thinkers influenced considerably the attitudes and values held by the common people. In our own day "scientism" tends to dominate the average thinking man's view of the world. He scarcely enjoys the comfort of an ancient metaphysics, which seemed to have all the answers, but he is convinced that somehow scientists will find the answers to the riddle of the universe if only they are given the time and equipment with which to probe the immense distances (and relationships) of the macrocosm of the stellar universe and the microcosm of the lowly atom.

For the Hellenistic world, however, man had to be modest in his struggle against nature and its power. Otherwise he ran the risk of being guilty of *hybris*, that overweening pride which, like Nemesis, was always ready to humble man. The gods of the Greeks had their way of imposing limits on man's exploits. If nothing less served, they would melt the wings of Icarus to keep him from soaring to the sun. For modern man even the sky imposes no limit.

Ancient society was based very largely upon institutionalized slavery, with an estimated three fourths of the population of the

Roman empire enslaved. In our own day, slavery has been outwardly condemned, at least in the civilized world, though it remains with us under the guise of "indentured labor" and "political re-education."

For the ancient Mediterranean world sex was very closely tied to fertility cult practices, with all their religious significance. Today, in the Western world, sex is quite another type of activity, involving personal gratification as much or more than procreation.

The ancient world was filled with spirits, demons, and black magic. Our own Western world believes somewhat in the occult, in ghosts and gremlins, and is even trying to make a scientific study of them under ESP (extrasensory perception), but our attitudes are very different from those of the ancient Romans.

The average Greek certainly regarded human history as the work of men and gods, while modern man is much more likely to think that it is the outworking of impersonal forces, often labeled as "economic determinism" or "dialectical materialism."

An even greater difference may be found between the distinctively Biblical view and that of modern secularized society. In the Bible, God is presented as behind and in history, with the ultimate course determined by His sovereign will; but, for modern man, biological evolution, with its corresponding parallels in other areas of human development, seems sufficient to explain all that has ever happened. The Biblical view is that God speaks to man; but present-day Western man insists that whatever is recorded of such communication is only man's reinterpretation of certain physical and psychological events. The Bible presents God as making man in His image; but contemporary man insists that man has made God in his image, psychologically as a parent substitute or a prop for failure, or philosophically as an excuse for ignorance or a sentimental label for the unknown.

The Bible describes creation as pointing to God, but men today think that things only point to themselves. From the Biblical point of view man's moral troubles stem from his positive rebellion against God and his rehabilitation can be accomplished only as he submits radically to the will of God. Most modern thinkers take the view that man's moral difficulties stem from his finite, weak character, which can be improved only through enlightenment and training. In the Bible the most important question for man is God; but many contemporary philosophers regard the question as irrelevant. They contend that since God cannot be submitted to any controlled experiments, His existence is, not necessarily deniable, but undebatable and for all practical purposes meaningless. The Bible views the future as in the hands of God, with certain decisive events still to be unfolded, in Messiahship and judgment; while the view of most modern thinkers is that from a physical standpoint the earth is ultimately doomed to the deep freeze of entropy, but that meanwhile man will go on evolving, unless he obliterates himself through his own folly.

These significant differences pose no small problem for the expositor of the Biblical message. At the same time, it would be wrong to give a false impression of the differences between the world in which Paul ministered and the world of our own day. Some people tend to speak as though the gulf between first- and twentieth-century man is so vast that some entirely new approach to Biblical truth is required if the concepts of the Bible are to be intellectually respectable or communicable to men of our day.

However, this point of view must not be assumed to be new. Philo in his time felt constrained to "demythologize" the Hebrew Old Testament in order to make it agree with the findings of Greek science; and the Gnostics, who accepted certain elements in Christianity, became adept in reinterpreting the New Testament account to make it more palatable to those who had adopted the philosophical presuppositions of the Greek world. One must not imagine, therefore, that the world in which Paul announced his message was a gullible, naïve sort of society, unacquainted with logical categories or unfamiliar with the practical skepticism of the Sophists or the erudite agnosticism of the Epicureans. True, in a city as sophisticated as ancient Ephesus a mob could be manipulated into bombastic shouting about their patron goddess; but much the same phenomenon is seen in modern times when crowds go into ecstasy over the image of a patron saint. On the other hand, the council of the Areopagus, made up as it was of the ex-magistrates of Athens, consisted of a highly educated group of men, thoroughly familiar with the contemporary canons of truth and quite prepared to question and to rule out as utterly absurd the idea that Jesus Christ arose from the dead.

It is true that the ancient world seems a little naïve in that they "deified" their emperors, but they did so only after "the gods had died." The Emperor Augustus was no Olympian Zeus, and no thinking person ever took seriously the divine claims of the pathetic Caligula or the overbearing Nero. When the gods are no more, almost anyone can be a god. We must not be deceived into thinking that man such as Cicero, Pliny, Lucretius, Marcus Aurelius, or even the Emperor Tiberius himself looked upon the panoply of state religion as anything other than a symbol of uncertain social solidarity, constructed on the broken foundations of antiquated beliefs. To that extent the spirit of the age was very similar to our own, even though the particular beliefs were different. Nevertheless, such orientations to life continue to make the matter of communication one of constant concern for the presentation of real, and not merely supposed, equivalences.

The Lack of Correspondence between Participants

It should be obvious that, despite certain cultural similarities, the participants in the Biblical communication cannot be equated with corresponding participants today. Accordingly, no present-day translator of the Scriptures into English, whom we might designate diagrammatically as ⑤ (i.e., the source of the message as it is communicated into English), can ever really be Ⓐ (i.e., a receptor of the Biblical message as a valid participant in the Biblical culture). True, the scholarly exegete or expositor of the Bible must have a tremendous knowledge of the historical backgrounds of the ancient world, for only within the context of that situation does the Scripture have immediate relevance. Moreover, the Scriptures are no collection of cabalistic writings, in the sense of messages whose meaning is purposely obscured, or intended to be meaningful only to others than those to whom they were historically directed. This fact does not deny the possibility of double application, or the so-called prophetic perspective, but the primary sense of Scripture must be determined in relation to the historical situation in which the message was given, for the writers of Scripture are not Delphic oracles.

However, we must recognize that despite our broad knowledge of Biblical backgrounds there are many matters on which we have little knowledge. In many instances we gain new knowledge and fresh insights as the result of archeological discoveries. Thus, from Nuzi tablets, found in northern Mesopotamia, we learn some of the reasons why Laban was so concerned that Jacob had run away with the *teraphim,* or household gods (Genesis 31). From the Qumran and related materials we have learned more about what Jesus may have meant by the "kingdom of heaven suffering violence and men of violence taking it by force" (Matthew 11:12); for it appears that, to a far greater extent than was previously imagined, various groups who were expecting the establishment of the Messianic kingdom were resorting to militaristic means to impose God's kingdom by force. We are now beginning to explore some of the rich treasures of the intertestamental period and to understand more clearly the cultural environment in which the Christian movement began.

If, however, we can assert emphatically that, even with all available knowledge, no person in our present-day culture can ever be a truly participating member of the Biblical culture (no possible degree of historical reconstruction could even approximate such a condition) it is all the more obvious that no ⑤ (a source in our culture) can possibly be identical with ⑥ (a source in the Biblical culture). In other words, no translator (as one form of communicative source) can ever be equivalent to the original writer of the Scriptures.

A Three-Language Model of Communication

Actual communication of the Biblical message is in many circumstances much more complex than the process we have just described; for the message, as given in Greek and Hebrew, is communicated to us in English, and we in turn must communicate it to others. For some this means the use of a foreign language, often in an utterly divergent cultural context; for others, it requires adjusting to the form of language used by some subculture or distinct ethnic, social, or educational group, each of which has its own distinctive use of language and its own peculiar adaptation of the "world view." We can, however, see the basic problem more clearly if we discuss it in terms of a foreign language context. For this purpose we may employ the following type of diagram, in which the triangles represent the communication in Bible times, the squares the corresponding communication in English, and the circles the forms which such a communication takes in still another language:

The third element in this diagram is the circular culture, with the included communicative event, symbolized as circular source, message, and receptor. In order to highlight the fundamental problems and contrasts, we can best describe the differences in terms of the

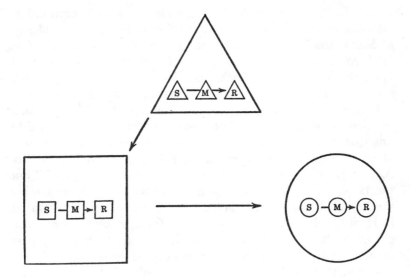

formal nonidentity of "square" and "circular" messages and cultures, and the distinctive relationship of the messages to the cultures.

The Formal Nonidentity of Messages

If the differences between the forms of messages in the Biblical and contemporary Western contexts seem to be of dissimilar kind and degree, then the contrast between the forms of messages in English and in other languages of the world will appear at times to be extremely great. Again, these differences apply to all levels: words, grammar, and events.

Almost everyone will admit that languages inevitably differ in the shades of meaning of words for such abstract concepts as "love" and "sin," but they are usually less aware of the wide range of differences which exist in all types of words and on all levels of meaning. *Repentance* in the New Testament is often explained as "changing the mind," and this is the literal significance of the Greek *metanoia.* Actually, however, the Greek word connotes a much more profound psychological transformation than is implied in merely changing one's mind, involving not only one's intellectual processes, but also and primarily the will and "heart." In other languages, however, there are many different ways of discussing such a psychological change. In Kekchi, a language of Guatemala, repentance is literally "it pains my heart." In Baouli, in West Africa, the same concept is expressed as "it hurts so much I want to quit." In the Northern Sotho language of South Africa, this spiritual experience is graphically described as "it becomes untwisted." The Chols of southern Mexico speak of "my heart is turning itself back," and the nearby Tzeltals express the same idea in the phrase "my heart returns because of my sin."

Even those who recognize that quite different types of expression may have very similar areas of meaning are nevertheless perplexed to find that the formal structure of certain languages prevents one from saying things which are routine in another language. In Hopi, a Uto-Aztecan language spoken in Arizona, one cannot say "my God." For the Hopis "God" is a word which simply cannot be possessed. He can be called "my Father," but the real equivalent of "my God" is in Hopi "God in whom I believe." There are, of course, many languages in which one cannot say "God is love," for there is simply no noun for "love." Not that people cannot express the concept of "love" —they most certainly can and do; but since it is regarded as essentially an event, not an object, it falls into the class of verbs. Hence one can only say "God loves" or "God is one who loves," but the abstract noun "love," without indication of when, how, where, or who loves, does not exist in many languages.

Many expressions naturally reflect the practical circumstances of life in which such terms have come to be used. The Hopis, for example, would never speak of weeds "choking out a plant," for in the ecology of Hopi farming weeds "dry out the plants." Moreover, the way in which people describe events depends not only upon the nature of their habitat, but often as well upon their beliefs about religious experience. The Hopi concept of the dead passing through the sky to the west prompted a Hopi child some years ago to explain the first noisy airplane he had ever seen as "a truck that has died and is going through the sky."

The Formal Nonidentity of Cultures

As already noted, the basis of many formal differences in messages is the distinctions that underlie diverse cultural traits. For us a dove often symbolizes "peace," for this is a long heritage, beginning with the story of Noah and the dove that brought back the token of new life. But for the Indians of America such a bird symbol would denote "haste" and "speed." For us virginity seems a highly desirable attribute in the bride, but in many parts of Africa a young woman who has already given birth to a child is regarded as a more desirable bride, for she has proved her capacity for childbearing. This preference for proof of fertility rather than virginity reflects the concept of marriage as centered in child production, while for us it is centered in sex relations. Our present Western world has become highly interested in dreams as symbols of a hidden reality. For the Kaka of the Cameroun dreams are a quite common means of prophecy, often with dire consequences, for a dream of incest means imminent death, but a dream about extramarital relations is regarded as a sign of the greatest good fortune.

While we here emphasize the important contrast between the "square" and various "circular" cultures, we must not overlook the fact that, in a sense, our diagram of triangles, squares, and circles is a distortion of certain relationships. The circular form seems entirely different from the square and triangle; but if we carefully examine the whole range of cultures throughout the world, we soon discover that our Western modern culture is actually the aberrant one. We are the ones who are so vastly different, with our highly involved technology, specialized division of labor, impersonal systems of communication, and unprecedented mobility (geographical, social, occupational and ideological). We ourselves often find it more difficult to understand the message of the Scriptures than do many peoples of other cultures, who are far more at home with such features as cities of refuge, blood revenge, sacrificial atonement, redemption of relatives, levirate marriage, polygamy, clans, paternal blessing, and government by a council of the elders. An attempt to determine why God chose the Jewish people as His channel of communication—any such inquiry must be highly speculative, for who can know "the mind of God"?—will certainly find no basis in the often claimed sublimity of Hebrew idioms or the elegance of Greek grammar. Chinese is far more flexible in idiomatic structure than Hebrew, and Zulu is formally a more precise language than Greek. The selection of the Jewish people can be understood in some measure on the basis that God chose to reveal Himself through a people who, there at the crossroads of so many cultural influences at that point in world history, possessed a culture with greater similarities to a greater number of other cultures than has existed at any other time in the history of mankind. It is, therefore, in large measure because of basic cultural commonalities that the message of the Scriptures is communicated with so much force and intelligibility.

In contrasting cultures we must not, however, restrict our point of view to an assortment of isolated traits. We need to see the differences in their broadest possible perspective, in terms of a people's "world view," or system of values. In the total system the contrasts between people become even more striking.

In Bantu Africa there is a welter of different beliefs, some seemingly quite contradictory, but out of these highly divergent sets of views about the world and reality emerge some highly significant concepts with wide acceptance and relevance. For example, these Africans do not distinguish as sharply between themselves and "nonman" as do we, who regard such a distinction as inevitable in view of the philosophical "revolution" introduced by Descartes. Rather, Bantu people in general relate themselves very closely to their lineage, the world of nature around them, and the realm of the supernatural. Each living person is conceived of as constituting merely a link in the chain which unites him with his ancestors before him and the descendants who will follow him. With these ancestors he is in very intimate contact, for they communicate with him in dreams and bestow benefits upon him. In return he must maintain a filial regard for these benefactors, must prevent them from becoming disgruntled or angry, and by proper offerings sustain them in their efforts to help the living from the realm of the dead.

In addition to this close tie with the ancestral spirits, who may in fact be reincarnated as a man's own offspring, many Africans feel themselves very much a part of the nature surrounding them. Some are related to the world of nature through ancestors who were animals, e.g., crocodiles, lions, leopards, turtles, vipers, buffalo, or gazelles; and such clan totems make a man personally conscious of the animal world, for he must avoid the flesh of his own totemic "relatives," must make proper atonement if perchance he kills such animal kin, and must depend upon his kinship with the animal world for certain types of protection and success. Not only are certain animals, and even plants and insects, totemically related to people, but certain individuals are thought to be able to transform themselves into animals. Thus some animals are believed to be merely men in disguise. Furthermore, the spirits of animals are regarded as not too different from those of men. In the whole world of nature live innumerable spirits, in gnarled trees, deep pools, strangely formed rocks, and re-mote mountains. These spirits are like people in that they are good and bad, helpful and malevolent, prank-playing and vicious, depend-able and irresponsible.

Moreover, man is linked not only with his ancestors and with nature, but also with the supernatural world. At one point this world is represented by ancestors, who may even be deified and thus bring men in touch with the gods. At the same time the nearby spirits of nature may serve to establish the close tie of man with the super-natural world, by means of which he can divine the future, guarantee abundant harvests, insure prosperity, and invoke blessings upon his descendants.

The view of the world held by many an African is based on some entirely false assumptions, but it serves to relate him to his world and to help him find his place. Though inimical spirits may haunt him and ancestors threaten him, both spirits and ancestors have one principal goal, namely, the maintaining of traditional values and patterns of behavior. He can therefore feel quite at home within the security of the ancestral village and the old way of life.

Unless we understand these different systems of values, we almost inevitably misjudge those who hold them. For example, Africans are often accused of crass materialism, even going beyond Westerners in this respect. But the African's quest for things does not arise out of the same cultural background, for in a sense he may be said to have a "spiritual reason" for his materialism. In terms of his ultimate values, what counts most is "life," but not in the sense of continuing exist-ence, as thought of by the typical European or American. Life for the African means "life force" or "life potency," which comes primarily from ancestors and is passed on to descendants. This force manifests itself during life by outstanding skills, exceptional leadership ability, and the control over spirits, people, and things. Things, then, become an obvious means of validating this "power," for wealth is a symbol of an inner power which brings victory in war, luck in love, and success in acquiring riches. Thus things are not mere ends in them-selves—as they may be with us—but instruments for confirming the possession of a *force vitale*.

There is a sense, however, in which the African's view of power and wealth is not much different from certain aspects of the Puritan ethic, in which it was presumed that the proof of God's blessing upon a man's efforts was to be found in his evident prosperity. Financial security becomes then not only an end in itself, but a means of proving one's spiritual capacities. In many respects church people in America have outgrown this unholy alliance of money and religion, but it still tends to haunt those of "lesser faith," who not infrequently assess the rightness of a program by the amount of money which is sent in "by God's children" or the success of a minister by the size of his salary.

In contrast with the view of the world held by many Africans, the philosophical orientation of the East, with the exception of the importation of Communism as an ideology from the West, is very different.[5] In the East there is no basic concern for progress as we know it, and no constant drive toward Utopias where life may be fitted to certain ideas. Rather, men strive for "release from everything," as characterized by the philosophy of India, "the wisdom of nonbeing" as taught in Taoism, and "the vast impartiality" as developed in Confucianism. Moreover, men believe that thought itself should not be so neatly discursive, so logically bound as it is in the "square and earthly" categories of the West, but should be "round and spiritual" as in the East. There one can fluctuate readily from the specific to the general and from the concrete to the abstract, with a free-flowing abandon of intuitive insight, and without having to be rigidly departmentalized by Aristotelian canons of truth.

In the East such a view of truth is necessary, for real existence is regarded as cultural, lived within the microcosm of the family and the macrocosm of humanity, but with constant reference to continuity, in respect to the past as well as the future. If man is to live within society, he can do so only because fundamentally he is in harmony with the universe and is capable of complete adjustment. At this point, of course, the East differs from the West, which conceives of man as essentially struggling against a nature that is basically evil and in need of regeneration. For the East there are many ways by which truth may be attained, and many paths which lead to heaven.

Hinduism has developed a special emphasis in the philosophy of the East, namely, the priority of spirit over matter. In philosophical Hinduism there is only one ultimate reality, and that is spirit. This reality is the transforming energy of the universe, which consists of matter and which is both inferior and evil. Thus all of life is to be judged on a scale of greater spirituality, but it is all bound together by the inexorable historical process of *karma*, which allots to each person a *dharma* defining his place and role in this matter-to-spirit development. Final escape from this process is the primary goal.

So different is this view of life from our own that it scarcely seems comprehensible, but the views held by those even closer to our society also present highly significant contrasts to our own. Latin American society, for example, has been traditionally authoritarian in religion, politics, and education.[6] Its dominant theme can be summarized as "error has no rights." Hence heresy must be detected by the church and prosecuted by the state, strong men will not brook opposition, and education must follow the "given line," with all the implications of censorship and indices of forbidden books. Concomitant with this authoritarianism is a kind of passive fatalism, which no doubt has its source partly in North African Islamic importations into the Iberian peninsula and thence to Latin America. However, it is also an indigenous and a highly congenial belief among many of the Indian groups living in this hemisphere. The ancient Aztecs believed, for example, that a man's destiny was determined at the time of his birth by a conflict between God and the devil, who fought it out in the open fire kindled in the room where the baby was born.

In Latin America a concept of irrevocable sinfulness of the flesh, rather than fundamental rebellion against the will of God, has led in some measure to a denial of moral responsibility. Hence religion becomes primarily a technique for helping man over the crises of life by paid professional assistance, rather than a means by which life may be transformed in such a way that one is enabled to withstand temptation and develop deep inner convictions of right and wrong.

Again, in Latin America the basic distinction between the sacred and secular, as symbolized by the altar rail, which excludes the non-ordained from the full benefits and mysteries of the church, tends to place a high premium on so-called "spiritual work." The result of exalting the "sacred" at the expense of the "secular" is ultimately to debase all of life. Nevertheless, this non-Biblical distinction does set the priesthood off as a special class of people who engage essentially in intellectual activities. Their work is thus regarded as inherently superior and for such a person to soil his hands with mundane activities is accordingly regarded as debasing and wrong. In Latin America the problem has been that this same distinction of the superiority of the intellectual over the manual has crept into the professions, and hence the engineer must not get his hands dirty, or the lawyer, if he is to maintain prestige, must not be seen carrying his briefcase. Professional privilege thus becomes a more dominant theme than the dignity of labor.

One key to the orientation of Latin life is the phrase *la dignidad de la persona*, literally, "the dignity of the individual." The difficulty is that the Spanish world has never quite decided just who is *la persona*, "the individual." At times the idealistic fervor for social justice would make one think that *la persona* means *cada persona*, "each person"; but in many instances typical behavior seems to indicate that the phrase should be *la dignidad de mi persona*, "the dignity of my person." The paradoxical dualism of Don Quixote, the altruistic idealist, and Sancho Panza, the sanguine realist, continues to this day as part of the basic conflict in Latin life, where so many initially well-meaning revolutionaries have ended up as intolerable dictators.

Running through the fabric of Latin life is a constant emphasis upon the human aspects of existence—the meaning of friendship, the ties of family, and the loyal attachment to personal leadership which gives rise to the "personalism" in government and politics making possible the rise of the strong leader, or *caudillo*. Such a leader is more or less expected to use the social structure of society as a means of giving it direction. In general, he does not wait for society to select him, much less to force him to run for office (Latin America rarely has a reluctant candidate); to fulfill his destiny he must express his leadership by building up a personal following. As he views the world, *un indio sin patrón es coma rueda sin eje*, "an Indian without a master is like a wheel without an axle." Nor can humanity without his leadership fulfill its true destiny, or his.

Another feature of Latin life highly significant in providing that distinctive quality so apparent in its intellectual life is the belief that truth is not to be found primarily by any tedious processes of discursive logic, but by the flash of insight, the intuitive inspiration, and the beatific vision. Reality is more fittingly expressed, therefore, in poetry than in philosophical discourse. The novelist is thus closer to social truth than the sociologist and the propagandist than the writer of tedious volumes of fact.

It would be wrong to conclude that all Latin American life fits precisely this framework. Many liberalizing influences have blunted the traditional authoritarianism, broken down the social barriers and the privileges of the professional caste, brought into leadership men of unselfish ambition, and developed a sense of responsibility and intellectual integrity in the administration of justice, in national leadership, and in scholarship. Nevertheless, for the masses the three principles of miracle, mystery, and authority, so penetratingly depicted by Dostoevski, constitute dominant elements in the social and theological outlook of Latin society.

Protestant missionaries in Latin America, in attempting to introduce quite a different orientation toward life and truth, are sometimes quite unaware of these fundamentally diverse viewpoints. They tend to pass off resistance to the "Protestant ethic" as merely moral perverseness or fanatical superstition. Often they fail completely to realize the tremendous cultural adjustment they preach as a part of the gospel, or to allow for the fact that, both in explicit content and implicit assumptions, they operate on entirely different premises from most Latins. For example, they declare the right of private judgment, even on such matters as ultimate truth. For them authority rests not in the tradition of the church, but in a book, the Bible, which all men are said to be able to interpret. Even though men may be in error, they declare, the right to maintain such error must be defended by those who know the truth. Furthermore, they say that man is actively responsible for every aspect of his life, and if his faith is not accompanied by consistent works—sometimes defined in terms of the special mores of the group—then not even the church can help him. In addition, they insist that all labor is ultimately sacred, for each man has his calling from God. Thus the privilege of the few is basically abrogated. Religion is presented, not as a technique for passing through crises, but of acquiring that moral strength which will enable one to meet head-on issues where not even the assistance of the priest avails. It is true that Protestantism lays great emphasis upon the individual, but primarily in terms of his responsibilities within society, not his prerogatives as a member of society. Truth is usually explained as discoverable by discursive logic, based on accumulated facts, not through intuitive insight.

If we ask whether most people, whether Africans, Orientals, Latins, or Americans, all of whom represent distinct orientations toward life, are conscious of the fundamental characteristics of their world views, we must of course say "No." A society rarely becomes aware of its traditional assumptions until they are seriously challenged or no longer seem adequate.[7] In fact, it is often the outsider who can best see some of the orientations we take for granted. Alicja Iwanska, a Polish anthropologist, has made some highly significant observations about certain aspects of the world view of many people in the American Pacific Northwest.[8] She has shown that many white American farmers unconsciously divide their world into three basic categories: (1) the landscape, including the beautiful scenery of that part of Oregon and Washington; (2) machinery, their investment in mechanized agriculture, including their farms (for the farms are not essentially part of the scenery, but an element in production—hence equivalent to machinery); and (3) people, including their neighbors, friends, and relatives. It is significant, however, that two types of people are not classed with other people, but with scenery and machinery. These include the Indians, who are regarded as properly placed on reservations, to be looked upon as part of the beauties of nature, but not to be associated with in the towns or rural communities. These farmers would never think of Indians as not being human beings, but in their unconscious view of the world as a whole, Indians belong primarily with the scenery, not in society. Mexican farm laborers, on the other hand, are classed with machinery. They are negotiated for on the same basis as any other farm tools and are taken care of on the basis that one must take good care of machinery if one expects to get satisfactory performance from it. The Mexican laborers are, of course, also human beings. No farmer would deny it, but nevertheless they are regarded as in a very different class from those persons with whom one expects to have interpersonal relations.

Our real problem at this point is to recognize the fact that theoretical classifications of phenomena and those which result from actual behavior are often very different. Any one of these farmers would insist that Indians, Mexicans, and whites are all human beings, and that they are really different from scenery and machinery. This view, however, represents only the ideal structure, resulting from what one has been taught about the logical categories of the world. The real structure, which determines value judgments and interpersonal behavior, rests upon quite different presuppositions.

Various surveys of religious opinion in America indicate that over 95 per cent of the people insist that they believe in God. Nevertheless, actual behavior would indicate that for over 50 per cent of these people belief in God has practically nothing to do with their behavior.

As far as they are concerned, God makes few if any moral demands, and they do not formally express this belief in any overt manner. Of course, for some of these persons God is nothing more than "first cause" or "ultimate reality," but these more sophisticated concepts are not shared by a very large part of the population which claims to believe in God. For the vast majority one can only conclude that there is a wide gap between ideal and real behavior; that is, between (1) saying that one believes in God (for that is quite the thing to do in our society) and (2) regulating one's life entirely without reference to God (which is secularism) or determining one's values without concern for God (which is materialism). We cannot, of course, overlook the indirect effects which "ideal behavior" or responses may have on people. But when the culturally acceptable masks are stripped away, one comes face to face with actual behavior and the basic concepts that ultimately govern what men do.

The Meaning of a Message in Terms of the Cultural Context

The essential importance of the real cultural context in which communication takes place is that only in terms of this setting does any message have significance. Protestant missionaries who first went to the Navajos assumed that they would of necessity have to use the English word "God" if the Navajos were really to understand the spiritual nature of God. Unfortunately, the English pronunciation of "God" was very similar to the Navajo word for "juniper bush." Even to this day many Navajos think of the white man's religion as the worship of the juniper bush. Later, however, missionaries learned that in order to communicate effectively they must change the name of God to the Navajo equivalent of "the eternal spirit," which then made sense, for it had relevance within the context of the Navajo culture.

On the other hand, early Roman Catholic missionaries to Mexico and Guatemala encountered a ready response to the symbol of the Sacred Heart, portrayed not only as the sacred heart of Jesus but also of Mary. However, this exposed heart had quite a different significance to the Indians. To them it was the sacrificial heart taken from human sacrifices and offered to the pagan deities. However, since the erroneous reinterpretation was nevertheless one that prompted deep religious sentiments, it became a powerful instrument in winning the loyalty of the untutored masses, who quickly identified *Dios*, "God," as the sun and *María*, "Mary," as the moon. In many instances they carved these symbols into the stone above the entrances to their churches.

No symbols can have meaning of and through themselves; they always stand for something else. This assigning of "meaning" is done by the culture. Thus there are no universal symbols immediately apprehended by all mankind. Even the masculinity of the sun and the feminine character of the moon, so widely recognized in many parts of the world, is not universal, for in some cultures the reverse interpretation is understood. The symbolism of sacrifice is widely known, but in some areas, e.g., among the Pueblo Indians of the Southwest, sacrifice was not practiced. Whether, therefore, a symbol is widespread or is interpreted in a particular manner is essentially a cultural matter, not inherent within the nature of the symbol, but dependent upon the way in which a particular people chooses to apprehend such an object or event.

The Purpose of Communicative Procedures

Since the forms of messages are quite different in diverse cultures, and since these messages are dependent upon utterly different cultures for the basis of their significance, it is evident that no great amount of communication can be effected by teaching a receptor in, for example, a "circle culture" merely to recognize the form of the message in a "triangle culture." Such a message would be quite irrelevant, for the receptor would not be able to reproduce the circumstances in which the earlier message had significance. On the other hand, it is equally false to assume that in order to communicate one must reproduce all the circumstances of one culture within some isolated segment of another; that is to say, to try to construct a square cultural enclave in the circular society, thus "detribalizing" the people in order to communicate to them. This, of course, is part of the theory which lies behind the tendency to "transplant churches" rather than "to sow the seed of the gospel."

We can describe the lack of correspondence in the formal structure of messages by saying that ⊡ ≠ ⚠ and that Ⓜ ≠ ⊡. In other words, the form of the message in a square culture does not equal the form of the message in a triangle culture. Similarly, the form of message in a circular culture does not equal the form of message in a square culture. However, these differences of form between messages in different cultures should not concern us unduly, for we seek, not a formal equivalence, but a functional one. In other words, we want to be sure that ⓡ is able to respond to ⓜ within the context of his own culture in substantially the same manner as ⚠ responded to ⚠ within the setting of the Biblical culture. Thus, in substantially the same way as the message which came to men and women in Greek and Hebrew could be designated as "the Word of God," so this message that comes to the people in English or any other language can be "the Word of God" to them, for it is by and through this revealing message that God speaks. We are concerned, that is to say, with a dynamic, not a static, equivalence.

If, however, this equivalence is to be understandable, two principal factors must be involved: (1) in speaking to those with limited knowledge of the total message the communicator must select from the revelation these features which are culturally relevant, and (2) he must find certain cultural parallels which will make such a message significant within the immediate context of people's lives.

The selection of culturally relevant material from the revelation of God has always been the practice of the church. In the early centuries, for example, the atonement wrought by Christ on the cross was generally spoken of in terms of the great conflict between Christ and Satan in which, through "the cross and the empty tomb," Christ gained the victory over Satan and death. During the time of the Reformation, and down until more recent decades, one of the most common interpretations of the atonement has been substitutionary, in the sense that Christ took upon himself our sins and died in our place as a substitute sacrifice.[9] This interpretation, true and valuable as it may be for many, is not communicable to many persons today, for they simply do not think in such categories. For these persons, many of whom are keenly aware of the tragic conflicts that divide and alienate untold millions of people, the presentation of the atonement in terms of reconciliation is more meaningful, since in this way they can understand more readily how God could be in Christ reconciling the world to Himself (2 Corinthians 5:19).

The fact that, in three different stages of the church's history, people have chosen to communicate the significance of the atonement in these different but complementary and Biblical ways, does not mean that anyone of these views is necessarily wrong. Quite the contrary, they are all true, for the Scriptures do not restrict the explanation of this supreme encounter of God with man to one set of symbols. Rather, the fact of God's grace is presented in several ways in order that something of its relevance may break through to our consciousness within the context of our lives, which are so diversely ordered and hence dependent upon different facets of divine revelation.

This same fact is true of many elements in the Scriptures. The 23rd Psalm, for example, is for us and many others a great source of revelation about God and his dealings with his faithful believers. But for many peoples this Psalm is quite meaningless, for either they have no knowledge of sheep or the sheep they have may be scavengers, as in many parts of Africa. Actually, the most popular Psalm, as far as different cultures are concerned, is the first, which contains an abundance of figures of speech which have almost daily relevance to the lives of countless millions of people: "walking in the counsel of the ungodly," "tree planted by rivers of water," "his leaf shall not wither," "the chaff which the wind drives away," and "the way of the righteous."

In addition to the selection of culturally relevant elements in the Scriptures, one must find cultural parallels which will make possible an apprehension of the Biblical truth within the context of contemporary life. A modern preacher in one of our urban centers can and does explain to people the meaning of the parable about the "Vine and Branches." But for all his explanations this parable is likely not to be too significant because most of the people have never pruned a grapevine and know scarcely anything about its manner of growth or the practice of burning the dead and fruitless runners. They can, however, appreciate the basic principle of the need of the branch to be associated with the vinestock if the preacher uses the analogy of electrical household appliances, which cannot function unless they are properly plugged in. However, he may go on to point out that in the same way that a short in the appliances will blow a fuse and thus prevent injury, so God cannot permit the power of His Spirit to flow through sinful lives. Such contemporary analogies are not substitutes for the Biblical message, but, rather, useful supplements to the communication, to help people comprehend something of the present-day relevance of the message to their own way of life. They must, however, be used with caution, for even as in the parallel just cited the Spirit must not be thought of as an impersonal force but as one who establishes a living relationship.

Much missionary work has been unduly hampered by lack of adequate parallels within the indigenous culture. Early missionaries to the Hopis in Arizona assumed (as did the missionaries to the Navajos, referred to above) that the Indians would have to understand God in terms of His English name. But this word never meant much to the people, except as a foreign name for a strange being. If, however, the missionaries had studied the Hopi religion—perhaps one of the most spiritual of the indigenous religions of North America— they soon would have discovered that behind the sacred powers addressed in prayer there are two principal deities: (1) *Pas-nap-qatuhqa* and (2) *Nukpan*. The second is "the destructive one" and roughly equivalent to the Christian concept of the devil; the first is the good deity who is the ultimate source of power and whose name means "the one who exists by virtue of his very existence" (strikingly similar to the interpretation of Yahweh in the context "I am that I am"). Present revisions of the Scriptures in Hopi are using this term, readily acceptable by several of the Hopi Christians with such comments as, "Why didn't you use that name before? Then we could have understood."

CHAPTER 4

Symbols and Their Meaning

> *So out of the ground the Lord God formed
> every beast of the field and every bird of the
> air, and brought them to the man to see what
> he would call them; and whatever the man
> called every living creature, that was its name.
> The man gave names to all cattle, and to the
> birds of the air, and to every beast of the field.*
> —·GENESIS 2:19–20a

Language As a Communication Code

IN a children's meeting on an Indian reservation in the United States, a missionary asked the boys and girls, "How are we saved?" to which everyone responded in unison, "By the blood." But what did this symbol, "blood," mean to them? Certainly it did not mean the same as to the missionary, as was evident in the fact that the children never spoke of "the blood," except in answer to that particular question in the catechism. The expression "the blood" is a very important one in the history of the Christian faith. But of what is it a symbol? What is its real meaning? What is the event in history for which it stands, and what conceptions of it are held by people who employ this term in a Christian context? These are vital questions, but they cannot be answered unless we first explore the nature of language as a code, the encoding and decoding of the message by participants in the communication and the meaning of the symbols used.

Language, the most complex and significant code employed by man, consists essentially of sounds, shapes, and a system. Of the thousands of perceptually distinct sounds the vocal apparatus can make, each language uses a limited selection of sounds to distinguish meaning.

That is to say, the human voice can make many hundreds of different types of sounds; but in any one language no more than a dozen to sixty sound distinctions (technically called "phonemes") are used as basic elements in the formation of the meaningful units in the code (technically called "morphemes"). These morphemes (minimal forms of speech which have meaning) are the elementary building blocks of the meaningful structure of the language. In English they consist not only of roots, whether "free," as in *boy, man, dog,* or "bound" to some other element, as in *-ceive, -sist,* or *lingu-* (cf. *receive, deceive, consist, insist,* and *linguist, lingual*), but also of affixes, such as *re-, con-, de- in-, -ist, -al.* Other languages may have quite differently shaped roots, and the affixes may include not only prefixes and suffixes, elements placed before and after the roots, but infixes, forms occurring within roots, and suprafixes, principally intonational features superimposed upon other "shapes."

However, a language code must consist of more than mere sounds and shapes. It must go together in a systematic way, or no two people could use the code. No one could possibly remember thousands of unique utterances. What is more, a language to be really useful must have the potentiality of endless generation of new expressions.

An obvious feature of any language system is that there are strict rules governing what can and cannot be said. Though people may recognize this in their mother tongue and are quick to notice grammatical mistakes, they may deny the existence of a grammatical system in certain other languages. In Bolivian Quechua, for example, one can produce very long words, which are perfectly proper and actually used, as in the case of the word *phiniquichipushallawarkanquichejtajchari,* meaning "I expect you caused me to continually jump around for some one"; but though this word is made up of twelve different basic shapes (i.e., morphemes) they are selected according to strict rules of the grammatical system. This word would be just as meaningless in an altered order of elements as *mentestablreish* is for English speakers, though this nonsense form is only *reestablishment* scrambled.

On the level of syntax we would not normally use the order *John away ran,* though we can say *Away ran John,* and *John ran away;* nor would we combine grammatical forms such as *This man am go,* for *This man is going.* Why is it that we must use certain orders, and that after some words we use one grammatical form and after others different forms? Why, for example, must we have eight forms for the verb *to be*—namely, *am, is, are, was, were, be, been* and *being*—while for another verb we rarely have more than four or five, e.g., *sell, selling, sells,* and *sold*; and *ride, riding, rides, rode,* and *ridden*; and in some cases only three, e.g., *hit, hitting, hits?* There are really no absolute reasons for these usages except the history of language development. However, the very arbitrariness of English, or of any language, is evidence of the underlying system of the code or set of rules, regardless of irregularities which govern the ways in which the code is and can be used.

The code of language is only one part of human behavior, but it is perhaps the most unquestioned of all our patterns of behavior because it appears so unchangeable. We are seldom aware of the actual changes going on continuously, if imperceptibly. This relatively unchanging character of language, in addition to the fact that it is essential to every aspect of our lives, from courtship to war and from calling pets to entreating God, gives it an exalted status in our thinking. We realize that we must use it constantly in the very process of thinking. Moreover, despite the arbitrariness and irregularities of language we usually become enamored of it, for it is the very tool with which we test reality. That is to say, we think about something and then we compare our manipulation of word symbols with our perception of the world about us. Soon we become convinced that here is not merely a code, but a canon of truth; not just a set of symbols, but a right way of perceiving the universe. Then the mechanics of sounds, shapes, and the system disappear, and we imagine we have pierced the veil of the ultimate.

We are, however, brought up short when we hear of animals and insects having "a language." We learn, for example, that when a bee returns to the hive, after having found a new source of honey, it can communicate to other bees not only the direction of the find but approximately the distance. If, for example, the distance of the nectar is less than 28 yards away, the bee does a round dance, if the source is from 28 to 200 yards away, a "waggle" dance is added; and if over 200 yards away, the dance is completely a "waggle." The number of turns and waggles of the abdomen from side to side is correlated with the distance. The direction, on the other hand, is shown by the direction of the dance, as it is related to the position of the sun.[1]

Similarly, jackdaws have a kind of rattle expressing anger. It excites other birds to attack a person, especially if he happens to be carrying some black dangling or fluttering object. Everyone familiar with chickens can soon distinguish the cackling of a hen when she has laid an egg, her clucking as she leads little chicks in search of food, the sound of alarm when a hawk swoops down from the sky, and the squawk of terror when a snake or raccoon steals into the chicken shed.

There is no doubt that these different types of sounds communicate. But do they constitute a language? If not, how do they differ from human speech?

Signs and Symbols

In order to understand the essential nature of a language code, we must distinguish carefully between signs and symbols, for though they are closely related, there is an essential distinction which must be carefully noted.[2]

A sign may be said to indicate the existence of a particular thing, event, or condition within a context. Wet streets are a sign that it has rained, rustling leaves are a sign of wind, smoke a sign of fire. All these are so-called natural signs. But there may also be cultural ones, e.g., crepe on the door (a sign of death), streamers and tin cans tied to a car (a sign that someone has recently been married), and a clerical collar (a sign that the wearer is a clergyman). We are in fact constantly surrounded by signs in our lives: barber poles, arrows, buzzers, numbers on houses, lanes marked on highways, illuminated shapes of ice-cream cones on the tops of buildings, and the odor of good food being prepared in the kitchen. All these signs point to immediate features in the environment. They are analogous to signs that occur in communication in the animal world, where the signals employed (barking of dogs, singing of birds, and dancing of bees) are all signs of an immediately evident element in the environment.

With symbols the situation is quite different, for a symbol can be used quite apart from its immediate context or stimuli. We may, for example, talk about rain without its raining, either in the immediate past, present, or future. Similarly, we can use the symbol *death* without implying that it is a sign of some immediate event. It is only a label we use to identify a concept. Signs identify some feature of our environment, but a symbol is an instrument by which we label and manipulate our conceptions. In other words, it is the conceptions, not the things, that symbols directly "mean."[3] By means of these instruments we can, so to speak, take hold of the objects outside of our immediate world and reorganize them into quite different combinations.

There are, of course, various types of symbols. The most obvious distinction we can usefully make is between (1) "pure symbols" and (2) "iconic symbols." The pure symbols in no way partake of the properties of their referents. That is to say, they are not like the things to which they refer, any more than *boy* by the very sound characterizes a young male human or *girl* stands for a corresponding female. These words, *boy* and *girl*, are completely arbitrary in form, and as such constitute pure symbols. Iconic symbols, on the other hand, do partake of some of the properties of their referents. For example, the cross is an iconic symbol of the death of Jesus Christ, for it duplicates in form the instrument by which Jesus was killed, since it has some of the physical characteristics of that event. Similarly, rituals, dramas, pictures, architecture, and dances are iconic in that they "portray" in one way or another some of the physical properties of the referents for which they stand. Some words, however, are also to a limited degree iconic, if the onomatopoeic character of the sounds is designed to imitate the sound of the objects to which these words refer, e.g., *bowwow, cockadoodledoo,* and *meow.*

The distinction between "pure" and "iconic" is not the only way in which we can distinguish symbols, for we are concerned not only with the referents, but also with the convertibility of symbols from one system to another. For example, if we arrange a set of mathematical symbols into a formula, we can always "translate" such a formula into language. That is to say, it can be put into a lineal "syntactic" order. These types of symbols we can speak of as "discursive," for they are translatable into discourse. But we cannot translate certain other types of symbols, e.g., the symmetrical lines of an elegant Greek vase, the startling imagery of a voodoo dance, or the thrilling score of a Beethoven symphony. These meaningful symbolic forms cannot be translated element by element into language, for their symbolism is of a different type. This type may be described as "presentational," in contrast with the "discursive forms" which are equatable with linguistic formulations.[4]

Characteristics of Symbols and Codes

Before we attempt to treat the meaning of linguistic symbols, we must consider briefly some of their fundamental characteristics. First, they are essentially arbitrary. Even a so-called "natural response" symbol, such as *Ouch!* is arbitrary in form, for in Spanish one says *Ay Ay!*, not *Ouch!* Moreover, the relation of form to referent is arbitrary. The *lion* belongs to the *cat* family, but there is nothing in the linguistic forms *lion* and *cat* to suggest this biological affinity. Certainly the arbitrariness of linguistic usage is nowhere better illustrated than in the way in which languages so diversely describe similar psychological phenomena. In Tzeltal, a language of southern Mexico, one can speak of faith as "hanging onto God with the heart," while in Valiente, a language of Panama, one must say "to lean on God." On the other hand, the Anuaks of the Sudan say that faith is "putting oneself in God's hands," and the nearby Uduks to the north claim that faith is "joining God's word to one's body."

This arbitrariness is not limited to the relation between symbols and types of referents, but is applicable as well to the ways in which languages dissect various areas of experience. Though experts are able to distinguish over half a million different tints of colors, in English there are generally only eight principal color words, and less than 4,000 descriptive labels used by the experts. In some languages, e.g., Tarahumara, spoken in Mexico, there are only five basic color words, and some languages in West Africa have only three. In many languages, one's relatives may be designated by literally scores of words, depending, for example, whether one's uncle is on the father's or mother's side or whether he is younger than one's father or older. Similarly, a cousin of the same sex as oneself may have one type of name, but if he or she is of a different sex from the speaker, then quite a different name is used. At times the "labels" of cousins can be reversed, depending upon whether the cousin is related through one's father or mother. In fact, there seem to be almost no limits to the minute classification of one's relatives.

Not only are symbols arbitrary; they must also have a certain amount of conventional acceptance by the community that uses them, while at the same time they must not be dependent upon the immediate context; that is to say, they are not signs, but can be used freely in all sorts of situations.

Another highly essential feature of symbols is the adaptability to certain individual differences of usage. In fact, word symbols as uttered by different persons are always different, often by quite imperceptible degrees. In most instances we can recognize that different persons pronounce the same symbol in slightly different ways, that is to say, with different tone of voice, pronunciation of vowels, speed of utterance, and general voice quality. There are limits to such individual variation, but within these limits such differences must be permissible or speech and communication would be quite impossible, for people's voices are simply not identical.

Not only do symbols have a wide range of slightly different forms; they must also have a range of meaning. That is to say, symbols are not of much use if they stand for one thing and one thing only. Rather, they refer really to classes of things, e.g., leaves, chairs, houses, poles, fish, and monkeys. Too often we imagine that a word has one meaning and only one, but this is an illusion, for a fundamental prerequisite of a usable symbol is that it may be used to refer to a plurality of objects or events. Even the word "God" is a symbol for a great many different conceptions of Deity, and even the unique proper name "Jesus Christ" is not a symbol for merely one concept, complex as this one concept may be. Scholars make distinctions, for example, between the concept of Jesus Christ as presented in the Synoptics and that presented in the Gospel of John. Certainly when a child speaks of Jesus Christ, his conception is quite different from that of a theologian or an average adult Christian.

These symbols, with all their arbitrariness, dependence upon convention, individual differences of form, and diversities of meaning, are the basic ingredients of a language code, which consists of symbols and a system for their arrangement. Such a system again involves arbitrariness, but this time in the matter of (1) order of arrangement (e.g., in some languages the subject precedes the predicate and in others it follows); and (2) the way in which the relations between the symbols are marked—whether, for example, by similar affixes or by the order of words. The important thing is that in any system the same symbols may be used in many different positions, for only in this way can new combinations be produced—and unless we can say something we have never heard, we are really only parrots, not human beings.

The Limitation of Symbols

One of the basic facts about symbols is that they are both useful and difficult to use; that they both reveal and obscure. On the one hand, they reveal truth, for they help us to identify, explore, and interchange conceptions; but they also obscure, for they have the pernicious tendency to be slippery, never meaning just one thing but several things, not standing for a definite object but symbolizing a conception. Since these symbols as the "playthings of the mind" seem to stand for reality, we tend to think that they are reality. And in the end, we deceive ourselves into thinking that if a person can recite the doctrines, then he must assuredly have experienced what these doctrines describe. Or it may be that we become very fondly attached to some word, and before long we have made an idol of it, even as the heathen make idols of wood. Words such as *blood, trinity, sanctification, authority, infallibility,* and *immersion* have been particularly subject to this kind of treatment by various people, who in all sincerity thought that they had found in these words a touchstone of truth or a symbol of spiritual reality. Moreover, it has been much easier for people to conform verbally than morally. If only the right words could equal right beliefs, and if right formulations could guarantee right relations with God, then the words would no longer be the words of life, but words substituted for life. In fact, the most grievous errors and pathetic failures in Christianity have resulted from a wrong understanding of its verbal symbols. In general, people have been unaware of how these symbols are encoded and decoded by those who communicate.

Encoding and Decoding

Encoding in speech is so nearly automatic, or so it seems, that we even speak of people "talking without thinking." Actually this never happens, except in so far as we apply this phrase to persons having certain types of mental disturbance. It is true, however, that the way in which we formulate our thoughts into words is so nearly automatic that we are scarcely aware of the process. However, the fact that we are unaware of what happens does not mean that it is any less complex.

Actually much is involved, for the way in which we encode our thoughts into sentences depends on a great many factors other than the nature of the object we may wish to speak about. For example, as we speak we inevitably reflect the attitude we have toward the receptor, our feelings with regard to the object we are discussing, our general emotional state at the time of speaking, and the purposes of the communication, i.e., do we wish merely to describe something, or to evaluate it, or to prescribe it for someone else?

The encoder is of necessity limited to his particular background of experience in terms of what he has done and the words with which he has become familiar, though, of course, this background comprises his total experience and the ways in which he has mentally organized and evaluated it. If he is to communicate, he can draw only upon these two sources. And in a sense these sources are different in some respects for every individual. On the other hand, every speaker knows that if he is to communicate successfully with people of other backgrounds and language experiences, he must make adjustments. First, he must make adaptations in the choice of words. For example, if he is an American in London he must speak of the bonnet of a car, not the hood; of petrol, not gas; and of Oxford Circus, and not Oxford Square, on the analogy of Times Square in New York. Secondly, he must be careful of the way in which he puts words together and proclaims them, for ponderous oratory is quite out of place in many places in the English-speaking world. Failure to adjust to one's audience is always the object of humor, well illustrated by the joke told about the scholarly British pastor who concluded a point in his sermon to a yokel congregation with the statement, "Now, of course, some of you may wish to quote Eusebius against me."

All successful speakers are aware—in some instances, painfully so —of the necessity of adjusting to the background of their audience. Even with this awareness, however, there are dangers in encoding, since people blindly assume that what they say is a faithful reproduction of reality, when it is not. In the first place, this encoding of our conceptions into a set of symbols has to pass through the grid of our own previously stored "experience." In this connection Gestalt psychologists have shown quite clearly that we do not perceive reality as it actually is. Rather, we reorganize and reinterpret our perceptions as they impinge upon us. At times we select one feature and at other times another, while overlooking many details. There are instances in which we concentrate, so to speak, on the background. At other times we see only some special "focus of interest" and the background is for all practical purposes nonexistent, as far as our memories of events are concerned. Our conceptions must, however, pass through two grids before they can be communicated to others: (1) the grid or "screen" of our own accumulated perceptions (including the ways in which our minds have organized them) and (2) the grid or "screen" of our language. In English, for example, we see objects linguistically in terms of singular and plural, while in some languages such a distinction does not exist. When we speak of events, we normally specify whether they are present, past, or future, but in many languages these distinctions are secondary to the nature of the event. In Navajo, for example, the event is conceived as happening once for all, repeatedly, or as completed, not completed, or hoped for. As long as we are communicating in one language only, the problems are not so complex. In a sense, however, this is even more dangerous, for under these conditions we are even more inclined to consider what we say as a faithful "picture" of reality. We assume the complete validity of our own perceptions and we take for granted the "logical" nature of our linguistic grid, never realizing the extent to which our conceptions are distorted by our own observations and further "skewed" by the arbitrary character of the language in which we must encode them.

If, however, the encoder is faced with a problem, then it must be evident that the decoder has an even greater problem, since the encoder and the decoder are not hooked up like two teletype machines matched for one-to-one communication. Moreover, the decoder's mind is not like a telephone exchange, in which an incoming call can be automatically switched to the proper circuit. Rather, our minds are like some of the huge so-called "thinking machines," though almost infinitely more complex; and any impulse, in the form of a word or sentence, must not only be decoded in terms of its linguistic forms but must also filter through the grid of our own background experience if we are to have corresponding conceptions.

The decoder must, of course, adjust his grid so as to take in properly (i.e., assign proper meaning to) not only the words used but also the supplementary features of the communication, e.g., the gestures, mannerisms, posture, type of voice, dialectal variants, and style. To do so, he needs to know something about the background of the source (that is the chief purpose for the introduction of a speaker); for if he is to adjust his grid to match that of the encoder, he should have some information on how best to interpret the form of the message.

Successful communication involves a good deal of mutual adjustment, for the source must consider the backgrounds of the audience, and vice versa. Moreover, in the very process of personal communication there is a good deal of what we may call social "feedback," to borrow a term from electronic engineering. Those in the audience, for example, express their reactions by nodding agreement, smiling approval, showing boredom, grimacing, hissing, stamping, and cat-calling. The alert encoder will attempt to adjust his communication to the reactions of the audience, but as he does so his auditors instinctively know that he is making allowances for them and their attitudes, and hence tend to discount these adjustments. He, in turn, knows that they are aware of his attempt to adjust to them and tries to make further adjustments to compensate for the extent to which they discount his adaptations. Communication thus becomes a two-way affair, even though one person is doing all the talking.

This problem of encoding and decoding is difficult enough for the preacher, speaking to a congregation from a cultural background similar to his own but of many different levels of intelligence. However, for a person who wishes to speak to an audience from an entirely different subculture, for example, a theology professor speaking to an average congregation or for a missionary who has to address persons with quite a different cultural heritage from his own, the differences in grids and necessary adaptations are enormous, and nothing can be taken for granted. It might be assumed that one could translate literally into Spanish the expression "to receive Christ," but in Spanish *recibir a Cristo* does not mean to the average Roman Catholic what it means to the Protestant missionary. Rather than carrying the sense of personal commitment to Jesus Christ, it more often than not means "to receive the wafer of the eucharist." The experience grids of the encoding missionary and the decoding listener are thus so different that the two conceptions have only a faint correspondence.

Information Theory

In the transmission of a message more than the formal content must be considered; there is also the "impact." Startling new metaphors have more impact than clichés, and a brilliant illustration is more dynamic than a dead generalization. These facts have always been known, but information theory (often referred to as cybernetics) gives us useful insights by which we may describe and evaluate just such features.

The fundamental principle of information theory is that the

amount of "information" (here used in a very special sense) carried by any item is directly proportionate to its unpredictability. In other words, if we can predict the occurrence of a particular word or expression, then the word carries relatively little "information," or impact. If, for example, a person is always saying everything is "terrific," the expression carries relatively little "information," for in this person's speech it is so largely predictable. Similarly, as noted on page 40, in classical Greek almost every sentence began with a conjunction. Since at least some conjunction is thus predictable, and since in the New Testament one usually finds such conjunction as *de*, "but," *kai*, "and," *oun*, "therefore," and *gar*, "for," these conjunctions do not carry the same amount of "information" as their equivalents in English, in which they occur so much less frequently.

The basic principle of information theory is understood in some measure by anyone who takes a course in writing, for one of the first things the teacher tries to correct is the tendency to overwork such words as *thing, object,* and *matter.* Such words are often thought of as highly useful, and they are, for they can be used in so many different contexts and under so many different circumstances. At the same time, this frequency and predictability of occurrence (factors which tend to go together) means that though the words have wide areas of meaning (i.e., can be used with many referents), they have very little dynamic, for they carry little "information."

We must remember that in information theory the term "information" is not synonymous with meaning, as it is in ordinary usage. In fact, if one should quite unpredictably utter some completely unexpected nonsense word such as *"skwitchka,"* the "information" would be very high, for it would be quite unpredictable, but the meaning would be virtually nil. We say "virtually," for the very occurrence of such a "word" in some syntactic arrangement would help us to identify it as presumably a verb, noun, adjective, etc., and to that extent it would have some meaning. "Information" is not, therefore, to be equated with meaning, but to be understood as the dynamic impact of a word—the extent to which it stands out in the discourse because of its individuality and distinctiveness.

Though in general we prefer to receive messages characterized by a high level of "information," nevertheless we could not comprehend speech too high in "information." The distractions of the situation and our own inattention would be so great that in such a message we would completely lose track of what was being said. In fact, it has been shown that in speech successive sequences are usually about 50 per cent predictable, or in terms of information theory about 50 per cent "redundant." In the sentence *these men want their hats* the fact of plurality is indicated five times, not only explicitly in *these, men, their,* and *hats,* but implicitly in *want,* for a singular subject would require *wants.* In such a sentence there is considerable technical "redundancy," but it is not equivalent to repetition or tautology, for while "redundancy" makes possible the predictability of what follows, repetition or tautology merely repeats what has preceded.

For one engaged in translating the Scriptures the implications of information theory are great, since it soon becomes clear that if one is to communicate effectively he must not overload the communication channel. If the translator employs not only lexically strange combinations of words, but also rare and unusual grammatical constructions, the unusual character of such a message (i.e., its high unpredictability) makes it extremely difficult to understand. The same is of course true when we undertake to read something prepared for specialists, e.g., in symbolic logic, quantum physics, biochemistry, or ballistics. It may even be that we understand the meanings of all the words, at least in certain familiar contexts, but when such terms are used in unfamiliar ways and combined in unfamiliar contexts the "informational" load staggers us. We end up by saying that it is entirely too deep for us. What has actually happened is that the communication channel is too heavily loaded for the nonspecialist. We might understand the message if it had been sufficiently "padded out" with a certain amount of explanation, unnecessary for technically trained specialists, but obligatory if others are to comprehend it.

The preacher must face the implications of information theory from two points of view. First, he must make sure that he is not using a host of strange words in unusual combinations. Otherwise, people unfamiliar with the gospel message will be completely confused. Such phrases as "saved by the blood," "our position in the heavenlies," "sanctified by his grace," and "heirs of the covenant" may carry too much "information" and too little meaning to many people who are unacquainted with these combinations of words. Without some understanding of the background of these terms—that is to say, except for some explanation within the sermon or for prior knowledge of their implications—many listeners will simply be lost, even as the average person is in reading about nuclear physics. The preacher also runs the opposite risk of producing nothing but a series of trite, warmed-over expressions which may flow out with incredible monotony and sound exceedingly pious. Here the "informational" content is exceedingly low, for after hearing such a preacher a few times one can almost predict what he will say on any subject.

The significance of this principle of unpredictability and its relation to the dynamic quality of communication are evident in the use of new translations of the Bible. One of the important reasons for the popularity of J. B. Phillips' translation of the New Testament, and especially of the Epistles, is that new and striking expressions have been substituted for those which through familiarity no longer have the impact they once had. In fact, once someone begins to read a familiar passage in the King James Version, many persons can almost quote it ahead of him—for them there is complete predictability or "redundancy," and hence little or no impact. However, with a new translation, and especially one which uses contemporary language and daring idioms, people generally react with keener interest and respond with deeper understanding because the "information" has been greater.

One further aspect of information theory must be noted at this time, namely, its relevance to the use of concrete, specific vocabulary and content in contrast with abstract, generic discourse. In brief, this principle may be formulated as, "The greater the specificity of detail the greater is the information." Thus, an account of specific events is much less predictable than generalized observations. The sociologist may, for example, write some important descriptions of class differences, well documented with statistical findings, but the biographer or novelist can take the same fundamental problems and weave all the observations into an unpredictable story. That is why we "get more out of" illustrations than we do from abstract statements, and why a picture, which is in many respects the most concrete kind of illustration, is sometimes "worth ten thousand words." It is this greater communicative dynamic in timely and homely illustrations that makes Jesus Christ's teachings so absorbing. In a sense he can be called the "master communicator," for he not only spoke the language of the people but also framed his teachings in forms which have optimum "information value" as well as truth. His words were truth with impact.

The Nature of Meaning

Having examined language symbols first in terms of their systematic
arrangement in a code, and then in the light of their impact or "information value," we must now probe somewhat deeper in order to un-
cover the more elusive nature of language symbols. For one thing, we
should never be presumptuous about the extent to which we are
successful in communicating a message. Martin Joos has estimated
that the most literate and well-informed people rarely understand one
another more than about 80 per cent.[5] If this figure applies to people
of the same general background and training in communication (by
virtue of their education), it is fair to assume that less than half of
what is said between people of widely different backgrounds and educational experience is understood in the way intended. Undoubtedly,
this is true as well for a good many sermons.

There is, of course, more than one approach to meaning. Even if
we concern ourselves primarily with the psychological orientation, we
are still faced with two different possibilities. Of these the older is
the description of meaning in terms of mental images, a method going
back as far as Plato. In this way of dealing with meaning the emphasis is upon the type of psychological "model" which corresponds
to the symbol. This approach, however, involves a host of problems,
for though it is quite easy to have a mental picture of a particular
friend, how can one have an image of an abstraction such as triangle
(when there are all sorts of triangles) or a mental "view" of infinity,
when one cannot picture "unendingness"? Moreover, this approach
tends to run down a blind alley, for there is absolutely no way of
getting at these images or of comparing and testing them.

Beginning, therefore, largely with Pavlov, the study of meaning
shifted from a preoccupation with mental images to a concern with
response to stimuli. Psychologists became less interested in what went
on inside the brain and more concerned with how people reacted.
Again, however, this procedure could go only so far, since one does
not have physically measurable reactions to highly abstract notions
such as *matter, essence, reality,* and the *Trinity.* Accordingly, psychologists shifted their descriptions to take into account what they
called the "response potential" or "behavioral disposition."

A somewhat different approach to the meaning of symbols has
developed among anthropologists and linguists, who are little concerned with what goes on inside people's minds, but are vitally in-

terested in how symbols are used in certain behavioral contexts; in other words, how symbols operate as elements in human communication. They have studied the distribution of symbols (their places of occurrence) within the practical context of human behavior and within the linguistic context of speech. They have discovered fascinating elements which suggest clues to the meanings of these symbols.

Actually, in the study of meaning one must combine both psychological and anthropological-linguistic orientations to meaning, for language has a double purpose. It not only symbolizes concepts but is also used for the promotion of purposes; that is to say, it has not only psychological but also cultural and behavioral functions.

In trying to understand what meaning is, we can perhaps best begin by thinking of a word as starting with a very wide area of meaning. For example, the word *table* can mean scores of things, including its various meanings in "table and chairs," "logarithmic table," "actuarial table," "table land," and "to table a motion." However, in the very process of listing these different "meanings" of *table*, we have begun to restrict the meaning to that employed by a particular source under specific circumstances. If we can identify the source— the person who used a phrase employing the word *table*—we already have a clue to the particular meaning involved. It would usually make a difference whether we heard the word *table* from a janitor, a mathematician, an insurance man, a geographer, or a parliamentarian. Moreover, if we knew the circumstances under which the word was uttered —whether in the basement of a church, a classroom, a business office, or a lodge meeting—we would know what meaning to expect. And finally, if we knew the two or three sentences that preceded these expressions, there would probably be no doubt as to the meaning intended in the particular sentence. That is to say, a word in isolation (i.e., without context) begins with a very wide area of meaning, for it may occur in many hundreds of situations and may be used as a label for scores of objects; but by means of the practical and linguistic contexts in which it is used we can "whittle it down" to precisely that subarea of meaning which it must have in any specific utterance.

In this process of seeing a word in its various specific contexts, and noting the manner in which it is used by participants in the communication, not only to label objects but also to symbolize their conceptions, we recognize that verbal symbols constantly have two basic functions: (1) a referent-function, by which the symbols become a label for some object, event, state of being, or abstraction, and (2) a conception-function, that is, a label for, or a stimulus to, a corresponding mental conception. This second aspect of meaning is really the important one, since it primarily affects our behavior. It is the conception-function that carries with it all the emotive responses. Expressions such as *mother, God, the precious name of Jesus, washed in the blood,* and *marching to Zion* do, of course, possess some referent-function; but our response to these words is determined not primarily by the referents labeled, but by our emotional responses to the conceptions labeled. When the Psalmist writes, "He shall cover thee with his feathers, and under his wings shalt thou trust" (Psalm 91:4) and "Thou shalt tread upon the lion and adder" (Psalm 91:13), what concerns us is not really the objective referents of the message, namely, the "feathers," "wings," "lion," and "adder," but the fact that through the use of these words in these special arrangements we sense an emotional response to the claims of divine protection and care.

The importance of the conception-function in meaning is further revealed in the fact that it is in this respect that people really differ. Things are things, but what makes us so different one from another is the manner in which we conceive of these objects; in other words, the ideas we have about them and the way in which we value such ideas and their implications. As has often been said, what makes the difference between people is not their actual histories, but what they think have been their histories. The conceptions a people hold in common are more important for their present behavior than are certain historical accidents or events in their common background.

If people are to be made over radically, as in a real revolution, each person must undergo a drastic reorganization of his conceptions. To accomplish such a reorganization is never easy, however, for we are what we think, in the sense of the values we attach to our conceptions, and no amount of mere additional information will radically alter our emotional responses. If, therefore, a people are to be taught a "new way of living," the revolutionary party must do one of two things: (1) brainwash the people or (2) control the education of the young so thoroughly that the values of the adults cannot be passed on effectively to their children. The first procedure is being adopted in China; the second is the primary technique in the Soviet Union.

The Chinese people subjected to this procedure have not lost all knowledge of the referents of the words they have known, and many of their conceptions have remained unaltered; but the emotional responses to these conceptions and the values attached to them have been drastically altered by a combined pattern of fear, social pressure, and subtle suggestion of a kind possibly unparalleled in the history of the world.

In Christianity, conversion involves a somewhat parallel process, in that it consists of a radical alteration of one's entire value system. Again, for the new convert the referent-functions of his language symbols do not change, and most of his conceptions remain essentially the same, but his values are completely altered. His world, which has been essentially self-centered, becomes God-centered, and thus the things he prized before become so much refuse (Philippians 3:8).

Meaning and Perception

In a sense it is quite true that "all thinking begins with seeing."[6] By this phrase Langer means that all thinking originates primarily in perception, not merely by means of the eyes, but by any and all the senses: hearing, smelling, feeling, and tasting, as well as seeing. But if thinking begins with perception, it does not stop there, but goes on to other levels. As it becomes more and more abstract, meanings become less and less "picturable." In English such terms as *reality, matter, substance, essence,* and *ontology* are certainly not relatable to any easily picturable object, for there are simply no perceptual models in the universe for such abstractions.

A child's speech begins almost inevitably with the concrete and the picturable, and hence the communication to children must be in terms of "graphic" vocabulary and concepts. As the person matures he acquires greater and greater capacity for abstractions, until as an adult he may conceive of *trinity, deity,* and *infinity,* for which there are no perceptual models in the world in which we live.

But even adults are essentially "children" in their craving for perceptual models—conceptions which they can "see with the mind," or even better, see with the eyes. Hence they make for themselves images, which begin usually as mere models of the real substance, but little by little tend to acquire all the features of the real thing. In the same way that dolls may at first be thought of by children as just things, but soon are conceived of as having personality, so images, which begin as symbols of something else, gradually come to possess the very properties they were once supposed only to model. At last they become idols.

The danger of turning images into idols is, however, no more dangerous than the construction of false models. For example, many Christians have a perceptual model of the Trinity which is really not monotheistic but tritheistic. The very use of the phrase "three persons" (with a very different meaning than the corresponding word *personae*, "masks," had in Latin) has helped to promote this view of the essential separateness of the three. Accordingly, the model most people have in mind is far more one of three-ness than of oneness, even to the point of claiming that Jesus in his pity for mankind was willing to take the initiative in offering to suffer the wrath of an angry God in order to reconcile us to a vengeful Father. But this is a completely false model of what the Scriptures are talking about.

The Meanings of Words As a Conceptual Map of Experience

In mentioning earlier in this chapter the fact that verbal symbols segment experience, even though in an essentially arbitrary way, we have indicated the fundamental principle underlying this occurrence of words as a conceptual map of human experience. The only difficulty is that, whereas we can speak figuratively of a map, the actual situation is much more complex, for human experience is far from being limited to two dimensions.

The traditional practice has been to describe the totality of human experience as a circle in which the various verbal symbols cover the entire territory, though often with quite irregular borders, as shown in the accompanying diagram.

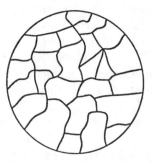

Several features of this type of diagram need explanation. As we have noted, the limits of territory are arbitrary. Furthermore, each area tends to represent, not a homogeneous territory with well-defined edges, but clusters or even constellations of meaning, often with a clear central vs. peripheral relationship, and frequently with fuzzy edges. This type of problem has been a constant source of difficulty for Bible interpreters in comparing such related Greek words as *agapaô*, *phileô*, and *stergô*, with their related meanings of "love." It is equally difficult for someone who is trying to evaluate properly such a series in English as *love, like, appreciate, have affection for,* and *be fond of.* Where does one expression leave off in the map of human experience and another begin?

Another aspect that tends to give difficulty is that the conceptual map of our experience is not on a single plane. It is actually a many-storied structure of great complexity. For example, on a relatively low level we may distinguish such objects as mouse, rabbit, fox, wolf, opossum, and kangaroo. (We recognize, of course, that there are words of even greater specificity on a lower level of analysis.) These symbols can be substituted for by such generic terms as *rodents, canines,* and *marsupials,* while all may be grouped as *mammals.* As we go up the multistoried structure there are words of even greater areas of meaning, e.g., *animal* (which can be used to include man), *object* (which covers the area of thousands of words), and even *it.*

The picture of meaning is even more confused by the fact that, though a general agreement exists among participants in any speech community, there is never an absolute agreement; for people differ from one another not only in their pronunciation of words but also in the meanings they habitually assign to them. This type of disagreement is inevitable, for a person's use of a term is dependent upon his experience with this symbol in the context of his own life. Since each of us differs to some extent in our experiences, conceptions corresponding to verbal symbols will inevitably differ.

Useful as this conceptual map of human experience may be, it is only a map and not the territory itself. That is to say, the symbols are not substitutes for experience. The tendency has always been to assume that if people knew the verbal formulations, that is, if they had conceptions about the truth, they would automatically have experienced the truth. In other words, ability to recite the doctrines was considered proof of having explored the Christian life. This attitude toward symbolism lies at the heart not only of much religious hypocrisy but also of the sterility of the spiritual lives of many.

The Range of Meanings of Words and Groups of Words

In general, the referent-function and the conception-function of verbal symbols are parallel, in that they have corresponding goals. For example, the word *house* has a referent-function, the labeling of a particular type of structure, and a conception-function, the labeling of a closely corresponding mental notion. But in certain contexts the normal and central referent-function and the conception-function of the term may not correspond. For example, in the phrase *the house of David* the Scriptures refer not to a type of building, which is the central (or more usual) referent of *house*, but to the lineage of David. This means that the conception-function of *house* in this type of context is not parallel with the usual referent-function. The same problem applies to the phrase *blood of Jesus Christ*. The immediate referent-function of *blood* is the physical substance which flows in the veins, but as it is used in the Scriptures this phrase in its conception-function points to the offering of life ("the life is in the blood") as atonement.

Another way of describing such figurative expressions is to say that the conception-function of such verbal symbols leads one not to the immediate, or central, referent but to another conception. Hence, in most instances the term *cross*, as employed in Christianity, signifies, not the actual instrument of execution, but the fact of atoning death. As such, it becomes a "metaphorical" symbol for the atonement.

In general, the meaning of a phrase can be determined by adding up the meanings of the constituent parts (such phrases may be called endocentric). The expression *Jesus was baptized by John* is such a phrase. On the other hand, many expressions in the Scriptures are not so easily understood. In these the meaning is not the sum total of the meanings of the parts, but something other than the totality of the parts. For example, *heap coals of fire on his head* does not have a conception-function corresponding to the sum total of the conception-functions of each of the parts; for this phrase describes not a technique for torturing persons to death (as some Kituba-speaking people in the Congo understood it), but a way of making people ashamed by being good to them. This type of expression may be called semantically exocentric, for the meaning of the whole is not the sum total of the parts.

Groups of words have two other quite different areas of meaning, namely, the grammatical and the stylistic. When one says *The Word was God* there is more here than merely the four verbal symbols. There is also a grammatical relationship of subject and predicate. Moreover, despite the order of the Greek expression, which is the reverse of the English, we know that *the Word* is subject and *God* is the predicate, because in Greek the predicate attributive *God* does not have a definite article. This absence of the article does not mean, however, that one can translate "the Word was a God." Moreover, the grammatical arrangement of these words, as indicated by the very absence of the article, is such that we cannot reverse them, as some people mistakenly try to do, saying, "God was the Word."

When one considers the totality of grammatical constructions, including their interrelations, frequency, and variation, and the selection of words and combinations of words, including their mutual compatibility and communicative significance, one comes inevitably to deal with the meaning of style. And style, for all its elusive character, is of the utmost importance in any communication. Sometimes our most serious failures to understand a communication are due to our reactions to its style. Some people find it very difficult to understand traditional translations of the Pauline Epistles, not because Paul's style is so poor in Greek (in fact, it is quite good and relatively plain), but because when translated literally into English the form becomes very heavy, cumbersome, and even misleading. If one is to communicate to a contemporary English-speaking audience some of the thrust and incisiveness of Paul's epistolary style, as well as the equivalent meaning of the message, the stylistic form of the message must be changed.

Combinations of words involve still another level of symbolization, for they may point not only to a series of conceptions which they normally symbolize but may also introduce the account of an event which in and of itself has a symbolic meaning. The story of the rending of the temple veil in Matthew 27:57 must be understood on two levels: (1) the literal meaning of the verbal symbols, which describe a specific event, and (2) the symbolic meaning of the event itself, which signified to the disciples of Jesus that they could now have access to the Father without priestly mediation, since the Lord had entered into the spiritual Holy of Holies to make atonement once and for all for the sins of his people.

However, the symbolism of events or of objects may be quite differently interpreted in different cultures. Matthew 7:10, "Or if he ask a fish, will he give him a serpent?" seems absurd to many people in Africa, who would often much prefer a serpent to a fish. If such an event is to be interpreted meaningfully to such people, one must use the name of an inedible serpent or add some explanation.

Perspectives of Meaning, Depending upon the Participants in Communication

Up to this point we have described meaning in terms of its referential and conceptual values on various levels and in terms of different cultural contexts. There is a further essential element in the problem of meaning, namely, the perspectives of the participants in the communication; for there can be no valid description of meaning apart from the ways in which the source and the receptor are related to the transmission of the message.

First, however, we must recognize that not all verbal communication is intended to convey the immediate conceptions implied by the verbal symbols. In other words, not all messages are supposed to be informative. Many, in fact too many, are primarily expressive rather than informative. That is to say, the source is concerned not so much with what he says as with giving vent to emotion. In such cases the immediate referential and conceptual meanings of the words are plainly secondary; what counts is the emotional state expressed. In some instances, the result is a flaming harangue; in others, it may be a lyric poem which speaks of "purvil of gold," "tissue of time," "shreds of Northern Lights," "fluttering life," and "oblivion's delight," while all the time expressing love.

Nevertheless, despite the difficulties imposed by such highly metaphorical language, where the message is purposely obscured in form in order to communicate significance in more subtle or indirect ways, all valid communication must involve to some extent an interchange between source and receptor. Except in the speech of dementia the source has some intention. However, in the communication of this intention through a system of symbols, a number of possibilities exist as to the meaning actually communicated. The following list shows some of the more important variations:

1. *What does S (the source) want R (the receptor) to understand by M (the message)*? This is the most generally accepted definition of meaning in communication.

2. *What does R understand by M?* Obviously, the receptor often misunderstands the intention of S. For example, the words of the communion *Drink ye all of it* are often understood to mean an admonition to consume all of the wine, or grape juice, in the cup, rather than a plea for all to participate.

3. *What ought S to have meant by M if he is to be in accord with the general concept rather than with his own particular conceptions?* A source may use verbal symbols in ways which are not in accordance with general usage; hence he may be misunderstood.

4. *What ought R to have understood by M if he is to be in accord with the general concept rather than with his own individual conceptions?*

5. *What do authorities in circumstances later than the original communication say that S wanted R to understand by M?* Absolute knowledge is here impossible, for it is impossible to reconstruct all the details of the communicative event, but lawyers, students of literature, the scribes of the Pharisees, and professors of theology have all been specially trained in this interpretation and determination of meaning.

6. *What do authorities in circumstances later than the original communication say that M ought to mean to R, quite apart from what S may have intended?* Here can be treated the exposition of the "holy kiss" and "tongues" in our present-day churches and the meaning of the Constitution of the United States for present-day American life. Few Biblical expositors interpret Paul's admonition of the holy kiss as immediately applicable to our congregations. And the judges of the Supreme Court know quite well that their interpretations have for many years gone far beyond what the founding fathers intended— though not necessarily different from what some of them would have prescribed were they living today.

There are, of course, other possibilities of meaning, e.g., *What R thinks S wanted R to understand by M* or *What S imagines R to understand by M.*

In view of the complex nature of meaning itself and the equally complicated interrelations between sources and receptors, perhaps it is not too difficult to see how a high measure of misunderstanding arises. In fact, it is quite remarkable that we do not misunderstand each other more often than we do.

The Problem of Meaning through the Centuries

It would be wrong for us to assume that only contemporary people have become aware of the problem of language and meaning or of the relationship of words to the objects they label. In fact, a fascinating insight (to which we shall refer again in the final chapter) is to be found in Genesis 2:19, where Adam is described as giving names to all the beasts and every living creature.

The Greek philosophers before Socrates, especially Parmenides and Heraclitus, also wrestled with these problems, but for the most part they postulated a more or less natural connection between the conceptual functions of the symbol and the object to which it applied. With Plato, reflecting the views of Socrates, the problem of language looms very large. In his dialogue entitled *Cratylus* he discusses at considerable length whether words are essentially logical in their structure and etymology or whether they are arbitrary conventions of man. Plato concludes that they are only labels and not reflections of inherent values or divine revelation. Aristotle developed the use of language as an instrument for the classification of experience and used it admirably to this end. Descartes in the seventeenth century clearly divided the inner world of sense from the outer world of phenomena and thus inaugurated a running debate among philosophers. For the next two centuries they would struggle with the central problem of epistemology, "How can one know?"

This concern for uniting the worlds of thought and of perception was renounced by the logical positivists, who during the last generation have been insisting more and more that the old arguments about meaning are irrelevant. Facts are facts, so they say, and the very fact that we can construct whole systems of symbols (e.g., mathematics) which have admirable utility in the practical world should assure us that all our hesitation about using verbal symbols as labels of reality is overdone. The existentialists would cut the Gordian knot in another way. They would fuse the past and the future, the subjective and the objective, in somewhat the same way as the pre-Socratic philosophers. However, they do so with much greater sophistication, putting human "awareness" in the crucible of the here and now, in which verbal symbols constitute man's most important keys to understanding and at the same time his greatest obstacle to true knowledge.

The modern approach to symbolism has thus largely swept aside the questions our grandparents asked. It has insisted rather that symbols be studied in terms of how they function in behavior. In one way or another, man is sidestepping questions about ultimate reality while he investigates how this amazing reality of the universe actually functions in the areas he can study and describe. He is content to recognize that symbols represent only certain selected phases of nature and society, and never the totality of reality, for "an essential distinction between language and experience is that language separates out from the living matrix little bundles and freezes them" into verbal symbols.[7]

The Restructuring of Meaning

When communication takes place between sources and receptors who have different cultural backgrounds, one must expect a high degree of restructuring of meaning. That is to say, whatever concepts are communicated are reinterpreted in terms of the total conceptual framework of the different context. People do not leave such conceptions floating about in their minds, unrelated to their total conceptual map of experience. People simply have to fit their ideas together into a whole or suffer the corrosive effects of neurotic tensions. Therefore, any new idea must be accommodated to the old, or the old must be modified to fit the new. And in most instances both the new and the old are changed.

The Shipibos of Peru[8] have an abundance of "How it came to be" stories, and they are constantly on the lookout for any further "mythological" explanations of the world around them. Accordingly, when they heard the story of the Gerasene demoniacs and how the evil spirits were sent off into the swine, who forthwith dashed down a cliff into the waters of the lake, they immediately decided that they had an explanation of the origin of dolphins, which they called customarily in their own language "water demons." The whole point of the Biblical story was lost, as far as the Shipibos were concerned, for they were much more interested in the presumed origin of dolphins than in what happened to the demoniacs. Similarly, when they heard the parable of the laborers in the vineyard, they interpreted the events as meaning that Jesus had established the feudal *patron* system and also confirmed the working day as being twelve hours long.

In the Kaka region of the Cameroun the Christian communion was restructured in terms of the Kaka conceptual world, for, in Kaka life, eating with a person is a way of solemnizing a reconciliation. Hence, in communion one is symbolizing this reconciliation with Ndjambie, "God." This conception is strengthened by the fact that when church members sin and are then excluded from church fellowship for a time, a symbol of their readmission into the congregation is their admission to participation in the communion. The Biblical concept of celebrating a covenant relationship by means of the common meal is quite foreign to Kaka Christians; it simply does not fit into the indigenous conceptual view of the world.

A single symbol does not necessarily have the same conceptual meaning throughout the history of a particular society or institution. Jesus Christ, for example, is symbolized by the early church as a man—the revelation of the personality of God and one who in full vigor leads the church to victory over its totalitarian enemies. After the institutional church had become victorious, there was a tendency to shift this symbol. Jesus Christ was then pictured more and more as the infant child, needing the protection of his Mother, in this case the earthly ecclesiastical guardianship of the divine personality.[9] It was only in the Reformation that the idea of the manhood of Jesus Christ was recaptured.

When the total conceptual structures of source and receptor differ, it is only to be expected that communication will involve an entire range of restructuring; for the parts fit into quite different configurations, even when the two systems have much in common. In Spanish-speaking Latin America, such words as *confesión,* "confession," *santo,* "saint," and *María,* "Mary" have quite different conceptual values to Roman Catholics and to Protestants. These three words mean to Roman Catholics confession to a priest, images in the church, and a divine protectress, respectively. To Protestants they mean confession of guilt in prayer to God, Biblical heroes of the faith, and an honored person. A Roman Catholic who fails to understand the communication of an Evangelical friend is not being stubborn or perverse; he simply has to fit ideas into his own structural framework. The same is true of the Protestant. To a greater or lesser degree, this same difficulty must be expected whenever communication across cultures is attempted.

Fundamental Facts about the Meanings of Words

The result of all we have said up to this point about the meanings of verbal symbols may be summarized in three statements about semantic correspondence:

1. No two people ever mean exactly the same by the same word.
2. No two words in any one language ever have exactly the same meaning.
3. No two words in any two languages ever have exactly the same meaning.

These statements may seem to be abnormally dogmatic, even highly pessimistic, for the possibilities of any communication. We need to examine them more fully.

If, as we have noted (pp. 35–42), the meaning of a word for any person is dependent upon his experience (both practical and linguistic) then it follows that the meanings must be different for any two people, because no two people ever have the same identical experiences. This fact is granted readily in such expressions as *dictator, communion, free love, desegregation,* but it is usually considered far-fetched to insist that it applies to such a common word as *apple.* Yet it does. For example, the word *apple* has for me personally a very special "meaning." I associate apples with my grandfather, whom I admired greatly, and who years ago had a large apple orchard in Idaho, where I visited as a child and there ate with him some of the best apples I've ever had. The word *apple* thus to me means something quite different from what it means to other people, who have not had these particular experiences.

That no two words in any language ever mean exactly the same thing seems to be denied by our popular understanding of "synonym," for we assume that all of Roget's lists of synonyms are sets of words which have identical meanings. This, however, is far from being the case. Synonyms can, of course, substitute for one another in some contexts, often quite limited, but they are in no sense identical. For example, one may speak of a *peace conference,* but not a *tranquillity conference,* even though *peace* and *tranquillity* are generally regarded as synonyms. Similarly, though *high* and *tall* are listed as synonyms one does not say *high tale* and *tall ball,* even though he can say *high ball* (or *highball*) and *tall tale.*

The fact that no two words in any two languages ever have exactly the same meaning is often readily granted for the more complex

or abstract words, such as "love," "hope," "faith," and salvation,"
but is almost as vigorously denied for such simple words as *cat* and
bird. Nevertheless, these words likewise are not identical in different
languages. In Spanish, for example, *gato*, "cat," has no correspondence
with English *hepcat*, while for English *bird* there are two Spanish
words: *ave* and *pájaro*. The first is a poetic equivalent, and *pájaro* not
only means bird, in common language, but is also widely used as a
name for a male homosexual, what we in English call a *fairy*.

The upshot of all this is that absolute communication is impossible,
for though a most rigorous semantic practice may reduce the essential
ambiguity of language,[10] such techniques cannot abolish the basic
lack of correspondence in meaning. Not only are the conceptual maps
of experience different as one goes from one speaker to another, and
even more as one goes from one culture to another; but no verbal
symbol can be completely understood without reference to the areas
of meanings of other related symbols. Not only are the specific parts
noncommensurate, but also the systems do not match.

The Possibility of Effective Communication

Even though absolute communication is not possible, nevertheless,
effective communication is always possible, even between persons of
different cultural backgrounds. There are three principal reasons for
this fact: (1) the processes of human reasoning are essentially the
same, irrespective of cultural diversity; (2) all peoples have a common
range of human experience, and (3) all peoples possess the capacity
for at least some adjustment to the symbolic "grids" of others.

There was a time when the ideas of Levy-Bruhl and others about
the "prelogical" thinking of primitive peoples were taken seriously,
and it was assumed that the minds of so-called primitives operated in
ways essentially different from our own. In contrast to this, Kluckholn
summarizes the contemporary view as follows:

> In a certain deep sense the logic (which means the modes of inter-
> preting relationships between phenomena) of all members of the human
> species is the same. The differences in thinking and reacting arise from
> the value premises and existential conceptions about the nature of the
> external world and of human nature.[11]

In other words, the fundamental processes of reasoning of all
peoples are essentially the same, but the premises on which such

reasoning rests and the basic categories that influence the judgment of different peoples are somewhat different. When, for example, a Kaka comes out with very different ideas about God from those a Christian has, one must remember that the Kaka begins with God as "spider," not as "Father." His reasoning about the nature of the spider—its ingenious ability to construct, its powerful poison, and its mysterious habits of life—is worthy of the best minds, given the same ideas about the world and the same outlook upon it that the Kaka holds. The fact that his "theology" is inferior to the Christian's is the result of having begun his judgment of reality with quite different presuppositions. Men differ, therefore, not so much in their reasoning powers as in their starting points.

During a devotional period after breakfast a missionary in Yucatan was trying to explain to an Indian servant what it meant to possess the Spirit of God—in itself a highly complex concept. He attempted to put his point across by saying, "If the Spirit of God enters into your heart, what do you have in your heart?" To which the woman answered, "I do not know." (After all, she was not used to thinking in terms of spirits in her heart.) The missionary then tried to make his point by picking up a glass from the breakfast table and asking the woman, "If I put water in this glass, what would I have in it?" To which the woman replied, "Milk!" At first the missionary was dismayed at what seemed to be a failure in the most elementary logic. A guest who was present reminded him that each morning at breakfast he, the missionary, had put some powdered milk into the glass, whereupon the servant woman had been asked to pour in some water. The result was not water, but milk. The earlier misunderstanding between missionary and servant was not the result of differences in logical processes of reasoning, but in what the two had started with: he with an empty glass and she with one having powdered milk in it. Whenever two persons fail to communicate effectively, it is not necessarily because of any superiority or inferiority of reasoning processes, but rather because the two begin with different presuppositions. It is because of these differing basic assumptions that discussions often leave people further apart rather than closer together.

The second basic reason for the possibility of effective communication rests on the fact that all peoples have similar human experiences. All peoples, for example, must make provision for such physical needs as food, clothing, shelter, and protection. In other words, they must manage to survive in their physical environment. They must also adjust to one another, and though the resulting forms of social culture may be very different, the same elemental features are present, namely, mutual responsibility, interdependence, and sanctions for behavior, whether on a family, tribal, or national level. Similarly, all peoples relate themselves to certain aspects of the supernatural. They may not believe in God, or even in gods, but they have some beliefs in the supernatural and they engage in rites aimed at communication with the supernatural. In addition, all peoples express themselves in certain esthetic media, e.g., plastic or pictorial art, music, dance, and drama. In view of these similar areas of human experience, all peoples can communicate effectively within a wide range of activity and symbolism.

Similarity in thought processes and areas of human behavior would, however, not be sufficient for effective communication unless people also possessed the capacity for mutual adjustment, including the ability to recognize differences and identify correspondences. This ability is perhaps best illustrated by what takes place when we listen to someone who speaks with a so-called "heavy accent." At first, it may be quite difficult for us to understand such a person; but after a short while (the length of time depends upon the degree of difference and our own experience in making such adjustments), we begin to understand what he is saying with much greater ease, often to the point of forgetting that he speaks with an accent. What we do is to adjust the "grid" of our own intake to acoustic impressions (the sounds, words, and grammatical forms), so as to make an identification between our own patterns and his. The forms do not become progressively more identical with ours; rather our understanding of them becomes more "equational." It is not he who changes, but we who make the adjustment.

What happens on a largely unconscious level in listening to others speak can be duplicated on a conscious level in understanding all modes of behavior, including gestures, posture, type of clothing, and mannerisms. Before adolescence the child generally adapts unconsciously to the patterns of behavior transmitted in an implicit way in the culture. Thus any normal child, irrespective of ethnic background, can become a thoroughly integrated member of any society, provided, of course, he is treated as a member of that society. Even after later adolescence, when such capacities of adjustment seem to be more nearly "frozen," one can nevertheless continue to adapt, and whether consciously or unconsciously, see things from another's point of view. Some persons who have lived abroad for a number of years find that they actually feel more at home in a foreign country than in their own. In most instances this means that they have adjusted their "grid" so successfully that they feel more at home with the grid in its "foreign position" than in its "home position."

Because of the vast differences among peoples and languages, a person may not always be able to communicate accurately or precisely. However, he can always, if he will only make the necessary adjustment, communicate effectively. The story of how this can be done, whether within or between cultures, is the theme of the remaining chapters.

CHAPTER *5*

Communication and Social Structure

> *Therefore its name was called Babel, because there the Lord confused the language of all the earth; and from there the Lord scattered them abroad over the face of all the earth.*
> —GENESIS 11:9

COMMUNICATION never takes place in a social vacuum, but always between individuals who are part of a total social context. These participants in the communicative event stand in a definite relationship to each other; for example, as boss to employee, son to father, policeman to offender, and child to baby-sitter. Moreover, in every society there are definite rules about what types of people say what kinds of things to certain classes of persons. On the other hand, what is quite proper for one class to say may be unbecoming for another, and even the same remarks from different persons may be quite differently interpreted. The same behavior interpreted as offensive arrogance in an underling may be considered charming insouciance on the part of the boss, and what is squirming subservience in the lower middle class may be interpreted as lovable modesty in the upper class.[1] Whatever different classes of people say is inevitably influenced by their respective positions in society. For man is more than an individual; he is a member of a very large "family," whether clan, tribe, or nation, and there are always important, though usually unformulated, rules that apply to all interpersonal communication.

This aspect of communication within the social structure is particularly important from the religious point of view. For wherever there

94

are tribal or national gods, these deities inevitably occupy special positions of importance in the social structure, either as mythical ancestors or as guardians of the social patterns and mores of the people. One thing is sure, these deities can usually be depended upon to conserve the *status quo* and in this way help to regulate the traditional relations between people. For this reason religion is always in opposition to any breach with the past, any breaking away of individuals from the "faith," and any presumed undermining of the prestige of traditional leadership. More often than not, a new convert to Christianity in a predominantly pagan society will feel very much like one Hopi Indian who returned to his own village after having been away at school, where he had been baptized a Christian. The first day of his return, when all the villagers went off to a dance and left him sitting in the shadow of the mission wall, he felt, as he described it later, "like a man without a country."

Unfortunately, some missionary approaches to non-Christians have involved the creation of a Christian caste or subculture. Almost unconsciously some well-meaning missionaries in India, before that nation's independence, felt that new converts, in order to become truly Christian and remain faithful to their new stand, needed full identification with the missionaries and the foreign community. But the result in some instances was the development of a wholly artificial, "hothouse" environment, where Christian converts might be protected, but could never really grow. In a sense (in terms of our diagrams in Chapter 3) they were being taught to be square pegs in round holes.

Well-intentioned missionary work has sometimes failed to communicate the gospel because the source adopted a role completely incompatible with any effective identification with those to be reached. In one mission to Indians in South America the role of the communicators is that of a rich landowner. Such a person can accomplish a good deal on the basis of his prestige. He cannot, however, effectively relate the Good News to the people he seeks to reach because the roles of the participants in communication block effective understanding. These missionaries have unselfishly done much *for* the people, but they have never been able to do anything *with* the people. Given the roles of landowner and peon, there is never a two-way traffic of meaningful communication about the real issues of life, and without two-way communication there can be no identification.

Types of Social Structures

Social structures, together with the networks of communication they represent, are very diverse. We shall attempt neither a detailed analysis of all the various types of social structures nor a discussion of the many factors that give rise to different patterns of social life. Here we are concerned only with a particular aspect of social structure—namely, that which is significant in terms of interpersonal communication. For this purpose two primary types of distinctions, intersecting on various levels, may be distinguished. First, we must distinguish between the urban (or so-called "metropolitan" society) and the rural (or "face-to-face" society) types of structures. Second, we must analyze these types of structure in terms of their homogeneous or heterogeneous character. The urban society is characteristic of the typical city dweller in large urban centers, whether in New York, London, or Calcutta, and the rural society is characteristic of the peasant community, whether it is an Indian village near Mexico City or a mountain hamlet in northern Thailand.

By a homogeneous society we mean one in which most of or all the people participate in the common life in more or less the same way. Such groups may have class differences and distinctions of leadership and positions of authority, but the society is nevertheless an integrated whole, sharing much the same system of values; it is not merely an aggregate of subcultures which operate along quite different lines. Sweden, for example, may be regarded as a more or less homogeneous society, in contrast to the United States with its large, heterogeneous population in varying degrees of "assimilation." It may be contrasted also with a country like Peru, which maintains an Ibero-American culture in its cities, but has a distinctly different culture in the villages of the altiplano and the eastern jungle.

In addition to these major distinctions, we must take account of: (1) the strictly primitive groups, of which there are relatively few left in the world, living in almost complete isolation from civilization; and (2) transitional groups, which were quite primitive up to the end of the last century but are now in process of being transformed into dependent folk societies. A high proportion of tribal people in Africa, India, and Southeast Asia are now in this transitional class. As far as their communication networks are concerned, they are to be classed as face-to-face and homogeneous.

Diagrammatic Models of Social Structure

In order to understand more clearly certain of the essential features of social structure, it is convenient to diagram such social patterns, using as a general base an "inverted" diamond jewel shape.

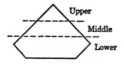

In this generalized and schematic diagram we indicate not only the relative positions and sizes of the different classes—upper, middle, and lower—but also something of the total configuration. This configuration suggests that the upper class tapers off into a relatively limited number of top leaders and that the lower class tapers in at the bottom, reflecting the fact that the lowest of the low class (which might be called the indigent section of the population) are generally fewer in number than are those somewhat higher in the social structure.

We have arbitrarily chosen to represent social structure in three classes. In some societies, however, one must recognize four, five, six, or even more classes. In such a case it is customary to speak of such distinction as upper upper, lower upper, upper middle, lower middle, upper lower, and lower lower. Haitian society, for example, can be described as having five principal classes. The élite, who constitute the upper class, are divided into two groups, called "first-class élite" and "second-class élite." The middle class, a relatively small group, is growing rapidly. The lower class is divided into (1) an upper-lower class consisting of the better-to-do tradesmen and farmers who own their own land, and (2) an indigent class who eke out a bare existence as tenant farmers and common laborers.

It would be wrong, however, to leave the impression that all societies have approximately the generalized structure, even within the diagrammatic framework we are using. The truth of the matter is that societies differ radically in structural configuration, so that one could describe diagrammatically certain of the over-all "impressionistic" features of certain societies in the following contrastive manner:

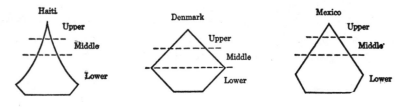

The forms of these diagrams are not based upon statistical data, for such data are not available in terms of class criteria. They are obviously impressionistic, but very useful.

It should be noted, for example, that in Haitian society the upper class constitutes a very narrow, stratified group, while the society almost bulges at the base. In the diagram of Denmark, the upper class does not tower proportionately so much above the rest of the structure, the middle class is rather large, and the lower tapers off to a very restricted indigent base. Mexico, on the other hand, represents a somewhat more "typical" structure, with a growing middle class, a somewhat attenuated upper class, and the bulk of the society in the lower class, though not with the proportionately heavy concentration at the bottom that characterizes Haiti.

Class differences in any society are based, not on a single criterion, but on a number of factors which usually combine to determine social position. These factors include such qualities and possessions as money, heritage, education, leadership ability, and special talents, for example, in acting, music, art, and oratory. Societies differ, of course, as to the value they place on one or another of these factors, and on different levels the criteria shift in importance. For example, for the determination of higher class status one finds that in Haiti family connections are exceedingly important; they are followed in weight by money and education. In Denmark one's family heritage and intellectual accomplishments are highly important. In Mexico money rates somewhat higher than education, provided one has the right family connections. For middle-class membership in Haiti, money is the principal criterion; in Denmark, it is education and personal ability, with financial rewards regarded as more or less inevitable consequences of the requisite education and ability; and in Mexico, money is again the principal criterion, with education recognized as an essential accompanying feature. For lower-class status the lack of money, education, and special gifts are generally definitive.

Communication within Social Structures

The significance of social structure for communication can be summarized in two basic principles: (1) people communicate more with people of their own class; that is, interpersonal communication of a reciprocal nature is essentially horizontal; and (2) prestigeful communication descends from the upper classes to the lower classes, and this vertical communication is primarily in one direction and tends to be principally between adjacent groups.

Truly effective communication, however, is not unidirectional. There must be reciprocity in communication (which we may call "social feedback"), or the results may be unsatisfactory. In war, for example, the general must know not only how to give orders to the troops; he must also know precisely how the troops are faring, or his orders are likely to result in bungling tragedies, as in the collapse of France in World War II. As a general must know where the men are and the type of resistance they are meeting, so in all types of organizational communication in which there is centralized source of communication, orders must go out, but information must be fed back continuously. It is interesting that organization and management engineers have discovered that, though the system of communication is usually well developed from headquarters to the front, or from the boss down to the man at the lathe, the reverse system of communication, whether in the military or in business, is often quite lacking, with resultant military fiascoes and bad labor relations.

Both in the ministry and in missionary work it is usual for the religious professional to do most of the talking. Too often the minister or missionary regards himself solely as intermediary of a superior message from God, and hence not aware of or dependent upon the feedback which should come from the congregation. He has gone forth to tell people the truth, not to listen to other people's ideas about the truth. If this attitude is pushed to an extreme, the message inevitably will become irrelevant. Even though it may be true, it does not reach its receptor, for the "master of the household" does not know the conditions under which the servants live and work. And even if he does know, his communication will be immeasurably strengthened provided those to whom he speaks are convinced of the fact that he knows and understands.

One reason for misjudging the harm done by the downward type of one-way communication is that we do not see its manifest effects.

But when, for example, an African insists on wearing a heavy, cumbersome overcoat on a hot day, simply to demonstrate that he has received such a coat from a white official and thereby has gained some measure of local status, it should be evident to the observer that what comes down from the top carries a tremendous amount of prestige. When African women insist on using a bottle to feed their babies, while their painful breasts drip with milk, they are demonstrating their determination to gain status by following the heavily valued prestige patterns of the higher social classes. In some instances, however, lower-class individuals have a surprisingly important influence on upper-class persons. This influence operates, however, only when the roles are in a sense reversed. For example, in upper-class homes of some urban societies it often happens that lower-class women are hired to nurse and care for the children. Not infrequently their attachment to the children and the children's dependence upon them are such that these women transmit to their charges many basic values of lower-class society, together with a host of concepts accepted primarily by the lower classes, e.g., bogies, ghosts, and magical penalties for disobedience.[2]

The Communication Patterns in
Totalitarian and Democratic States

In a totalitarian society the predominant patterns of communication may be diagrammed as follows:

The vertical communication line represents the orders of the ruling class, particularly the "party line" and the "accepted doctrines." Often there is considerable latitude for horizontal communication, especially in matters regarded as peripheral or as not conflicting with the accepted body of truth; but always there is a core of beliefs and doctrines which must not be challenged—books which must not be read, and ideas which must not be voiced or even thought. The two principal totalitarian structures in our contemporary world, Communism and Roman Catholicism, share a number of these characteristics.

It must be recognized, of course, that there is communication from the masses to their leaders, for the demand for consumer goods in the Communist world and the popularity of Mariolatry in Roman Catholicism do undoubtedly reflect sentiments that come from the people. However, in totalitarian systems the mechanisms for communication from the lower to the upper levels are not institutionalized. There are seldom any consumer surveys, or market studies, and few attempts to obtain effective representational or random sampling of opinion in order to incorporate effectively such "feedback" information into the communicative system.

In a democratic state, communication is institutionally developed as a reciprocal interchange on both the horizontal and vertical axes:

Such a system of communication of course requires a more equalitarian structure, not necessarily in terms of social status, but in terms of rights and privileges. The democratic leadership must be more responsive to the communications rising from the people, for the people have an effective means of expressing opinion. Furthermore, since the structure is numerically weighted in their favor, they can control the leadership if they are organized. When control is taken over under irresponsible leadership, as sometimes happens in democratic systems, demogoguery is the result.

For the most part Protestant churches are organized along the lines of a democratic society, for though the pastor speaks as the representative of God in his prophetic ministry, it is usually the congregation or the church that calls the pastor, pays his salary, and owns the property. The laymen of the church are not just "adherents" to the church, as in the Roman Catholic system; rather, they constitute an integral part of the corporate structure.

Communicative Approach to Urban Society

The importance of distinguishing between totalitarian and democratic social systems is that in communicative approaches to various
societies there have been, in the recent past, three main types of
orientation. These can be called generally Roman Catholic, Communist, and Protestant, though one must immediately raise a caution
against a tendency to identify a "missionary approach" with a particular institutional structure. Nevertheless, these distinctions, as we shall
see, reflect in general the manner in which for the most part Roman
Catholics, Communists, and Protestants have set out to influence
significantly the social structures.

In the Roman Catholic approach to a new society, primary consideration has usually been given to the upper class, though a number
of instances can be cited in which a broad segment of the society has
been approached. The tendency, however, has been for the Roman
Church to identify itself with the leadership of the society and
through it to influence the lower classes. In exchange for partnership
in controlling the society, the Church always provides the upper class
with many benefits, including the best professional religious services
and facilities for the education of children. Moreover, the leadership
of the Church is generally drawn from the upper class. (The present
Pope John XXIII is a notable exception.)

The typical Roman Catholic approach may be schematically diagrammed as follows:

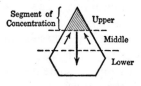

The shaded area indicates the class with which the Church has primarily identified itself, and the arrows indicate both the direction of
control (downward) and the pressures of opposition (upward).

In Latin America, where the Roman Church has traditionally
dominated the social and political structure of society, most of the
opposition to the joint control of society by the upper class and
the clergy comes from members of the upper-middle class, who see in
the coalition of the rich landed aristocracy and the Church a threat to

their ambition to improve their status. Hence, thwarted middle-class leaders often compete for the loyalties of the lower classes, especially the more aggressive elements of the upper-lower class, and by means of revolutions have from time to time overthrown clerical control. Such a revolution has occurred at one time or another in all the independent Roman Catholic countries of Latin America. However, it has often happened that after winning the revolution the leaders of liberal movements have failed to reorganize society with a new set of values. Because of the resulting vacuum, the Church has consistently returned, though usually not with the same degree of control, and often making a broader appeal to the masses who deserted their earlier masters.

The Communist technique in approaching a society is to draw out a segment from the middle and lower classes, usually the lower-middle class and the upper-lower class. In this segment there is usually a small nucleus of frustrated middle-class intellectuals, who may have been thwarted in their attempts at social climbing or who represent minority group disabilities. These intellectuals then combine with the economically, socially, or politically disenfranchised lower-class elements and by revolution capture the leadership. The former upper class must then be liquidated, either by confiscation to destroy its economic power, or by physical destruction, or by brainwashing. The main features of this development may be diagrammed as follows:

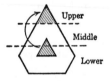

Having taken over leadership, the new upper class of party members and certain technicians then establish a heavy barrier between themselves and the middle classes. Leadership is not recruited from the middle classes (except in so far as certain experts may work for the state); the decisions and the control of communication continue to be exerted by an élite drawing its membership from the lower-middle and upper-lower classes. For example, in East Germany during the last few years the often brilliant sons of professionals are discriminated against in obtaining advanced educational opportunities, while the less intelligent sons of working men are given preferential treatment.

Persons who have been selected according to this system, and cata-
pulted by means of party membership from a lower-class status to one
of the highest priority, naturally owe all they are to the party, and
not primarily to personal achievement or background. They are thus
far more obedient to the party than would otherwise be the case; for
expulsion from it means not a somewhat horizontal movement, as in
our society, but a severe loss of all privileges and status. All this
centralized control is made possible in our modern society because of
the highly specialized nature of communication and transportation,
by means of which a relatively small group of people can control
millions. There is no longer any possibility of successful pitchfork
rebellions.

The present Protestant approach to society, especially in its missionary aspects, is quite different from the Roman Catholic and
Communist orientations. It must be recognized that, in the past,
Protestant developments were closely related to broad political and
social movements in northern Europe, in which significant changes
in church affiliation were considerably influenced by the loyalties of
certain princes and rulers. However, it is also possible to read too
much significance into the actions of individual kings and to forget
that they reflected as well as molded the events that precipitated the
break with the Roman Church.

If, however, we are to judge the Protestant approach to society as
evidenced both in the mission field and in certain aspects of important Protestant movements in England and America (e.g., the development of Methodism), we may say that Protestants concentrated
their efforts on the diagrammatic bulge in society, that is, on the
lower-middle and upper-lower classes—even as, in a sense, Communists
have done. In such areas as Latin America, for example, persons of
the lower-middle and upper-lower classes often have little to lose by
identifying themselves with the Protestant cause, since they belong
largely to a socially "disinherited" group. On the contrary, they often
feel that they have much to gain, quite apart from the benefits they
believe are derived from a direct personal relationship to God rather
than a relationship through some mediating person or institution.
These supplementary benefits often involve educational opportunities
for their children, medical assistance for themselves and their families, and a new sense of dignity and "belongingness" in a fellowship
which is highly interdependent and mutually helpful. The major

aspects of this development may be diagrammed as follows (but note that on this diagram the arrow indicates direction of mobility):

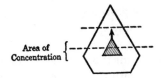

It should be noted that the constituency thus formed tends to have an upward movement. This upward mobility results almost inevitably from a greater sense of personal responsibility, accumulation of capital (for the convert does not spend so much money as formerly on certain forbidden "pleasures"), increased concern for and appreciation of education, a new attitude toward work as a virtue (part of the "Protestant ethic"), and opportunities for the expression of leadership within the Protestant fellowship.

However, this same upward mobility tends to separate those concerned from the very groups out of which they have come. The Methodist movement in England was a typical Protestant approach to the lower bulge of the social structure. It came as a reaction against the more or less authoritarian structure of the British religious system, which had been inherited from Roman Catholicism. The principal appeal was made to the lower-middle and upper-lower classes, including some of the very lowest classes, especially the miners. This movement is now, however, distinctly upper-middle class and even lower-upper class. In the United States, Methodism has experienced the same type of upward movement, but with an interesting series of successive waves of related movements. These "waves" have progressively sought to reach out to bring in those who were being left behind or neglected, and who, as they were included, have in turn moved up in the social structure. As Methodists moved up, such groups as the Nazarenes came in to reach those "left behind," and as the Nazarenes in turn moved up, the various types of Pentecostals made their special appeal to the lower classes.

A number of persons have compared the current rebirth of interest in religion in America to the wave of religious devotion that swept over England in the Victorian period. There is, however, a striking difference. Whereas the Victorian religious revival in Britain was concentrated in the better-to-do classes, and in considerable measure left the working man out in the cold (a fact which helps to explain the present irreligion of the masses in the United Kingdom), the development in the United States has included the so-called "third force," the rapidly growing and appreciably improving Pentecostal sects, which principally appeal to and have their strength in the lower classes.

There are valid reasons for this so-called "Protestant approach," for the future is ultimately with the masses, as it has been throughout history. The upper classes finally disintegrate because of what we might term social "dryrot." Their primary orientation is to preserve the *status quo*, in itself never a sufficient dynamic for creative development. "Where there is no vision the people perish." On the other hand, the creative minority is almost always to be found in the middle class, and this group provides leadership to the Protestant dynamic. Moreover, there is a third operative factor, namely, that it is possible to uplift people only by identifying with them through vertical communication. The control from a position of social dominance, as is usually the case in Roman Catholicism, is well calculated to produce continued loyalty and adherence. However, only by a true identification with people and by communicating with them on an essentially horizontal plane can one effect a real transformation of individual lives and of society as a whole.

Protestant missionary programs to reach the intelligentsia in various countries are of course very worthy, and most certainly the upper classes should not be neglected, for they are likewise objects of God's constraining love. Nevertheless, it must also be clearly recognized that not infrequently the leaders adopt the religion of the masses, even as Donald McGavran has pointed out,[3] basing his observations on Arnold Toynbee's analyses.

To our thesis that Protestants generally approach the lower-middle and upper-lower classes there is one seeming exception; namely, that in India Protestant missionaries have concentrated their attention upon the outcastes and have had a notable response from them. There are two important reasons for missionary success among such groups and for the high quality of leadership displayed by so many of these people. First, these people usually have had everything to gain and nothing to lose by identifying themselves with a foreign religion, since for all practical purposes they have been excluded from Hinduism itself. At the same time, however, the outcastes must not be regarded as merely an accumulation of indigent people (the equivalent of "poor white trash" in the United States) who, having never made good at anything, finally drifted into the outcaste groups. On the contrary, many of these people came from indigenous groups forced into various types of occupations that made them ceremonially unclean and hence outside the pale of Hindu ritual. Other persons became outcastes because they violated taboos. These outcastes, despite their miserable lot, are thus not just the dregs of society, but rather a religiously excluded class that included many persons of unusual gifts and capacities, as they have shown, once they were given an opportunity.

One reason for Protestantism's lack of appeal to many elements in the strictly indigent class—which is not only poor, but content with its status—is that it demands too high a standard of personal accountability, while at the same time failing to adjust its approach to different constituencies. Moreover, the Protestant church has had from the strictly indigent, drifting classes few who could provide leadership to reach out to bring in other persons of the same groups.

The Structure of Face-to-Face Societies

To the structure of urban societies, the rural, peasant, and primitive face-to-face societies present certain striking contrasts. There are, of course, many important differences between, for example, a small rural community in the hills of Kentucky and a village in the northern part of the Belgian Congo. Nevertheless, certain significant features are characteristic of most nonurban groupings, and these features are particularly relevant to the problems of communication.

In general, there are two main types of face-to-face societies: (1) folk and (2) primitive. The first is a dependent type of society which looks toward the urban center, derives considerable benefits from it, and also contributes much to it, especially by way of raw materials. The primitive society, on the other hand, is also a strictly face-to-face grouping, whether loosely or tightly organized, but its economy and orientation are almost completely independent of outside influences. Such a group, with its own laws, is quite homogeneous, with little division of labor, except as between sexes. Actually, strictly primitive groups—in this sense of the term—are now few. They consist primarily of small tribelets in Amazonia and New Guinea, as well as certain more isolated parts of Africa. Societies often spoken of as primitive, e.g., Indian tribes in Mexico and the altiplano of South America, are basically "peasant" or dependent societies; and many African tribes south of the Sahara and indigenous groups in India, Southeast Asia and the Islands of the Sea, are rapidly becoming such, though at present they are in a transitional state. The rapid development of transportation and communications and the economic exploitation of so-called primitive areas and peoples have in many instances changed these people from independent to dependent societies.

A typical folk or peasant society is not only economically dependent upon the urban center, whether it looks to the mining area around Elisabethville in the Congo or sends its produce into a *ladino* town such as Cuzco in Peru; it also exists in cultural dependency to the prestigeful urban center from which so many cultural influences radiate. In contrast to the large, often heterogeneous and impersonal city society, with its lax morals, softer life, secular attitudes, and aggressive manner, the peasant, folk society is generally small, usually quite homogeneous, and intimate, with a milder, more passive manner, and with emphasis upon strong concepts of traditional morality, capacity for physical endurance, and deep religious sentiments. In such a face-to-face society, everyone knows everyone else, and also knows almost everyone's business, including a good deal about everyone's private life—in fact nothing is hidden from the prying and watchful eyes of neighbors. There is very little formal codification of law, but the customs are generally adhered to with an almost fanatical loyalty. By and large the people are more honest, especially within the in-group (the rural society with which the people identify themselves); but they are also more defensive against outside influences, and hence more likely to suspect ulterior motives and to react with blind stupidity and recalcitrance. In some ways long-established folk societies (though not "transitional societies") are more resistant to change than are strictly primitive groups, to which the outside world is less familiar. Furthermore, the folk society has generally discovered that the only defense against being overwhelmed by the outside world is to resist, passively but stubbornly, any changes sponsored by the outgroup (the social grouping of which they are not members). This fact partly explains why Protestant missionaries have generally been more successful in dealing with primitive societies, for example, those in Africa, rather than with such a society as the Andean Indians of South America, whose patterns of resistance have been crystallized in opposition to the threats of domination by the white-sponsored culture of the urban centers.

In contrast to the inverted diamond structure with horizontal class cleavage which is typical of urban cultures, folk societies and, to a considerable extent, primitive societies as well may be diagrammatically described as broad-based, pyramidal forms, with roughly parallel rather than cross-sectional divisions:

The pyramid in this instance is quite broad-based, for in general the distinctions between those who lead and those who are led are not great. At the same time, there are no simple higher, middle, and lower classes, or elaborations of these distinctions. Rather, the structure of the society breaks down essentially into family groups related by birth or marriage, and consisting of clans, tribelets, phratries, or moieties, depending upon the particular form which any particular social structure may take.

The apex of the diagram indicates the leadership of a small group, the elders of the society, who form an oligarchical control, but who also, as suggested by the dotted lines, individually represent their family affiliations. Such a society has a strong sense of cohesion and presents a more or less uniform front against intrusion. It must be conservative in orientation in order to preserve itself. By and large it makes collective decisions, not by any formal parliamentary techniques but by the kind of informal discussion and interchange of opinions that characterize most types of "family decisions." The effective spread of information in such a society is not describable as along either horizontal or vertical axes (as in our previous diagrams), but rather primarily along family and clan lines. McGavran makes a point of the necessity of using these effective channels of communication as the "bridges of God."[4]

Communicative Approach to a Face-to-Face Society

The methods by which we can best reach people in an urban type of society are quite evident to us, because most of us belong to such a social grouping. But the best type of approach to people living in a face-to-face society is for the same reason strange to most of us, since the social and communicational lines and structures are unfamiliar. However, once we have recognized the fundamental structure of such societies, we can see that the approaches which have proved to be most successful in them are the ones that make optimum use of the natural flow of communication. The basic principles in such an approach are four: (1) effective communication must be based upon personal friendship, (2) the initial approach should be to those who can effectively pass on communication within their family grouping, (3) time must be allowed for the internal diffusion of new ideas, and (4) the challenge for any change of belief or action must be addressed to the persons or groups socially capable of making such decisions.

In a face-to-face society it is essential to establish a personal basis of friendship and acceptance before communication can become effective. An outstanding early missionary in Peru, John Ritchie, instrumental in establishing more than two hundred congregations among the Indian population, made it an invariable rule never to go into a village except by personal invitation. He went to the home of the villager who had invited him and there remained during his visit of two or three days. In other words, he never went unannounced and unexpected into any Indian community to "evangelize," for he had concluded on the basis of years of experience that this course was simply not to be followed in an Indian community. Indians who were Christians might do so, for they could always establish some "family or clan" connection with the inhabitants, but the missionary, a stranger to the group, always felt that his message could be made acceptable to the people only if he was personally "sponsored" by someone belonging to the village. His host, though not necessarily a Christian, must be someone sufficiently interested in the Good News to invite the missionary to come as his personal guest. Such an approach also meant that there was little or no danger that other villagers would organize an attack to drive out the missionary, for as a guest of a member of the face-to-face community he was relatively immune from the overt opposition of hostile religious elements. The primary purpose of this invited approach, however, was not self-protection, but effective communication.

For this missionary invitations to visit new villages were not difficult to obtain, for interested persons, whether or not they had become believers, had relatives and friends in other villages who would invariably pass on the word about this remarkable new message. Moreover, the people learned that the missionary would not impose himself upon anyone, but in typical Indian fashion approached them only on the basis of friendship, and not as a campaigning politician or a dubiously motivated rabble-rouser. It then became a matter of distinction for the leading men in various villages to invite the missionary to come and stay with them, while he shared his personal message of what God had done for all people, including the Quechua-speaking Indians of the altiplano.

A similar approach has been followed by a mission doing highly successful work among certain Indian groups in Mexico. A Mexican evangelist, sometimes with the help of an American missionary, goes into a village and establishes friendship with some leading people in one of the *barrios* of the village. (The *barrios* are geographical divisions of Mexican towns and villages, reflecting earlier Indian distinctions of family or clan relationships.) Within each *barrio*, especially in completely Indian towns, the people feel an even closer face-to-face relationship than they do with others in the town as a whole. Hence, when work begins in a particular *barrio*, it is normal to keep the "communication" limited primarily to this group until it is well established. There are two reasons for this procedure. First, once the evangelist has made the friendship of some leading person in the *barrio*, he is likely to have ready access to a number of families related to one another in some way, either by birth, marriage, or the *compadre-comadre* relationship (the "godfather-godmother" system). Second, extension of the communication will probably be unopposed, provided it stays within this interpersonally related group of people. If, however, religious beliefs contrary to the traditional Christo-paganism of the region are proclaimed to the entire community by outsiders who have not first obtained significant acceptance by a recognized community group, the leaders of the society as a whole will feel that a serious intrusion has been made. Their normal reaction will be to persecute the carriers of the message in order to preserve the solidarity of the community structure. Thus an initial proclamation to the entire community is likely to result in a strongly negative reaction, while a quiet approach to a closely related segment is much more likely to be favorably received. Later, when the entire community recognizes the message as foreign to its tradition, the movement will already have become established among respected members of the community, and hence persecution in its more violent forms may be regarded by the community as either inappropriate or too late.

The second and perhaps the most important principle to be followed in approaching such a community is to make the initial approach to those able effectively to pass on the communication. In some instances, the missionary is able to appeal to the chief of the tribe. In the United States, the rural "missionary" may be able to get the backing of the richest farmer in the region where he works. Usually, however, the unqualified support of the "top man" cannot be obtained immediately, for the leaders in a face-to-face society are generally slow to move ahead of their people. In fact, a man's position of leadership in a face-to-face society depends more upon the intimate and knowledgeable support of his followers than is true of a leader in an impersonal, urban society, where "money talks" more successfully. Thus the chief or headman in such a society is likely to be cautious about accepting any new thing; for the society itself is highly conservative and the leader is usually even more traditional in orientation than the majority of the people. In such a society strength lies in conservatism. Accordingly, those successful in reaching people in folk societies have usually approached a key person near the top, but not quite at the top—someone who, though respected within his own family and clan, has not yet assumed responsibility as an elder of the people. This person is usually a strong personality, well liked by the people. Not infrequently he feels that sponsorship of new ideas may be to his social benefit. However, a word of caution should be added here. It must be recognized that a truly "marginal person" in the cult will not prove satisfactory for this purpose. Such a person's status may mean that he has been ostracized by his own society because of some affront to traditional leadership, or because he has violated the ethical standards of the people. It may mean that he is really an outsider in the face-to-face society, but hangs on in parasitical fashion because he derives economic benefit from exploiting the folk society.

Nevertheless, we must not leave the impression that only such persons as have been described as helpful are indispensable to evangelistic endeavors. In many instances persons apparently lacking in these qualities have compensated for their liabilities by unusual sensitivity to the people, evident devotion to the cause of Christ, and remarkable transformation of their own lives, with the result that many have been attracted to the message through them. But when we analyze developments throughout the whole range of work with face-to-face societies, it becomes evident that the social and personal qualities of those initially won to the new faith are of high significance in assessing the probable effectiveness of the communication and its extension to others.

Whereas in our own churches we often think in terms of high-pressure, dynamic programs intended to reap results overnight, the approach to face-to-face societies must be of quite a different order. Traditionalists living within the comfortable emotional security of their "extended family," which maintains itself primarily by resistance to ideas from the outside world, cannot be pushed into making quick decisions. Such people, confronted by a "crash program," will be inclined to reject it at once. Just as a family must be given time to make up its mind, so a face-to-face society must be carefully nursed along until the people are ready to act. At this point, an acute problem arises, for the missionary's tendency is to encourage some especially responsive persons to step out, repudiate the traditions of their tribe, and declare themselves for Christ. Such a procedure often causes the people as a whole to reject the message. For until a people are able to make what seems to them a valid decision, any pulling out of members from the ranks of the closed society immediately raises the fear of loss of solidarity. An instinctive resistance to assault upon the tight-knit social structure follows. By far the most effective work among folk societies has been done by those sensitive to the "timing" of the first converts. Allowing sufficient time for the making of decisions is the indispensable third principle in communicating with face-to-face societies.

This discourse may seem to imply that the missionary's efforts involve nothing more or less than a diabolical assault on traditional cultures; that in a Machiavellian manner the missionary is to decide astutely and act on the most successful techniques to accomplish his purpose. What we are trying to say, rather, is that the missionary, or anyone for that matter, must avoid the overurging and pressuring of genuinely interested persons. After all, the people within a folk society will know full well whether a new convert comes to his decision as the result of his own careful and full deliberation, or whether the missionary in his zeal has overstepped the bounds of propriety for the sake of registering a "triumph for the cross." If a man comes to a genuine conviction about the new faith and decides to make an independent and clean-cut break with past tradition, he is to be encouraged. We cannot and should not dictate the way in which the Holy Spirit works in the hearts of people. But we must be certain that the decision made reflects a man's honest, thoughtful response to the total claims of Christ, rather than an emotional reaction and mixed motives that will be read only too plainly by other members of the society.

In one unusually fine piece of work among Indians in Latin America, I was personally surprised to find, on visiting the region, that the missionary never extended public invitations to people to "accept Jesus Christ." I had more or less expected that the missionary's background would prompt this type of approach. When I asked why he did not use such a method, he explained frankly that he never gave such an invitation because he was certain that a number of Indians would then make a public "confession"—not so much because of personal conviction, but because of their desire to please him. Moreover, he explained, he tried to keep close to these people so that he would know when the Spirit of God was dealing with them. Then they would either come to him of their own accord, or he would provide an opportunity whereby, in a natural context of friendly conversation and without the evangelistic trimmings of group pressure, they could be led to an effective decision for Christ. This work, though not spectacular, is well founded and growing rapidly. It will continue to expand for years to come, for it has won its way into the very life of the tribe.

The fourth principle in approaching face-to-face societies is to present the challenge for change of belief to persons socially capable of making valid decisions. We who do not know the meaning of clan life, since we are not ourselves members of such a society, can rarely imagine the pressures upon the individual in such an organization. We take it for granted that anyone can and should make up his own mind about what he believes and what he should do. But this is not true in all cultures. Members of such a society feel an instinctive loyalty to the extended family unit. The individual derives his personal and social security from it, and usually gives it his complete and often unthinking support. Even an adult man may find it impossible to break with such a family unit. It is as though we invited a neighbor child to go to the beach for a day with our family, without consulting his parents. In general, his first response will be, "I'll go ask my mother." In fact, if we handle such an invitation rightly we would ask his mother for him, so that she would recognize the conditions as well as the genuineness of the invitation. Something of the same situation exists in face-to-face cultures, where individuals do not act on their own, but respond as members of families, clans, and tribes.

This group response to the gospel message lies at the core of the so-called "mass movements," called "people's movements" by McGavran. He pleads, and rightly so, for a more intelligent appreciation of the structure of societies in which people normally act as groups. He therefore insists that the process of Christianization must be divided between initial "discipling" and later instruction, and that the importance of initial commitment by the people to a new way of life must be fully recognized and built upon. The motives of such a people in mass response should no more be suspect than are the often mixed motives that prompt many individuals in an urban society to declare themselves for Christ, only to find later that they have committed themselves to more than they had earlier thought. In either case the initial commitment of either group or individual provides the basis by which instruction in the faith may be given and through which full maturity of Christian discipleship may be reached.

The Problem of Heterogeneous Societies

Heterogeneous societies are primarily of two types: (1) urban societies that contain urban-structured minority groups, similar, for example, to the Negro subculture within American life; and (2) urban societies that include face-to-face subsocieties.

In the first type one must recognize three factors: (1) the basic differences, which mean that one cannot, for all his idealism, use identically the same approaches to the various groups; (2) the immense prestige differential, which means that the people in the less prestigeful groups try to follow, or think that they are following, the norms of the higher group; and (3) the priority of intragroup communication, if effective communication is to be attained.

The relation between two urban-structured groups in a single society can be diagrammatically represented as follows:

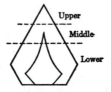

Assuming that this diagram represents in rough outline some of the relations of the Negro subculture to the dominant white culture, there are several important factors to note: (1) though some Negroes have achieved relatively high status, there are proportionately fewer in this category than in the white majority; (2) the Negro position is more that of a caste than a class, for disabilities from birth generally preclude mobility of the Negro from his own culture to the white culture (even though many thousands of Negroes "pass" each year); and (3) communication about everyday economic matters may involve participants of both white and Negro groups, but communication about ultimate life values, social relations, and basic world view are restricted largely to the two isolated segments of the society.

Such a minority group as the Spanish-speaking constituency in the American Southwest has a somewhat different status and role, for though distinctly a "minority" group in most places, it is not always urban structured, especially in small communities, and its members can pass more readily into the prestige group. On the other hand, Puerto Ricans in New York have a much more difficult status and their language problem combined with racial traits constitutes a segregating liability.

Communication to the Negro society in the United States is beset by a number of severe problems as the result of the fundamental social structures and outlooks involved. We must first of all face squarely the fact that between the Negro and white segments of the population there are significant differences that make communication at times seem irrelevant. For example, the typical white Protestant view of work as the logical fulfillment of life's purposes is not consistent with the view of Negroes, many of whom regard work as a means whereby one insures a livelihood in order to enjoy "non-work." The Puritan concept of the righteousness of work for work's sake does not make too much sense in the Negro world view. Nor does the Protestant view of the dignity and responsibility of the individual seem to have much meaning when the Negro is socially barred from the very system that preaches this dignity and at the same time gives him little or no opportunity for the development of wider responsibilities than his own restricted group affords. On the other hand, many Negroes exhibit an appreciably greater religious sensitivity than do whites, for religious expression is far more central to their way of life. Similarly, they often have a more profound capacity for human friendship, for they are more "people-centered" than "thing-centered." Moreover, they also have a greater capacity for the "joy of life" (certainly in terms of their opportunities), and their laughter is not just a nervous mask for intolerable tensions (though such tensions may at times be involved); they are in general simply more given to seeing and participating in the humor of life than are more "deadpan" whites. This analysis of differences is not intended to imply that one type is essentially inferior or superior to another. The two are simply different. But these differences are vital to any understanding of intergroup communication.

The wide differences in relative prestige of the white and Negro groups have inevitably led Negroes to be suspicious of outsiders. As a group they have suffered greatly from those who sought to exploit them economically and ideologically. The ideological exploiters have included some militant social reformers of the old style, more interested in proving their theories right than in helping people. Rarely, if ever, do such reformers identify themselves with their "guinea pigs of social change." It must be said, however, that this class of professional reformer, handicapped by an acute lack of empathy with the people, appears fortunately to be passing, and others with a sounder understanding of social problems and a realistic appraisal of their own legitimate roles in such engineered change are assuming much needed leadership. Nevertheless, it is evident that a people restricted in the spheres in which they are allowed to express their capacities are understandably jealous of the opportunities they do have.

In some instances the problem of prestige seems strangely reversed. In Cuba, for example, a young Negro of unusual personal gifts and ability was specially trained for the Protestant ministry among his own people. However, several predominantly Negro churches which he might have served effectively did not want a pastor of the Negro race, for they felt that he would lower the prestige of the congregation. They contended that a Negro pastor of a predominantly Negro congregation would not only make the white people reluctant to attend the church, but that Negroes themselves would go to other churches having a white pastor and a predominantly white congregation, where they would not suffer from discrimination or implied inferiority. The Negro pastor was finally accepted by a predominantly white congregation which appreciated his capacities for leadership and had no fear that their predominantly white membership would suffer loss of prestige from having a Negro minister.

Given the circumstances that prevail between white and Negro segments of American society, religious communication is undoubtedly more effective within each group than between the groups. This argument is not one for the continuance of legal segregation in any form; the legal inequalities are not only unchristian but thoroughly antithetical to a democratic way of life. Moreover, it is only after the removal of legal discriminations that other and equally wrong forms of discrimination can be righted. Much of our present flurry about racial integration is only a passing mood to relieve a bad conscience. It is interpreted by many Negroes as being nothing more or less than a compound ailment of guilt and old-fashioned paternalism. The real answer to interracial communication is for each group to have something relevant to say to the other. Such a condition comes only as a result of effective identification. (See Chapter 7.)

In the second principal type of heterogeneous society the dominant urban structure includes a minority group having a face-to-face type of society. A typical situation of this kind may be illustrated by the following diagram:

Several significant features of this diagram should be recognized. First, the included face-to-face group may penetrate into the middle class, if one takes into account economic resources and general prestige. Second, the base of the included face-to-face group is usually not so low as that of the urban culture, for in general the poor people of the urban slums are in far worse circumstances than are the poor people of the smaller rural communities. This is certainly true, for example, of the poor Indians of the altiplano in South America as compared with the indigent urban population. Sociologists in Mexico also regard the poor people of the slums around Mexico City as in much more desperate circumstances, and often less amenable to effective help, than are the Indians of many tribes living in remote areas of the country.

It should not be concluded that all face-to-face societies of this kind are more or less the same. This is far from being so. In Mexico, for example, the Zapotec Indians of Tehuantepec and the Otomi Indians of the Mezquital represent entirely different types of circumstances. Many of the Zapotecs are rather well-to-do; a number have completed their university education and have professional positions in Mexico City, though upon their return to their homes in Juchitan and surrounding towns they are still accepted as members of the Indian society. On the other hand, among the Otomis very few are regarded as any higher than lower low in socioeconomic status. These relative structures of two contrasting groups can be diagrammed as follows, each within the general context of Mexican life:

Included folk societies have always been recognized as in some degree different from their urban neighbors, especially if they happen to speak another language and wear different types of clothing. But rarely is it recognized that such folk societies have fundamentally different orientations toward life and are usually structured along quite different lines from the urban society, so that any communication to them must be specially formulated and transmitted if it is to be relevant. The Indians of Mexico are not simply Mexicans who happen to live a long way from the city; nor are the Cebuanos in the backwoods villages of Cebu in the Philippines the same as the throngs in Manila. Of course, many peoples in the world are now in process of drastic change. The Zulu who alternates between the mining compounds of Johannesburg and his own village in the bush is in a sense a part of both societies: the urban and the rural, the impersonal city and the face-to-face village. However, he is really not a fully participating member of the urban society, except at the lowest levels. Actually, he is primarily a substitute for machinery and socially is not really considered a human being. In his village, however, he belongs, has a role, and performs a valid social function. But the standards of his two worlds are very different and he is caught in a maelstrom of tensions, where economic necessities force him, regardless of personal preference, to play a double role. Accordingly, he suffers the emotional instability that always comes with the conflict of double standards and uncertain position.

Communicative Approach to a Heterogeneous Society with Included Face-to-Face Constituency

When a single over-all social structure involves not only a dominant group but an included face-to-face constituency, it is essential to recognize not only their differences of structure, but also their interrelations. One of the most serious mistakes in missionary work has been to imagine that Indians in the Americas, for example, should be reached as a separate constituency and developed as an isolated community, when all the time they are in highly dependent relation to the urban center. The result of such efforts is usually to set up a church organization, incapable of relating the people to the larger national constituency. The people thus never feel a part of the larger fellowship and often dwindle away since they are obliged to depend exclusively on their own resources. Moreover, without the support of outsiders (other than the missionary) their status in the urban center is jeopardized. As a result they feel that in some way or another their religion is a foreign thing, imported directly from the United States and without any affiliation with other Christians in their own country. In one center in South America an enormous amount of money has been spent to reach the poor peon population, almost to the complete exclusion of the town community. The result has been that the peons, the ostensible object of all this economic assistance, have spent a good part of their income to provide their former bosses and town friends with liquor, by way of demonstrating that they are really not a part of the Protestant mission effort, but are still loyal dependents of the urban center even though in the past they have always been insecure and exploited.

It is just as possible, however, and more frequently the case, that missionary effort fails to recognize the need of devising different approaches to the urban and folk societies, but lumps them together without regard to their different structures. The probable reasons for this lack of discrimination are that American missionaries mistakenly think that the urban and rural areas abroad are equivalent to the corresponding areas in the United States. Even though Americans living in small towns and rural communities have a number of characteristics typical of a face-to-face community, farmers in the United States are by no means "peasants." Except for people in certain very isolated communities in mountainous areas, their world view, standard of values, general orientation toward life, and educational opportunities are substantially the same as those of the city dweller. There are of course differences between the "hayseed" and the "city slicker," but except for certain very restricted cases, in American life there is no peasant culture, with its emphasis upon family structure and clan relationships, and its highly traditional and resistant attitudes. Certain of these tendencies do exist, but they are by no means so pronounced or so significant as in a true peasant culture.

When an American goes to a foreign country, however, he tends to judge all situations by what he has known at home. He does not appreciate the significance of the existing contrasts, because his eyes have not been opened to them. He therefore lumps all groups together and proceeds without reference to basic differences. If, however, he is to be successful in communicating, he must recognize the distinctions that exist between various classes of people and make his message applicable to their circumstances and transmittable by means of their traditional networks of communication. Each class or subculture must be reached within the contexts of its own life, and in so far as they are interdependent, the Christians among them must be helped to recognize their mutual responsibilities.

The church in the folk society must learn how to receive and profit from the help obtainable from the church in the urban society;

similarly, the urban church must learn how to give help to the rural group without overwhelming its leadership and quenching its spirit. It is not enough to train the tribal peoples for participation in national life—even at best, this cannot be done in a single generation. Hence, the urban churches must be taught how they can help without hindering, how they can lead without dictating, and how they can encourage without stifling local enthusiasm. The way in which urban churches tend to dominate rural churches and ultimately to snuff out their fire and vigor is tragic. At times, for example, it seems even harder for the leaders in Manila to understand what is needed in the mountains of Luzon than for the Kankanaey tribesmen to tell their city "cousins" how their work should be conducted. In any national church organization, however, it is usually the city churches that do the dictating, though it is often in the rural areas that the church has its growing edge. Not infrequently the urban church would die if it were not for the steady stream of rural people who flock into the cities to find new opportunities for work and advancement.

When a missionary faces a bilingual situation, his immediate instinct is to find a bilingual person to carry on the work, either as full-time evangelist or as his interpreter. The difficulty here is that bilingual people are not necessarily "bicultural"—often quite the contrary. Often they are really allied with the dominant culture which tends to exploit the peasant classes; sometimes they have been ostracized by their own community. In still other cases they may have left their own society when relatively young; and while they may still speak the language, they do not know the cultural features in which these words actually have significance. They thus know the vocabulary, but not the life and the value system. There is a possibility that even the young person specifically prepared by the mission schools for work among his own people may not succeed, for he has usually been educated away from rather than toward his own culture. The new way of life he has learned—for education is by no means confined to books—ultimately alienates him from his people. Furthermore, by going back to his village he risks losing status with the dominant culture, for his identification with the prestige society is probably still insecure. Actually, it is often emotionally much easier for a missionary to adjust to the peasant or indigenous culture than for a national of the country to do so, for the missionary's education and secure social position—he is after all a hero to those who have sent him out—make it relatively easy for him to make an open identification with the people. He feels quite certain, though he might not admit it to others, that no one will be deceived about his real status and position.

In a heterogeneous society with an included folk culture there is always the acute problem of dealing with people in a state of transition. How are they to be ministered to—in terms of their rural circumstances, or in their city setting? In a sense, it all depends on where they are and how they view themselves. A Tarahumara Indian in northern Mexico usually expects that, when he is wearing pants, outsiders will address him in Spanish; but the same Indian, dressed on the next day in his tradition breechcloth, and meeting the same people, will expect to be greeted in Tarahumara. Something of the same situation holds with respect to groups in transition, for the people themselves are living a dual role. In the metropolitan center of Leopoldville in the Belgian Congo such people are caught up in the system of thought, the types of reactions, and the impersonal business of city life. These same people back in their villages—though if they can possibly do so they try to remain in the big city—usually take up their traditional roles again, but not without some strain and frustration. They are like the farm boy who went away to the city to make good but could not quite make it. He may still put on the airs of city sophistication, but unless his exposure has been long and thorough, he still looks at his world through "country eyes."

Orientations of Societies toward Life

It is one thing to analyze the structure of a society, whether homogeneous or heterogeneous, and to point out the fundamental lines of communication; it is quite another to develop a message relevant to different social groups that takes into consideration their orientation toward life in terms of their interpersonal relations.

David Riesman in *The Lonely Crowd*[5] has developed a highly suggestive thesis about certain fundamental social orientations. In considerable measure the following analysis is derived from his unusually helpful insights; though in religious matters he touches only on certain limited factors and of course does not take up the problem of relevant themes of communication, and in these respects the analysis is my own.

In general, Riesman argues that societies tend to be classifiable into three groups: tradition-directed, inner-directed, and other-directed. The first type of society is characterized by the outlook, "We have always done it this way" (or in Spanish, *Es costumbre*). This type of society, which might be called the "beaten path" society, may be illustrated by hundreds of primitive and folk societies, as well as by some larger groups, e.g., Thailand, India, Cambodia, and Burma, especially as they were fifty to seventy-five years ago. The inner-directed society takes the position, "We ought to do it this way, for it is right." Such a society might be called the "gyroscope" society, for its members have as a stabilizer a well-functioning, built-in conscience, based primarily upon the direction given them by their elders, but directed toward an expanding frontier with growing population and the concept of new horizons and a changed way of life. This pattern was typical of the United States a generation ago, and is still more or less true of most of the larger societies of Europe. The other-directed society takes the view that "Everyone is doing it, therefore it is O.K." This type of society may be described as a "radar" group, in which the members of the society are constantly trying to determine norms of behavior by seeing what others are doing and how others are responding to them. It is typical of what is happening in many phases of contemporary American life, in situations in which the horizons seem to have been reached, the frontier is gone, and the society is settling back into a stage of "getting along together."

A cyclical or dynamic pattern of change appears to operate in all societies. Ancient Greece in many respects went through these same three phases. The traditional period was before the time of Pisistratus and Solon in the sixth century B.C. The inner-directed period extended from Solon to Plato in the fourth century B.C. The third, or other-directed period was typified by the Hellenistic Age, especially from the time of Aristotle to the conquest of the Eastern Mediterranean by Rome. A similar series of changes occurred in Roman society, beginning with the tradition-directed society before the establishment of the Republic in 509 B.C., to an increasingly inner-directed society during the period of the Republic, until about the time of Julius Caesar, at which time Roman society began to shift more and more to an other-directed type of social structure.

Of course, these changes do not occur abruptly in any society, and they may affect one level of society faster than another. However, Riesman seems to have found some highly significant contrasts between social orientations which are not only relevant for individual outlooks within a society but are also descriptive and diagnostic of groups as a whole.

To appreciate some of the differences in communication and approach to social groups having such diverse orientations, we must examine some of these contrasts in greater detail. Though we cannot treat all the significant distinctions discussed in *The Lonely Crowd*, there are some of particular importance for our emphasis upon communication. The tradition-directed society, for example, seems to look toward past behavior for its norms, the inner-directed group looks to its built-in conscience, and in the other-directed society persons look to their contemporaries for clues as to whether they are "doing all right." The tradition-directed society is essentially a static one, with a stable birth rate over a period of years. The inner-directed society has a rising birth rate and increasing population. The other-directed society has begun to settle down. Even though the birth rate may be increasing, the total increment has begun to taper off, and men are concentrating more on running the machine than on making a bigger and better one. Their primary considerations are thus human adjustments within the society, rather than adjustment to the world outside.

The tradition-directed society has little doubt about how children should be brought up; they are brought up as the parents were. The inner-directed society is likewise without much doubt as to child rearing, for it has confidence in its own norms of conduct. The other-directed society, however, is in considerable doubt, since there seem to be no clear rules. The primary reasons for these differences are that the tradition-directed society looks to the clan for guidance; the inner-directed person, to the family; and the other-directed group, to its peers. Thus the lines of guidance for the other-directed are indistinct and conflicting; for while the tradition-oriented people are living out their role, and the inner-directed person is acquiring a better role, the other-directed individual is very much concerned about finding his goal.

In a sense it can be said that the tradition-directed society looks to its culture heroes for the established ways, the inner-directed society finds its course by following the pioneers (*Robinson Crusoe* and *Pilgrim's Progress*), and the other-directed society looks for solutions in the soap-opera dramas of human adjustment. Thus, in a sense, the tradition-directed group looks to myth, the inner-directed society takes inspiration from sermons, and the other-directed man may be said to seek corresponding help in counseling and psychiatric interviews. Actually, the tradition-directed society is primarily concerned with shame when it violates tradition; and the inner-directed person bears a load of guilt, whether he is apprehended or not, for his conscience is his ward and his master. The other-directed person, on the other hand, may be equally anxious about his failures, but the anxiety is of of a more diffuse nature and centers about his relations with other people.

In the specifically religious context, one may contrast these three types of societies and orientations toward society from a number of points of view. The tradition-directed group may be said primarily to fear supernatural sanctions in the form of ancestral spirits and society-conserving gods (or God). The inner-directed person is more fearful of punishment, whether here or hereafter, from a personal devil or a conscience-supporting God. The other-directed person is more afraid of social ostracism than of any divine expulsion, and he regards his worries more as a psychosomatic disease than as induced by any outside supernatural considerations. In all such moral and religious issues the tradition-directed person looks to what "they" would do, the "I" is important to the inner-directed individual, and "we" to the other-directed person.

In terms of our own culture, and within the context of religious practices and behavior, we can describe the inner-directed person as Bible-reading, given to spontaneous prayer, concerned primarily with the content of the message, and sensitive to "divine guidance." The other-directed type of person, on the contrary, is more concerned with television watching, responds more to group liturgy, reacts more to the personality of the preacher, and seeks for "group guidance." While the inner-directed person becomes interested in Christianity because of what "the Word of God says," the other-directed individual may be attracted to a church because of its social emphasis and his need for "belonging." He becomes religious because it is what everyone else is doing, rather than for the motives of the inner-directed person, who is religious because to be so is inherently right.[6]

Because of these differences in viewpoint, effective communication to inner-directed and other-directed persons must be different. The inner-directed person, for example, with his relatively strong feeling of guilt, is much more likely to be appealed to by the doctrine of substitutionary atonement; while the problems of social maladjustment are so central to the other-directed person's world view that he responds more meaningfully to a presentation of God being in Christ reconciling the world to Himself, since estrangement is so much a part of the other-directed person's involvement.

At the same time, "The Bible says . . ." is fully authoritative to the inner-directed person and generally rings a bell of recognition in his conscience; but the other-directed person may be more attracted to Jesus Christ as the one uniquely divine person in all of history who as God meets men personally. The inner-directed person usually works up to a crisis in his religious experience, for his strong inner convictions may hold out a long time against the claims of Christ. But once he has made up his mind he joins the church to register this commitment. The other-directed person, however, is very likely to join the church with few or no personal convictions, but simply because it is the thing for respectable persons to do. However, contact with the message of the gospel may little by little so influence his total view that, almost without realizing what has happened, he becomes truly Christian; he then acknowledges Jesus Christ as Lord and Savior, with all that it means in his total life experience.

Though there are very evident contrasts between the personal inner-directed and other-directed orientations toward social life, the distinctions between tradition-directed and other-directed societies are not so clear. The reason is that in each case the people are looking to other people. In the tradition-directed society they look toward people of the distant past, while in the other-directed group people look to their contemporaries. At the same time, both types of social structures have a "leveling" influence, for the heavy hand of social pressure tends to crush any unusual outbursts of nonconformism. In both types of societies, for example, there is not too much interest in progress or fundamental cultural change, for the traditionalists do not see any possibility of progress and the other-directed persons do not regard progress as worth all the effort. Neither society tends to produce particularly strong leaders or typical "prima donnas," for the traditionalists do not know where to go and the other-directed individuals presume that they have gone every place worth going.

These differences in orientation between tradition-directed and other-directed groups mean that in some measure communication of the gospel is and should be different for them. In the case of traditionalists, especially those so-called primitive peoples with a typical mythological view of the world, one usually communicates more relevantly by beginning with God, then the world, and finally man. These are then brought into a meaningful synthesis by explaining the work of Jesus Christ.[7] Almost invariably people in primitive and folk societies want to know about God: What is He like? What has He done? Where does He live? How can one know Him? In other-directed societies persons usually become interested in the Good News if one begins with people, their problems and vital needs, and explains that these problems can be solved only through knowing God as He is revealed in Jesus Christ. Here the order is man, world, and then God, but in every instance one points to the uniqueness of God's revelation in His Son. The typical questions of the other-directed person are: What is man, anyway? What is the purpose of existence? Why should the world be as it is? Is it possible that this world was made by God? If so, how has He revealed Himself? Many of these questions would seem irrelevant to the tradition-directed person, while questions that presuppose God's existence seem entirely meaningless to many people of an other-directed society. The ultimate truth is the same, but the way in which one enters into vital conversations with differently oriented peoples often requires special adaptation.

Similarly, if one wishes to discuss with tradition-directed and other-directed persons the importance of following the new way as found in Jesus Christ, one must clearly distinguish the approach. To the traditionalists one can say: "But there is a better way. Now it has been made known. In the past it may have been hinted at by wise men, but in these days we have the full truth. Blind adherence to the past only leads to a tyranny over one's ultimate capacities. Only as we are freed from the shackles of the past by Jesus Christ, who showed us this new way, can we possibly enter into the fullness of life."

To the other-directed person, who thinks he knows all the ways and who rejects them all by not wanting to commit himself to any, one can say, "You have robbed your life of meaning because you have refused to commit yourself to anything, much less to God. In a sense you have been tyrannized by the crowd, by seeking a guide who is as blind as yourself. Moreover, you can't find yourself by losing yourself in the group; this can be a very sterile identification, for it is just a projection of your own limited self. If you want to find the way, it can be only through Jesus Christ, who is 'the way, the truth and the life,' who not only went ahead as 'the pioneer of our salvation,' but has thus shown us the way in his atoning work on the Cross. By reconciling us to God, he has made it possible for us to be His children. This is life."

It is not to be assumed that all persons within any predominantly tradition-, inner-, or other-directed society are essentially the same in their responses to the social context. In fact, Riesman points out that there are three different kinds of reactions to each orientation "type": (1) the adjusted persons, those who "run with the crowd" and who are always in the majority in any such system (in fact, they may be so overadjusted that they respond with almost unthinking reactions), (2) the anomalous persons, those who simply "refuse to run the race," e.g., the bums, alcoholics, and recluses (these occur predominantly in the inner-directed society, which puts a high premium on success and exacts heavy penalties for failure), and (3) the autonomous individuals, those who insist on "running their own kind of race," whether in a different direction or at their own pace. In a totalitarian society these people are the deviationists and the heretics. They are often ahead of their own day and are incorrigibly nonconformist. They do not, however, make a fetish of their nonconformity, for those who do so find themselves merely in an exclusivist cult. They are what they are, though not as an escape from reality, but as a mode of being their fullest selves. They are not preoccupied with trying to measure up to the stature of a haunting conscience (which the fully adjusted man in the inner-directed society must do), or with responding with anxious fears to others' estimates of themselves (as an adjusted person in an other-directed society must attempt to do), or with plodding along the path of one's ancestors (as in a tradition-directed group).

As Riesman has carefully pointed out, the future hope of any society rests with these autonomous persons, for only in this type of individual can there be a creative minority, in Toynbee's sense, which can effectively change the direction of social development.

These different orientations of society are not relevant merely to our large cosmopolitan nations of Western Europe and America. Such differences of "social direction" exist in areas all over the world, for the impact of rapid social change upon previously tradition-directed societies has resulted in a number of violent social eruptions, with all their disastrous consequences for large groups of people.

Vilakasi[8] describes the emerging Zulu classes of South Africa in terms of three social types: (1) the traditionalists, (2) the Christians or "school people," and (3) the "flotsam and jetsam." The traditionalists are those who stay by the old patterns of life and for the most part remain in the villages or are at least emotionally tied to them. The "school people" are those of relatively superior education who are trying to adjust to the ways of the predominant culture, namely, the white way of life, with its avowedly Christian world view. The "flotsam and jetsam," caught in the cultural squeeze, deny that they believe in the indigenous customs and completely repudiate traditional African authority and leadership. At the same time they have refused to assume any responsibility and are often spoken of as "lawless people who have no heads or addresses." Not that they are nomadic wanderers or wandering indigents; their lack of "addresses" is a way of saying that they have no cultural homes. These three classes roughly parallel the division into tradition-, inner-, and other-directed societies, though the particular social context of Zulu life results in certain special adaptations. The reasons for the difficulty of simple identification with Riesman's classes is that in South Africa there is a mixed social base to begin with, for one must think in terms of two conflicting social patterns, not merely one that is in process of internal change.

Despite the fact that we usually sense the strangeness and sometimes the importance of different social structures and their orientations, we rarely recognize the degree to which these factors influence a people's religious thinking and tend to condition their response to new ideas, especially to the presentation of the gospel of Jesus Christ. Perhaps one of the most significant illustrations of the interpenetration of religious and social concepts is to be found in the Roman Catholic doctrine of the Virgin Mary as it works itself out in Latin American life. Protestant missionaries have found, for example, that almost any doctrine of the Roman Church can be challenged with comparatively greater impunity than can the dogma concerning the Virgin Mary. Why should the people be hypersensitive to this issue? Why should it happen that even those who are anticlerical and antichurch should become emotionally inflamed by any questioning of the important status accorded the Virgin? The reason, of course, is that the Virgin Mary is not merely a religious symbol, but a social one as well, and as such a focus of Latin life.

First and foremost, the Virgin Mary is a kind of symbolic "mother" in a female-oriented society; for in Latin family life the father is more or less expected to be unfaithful to his wife. Moreover, in some places his social reputation depends in considerable measure upon the number and quality of his mistresses. The mother, however, remains faithful to the family, and she is the continuing symbol of family loyalty. Furthermore, in the pattern of Latin family life the father is expected to be more or less the domineering head of the household, though subject to the entreaty of the mother, who generally serves as a mediator between him, as authoritarian father, and the children. She thus becomes for the children not only the emotional center of the family world, but also the means by which the "good things of life" are procured.

In the corresponding religious context, God is cast largely in the role of the substitute father, as the judge and ruler of the universe. Christ, who in Protestant theology is the mediator and intercessor, is symbolized in Roman Catholic theology as the suffering, dying one, who, for all the sympathy he may elicit, never succeeds in creating a desire for identification and emotional attachment, for a healthy-minded person cannot emotionally identify with a death symbol. Mary, on the other hand, is the symbol of life, beauty, and the benefits of existence. She is the one who is the mediator of good from God, and hence serves as a kind of mother substitute.

Moreover, the Virgin becomes identified not only with the personal blessings obtainable from God through petitioning the "Mother of God"; she becomes also a symbol of the welfare of the whole society —a religious emblem of the nation (each nation has its patron Virgin), the symbol of fertility and blessing, and the object of "survival identification." (Witness the pathetic fear of the crowds in San José, Costa Rica, a few years ago when someone stole the image of the national Virgin.)

Latin women, and especially wives and mothers, instinctively feel the need for supporting the Roman Church, for it maintains their status as wives by not permitting divorce (under threat of excommunication), though it does not exert the same influence against men's having mistresses by similar threats of excommunication. However, the earnest and understandable support of the Roman Church by women naturally further enhances the prestige of the Virgin Mary, who becomes for them a symbol of their identification with the

Church. The Church in turn reinforces their status in the home and thus helps to preserve the meaning of this female-focused family attachment.

Under these circumstances it is quite understandable that the sanctity of the Virgin Mary must be preserved at all costs, for it is an instinctive reflection of all that is nearest and dearest in life—home, mother, and family. Moreover, any attempt to argue the theological presuppositions of doctrines concerning Mary is almost never received with objective understanding. Communication on such subjects is virtually impossible, overcharged as it is with emotional attachments and unrecognized filial loyalties and personality projections. No denunciation of the Virgin's claims to divine status or of her intermediary role can ever convince the average Roman Catholic in Latin America that he should instead recognize the uniqueness of Jesus Christ and his exclusive prerogatives for worship. Rather, he must be introduced to Jesus Christ in such a way that he recognizes that only he is Lord. Then, and only then, will the Virgin assume her rightful place in the thinking and emotional structure of the believer's personality. In other words, Mary cannot be driven from her place, but Christ can be so reinterpreted to Roman Catholics that he takes his rightful place as the "only mediator between God and man." Only when such an interpretation is accepted will Mary reassume her rightful, Biblical role.

Principles of Communication and the Social Structure

Obviously in view of the fact that the social context not only affects the ways in which messages are transmitted, but also involves the manner in which they are decoded, the encoding of messages can be done effectively only when these social factors in communication are considered. The basic principles which may be derived from this study of social structure can perhaps best be summarized as follows:

1. The response to the preaching of the Good News may at times reflect a social situation, even more than a religious conviction.
2. Opposition to the communication of the Christian message may be in many instances more social than religious.
3. Changes in social structure may alter the religious view of behavior.

4. Effective communication follows the patterns of social structure.
5. A relevant witness will incorporate valid indigenous social structures.

The social motivations for adherence to Christianity are almost innumerable. In the village of Lolo in the Cameroun,[9] men who had several wives found themselves in considerable trouble, for they discovered that they could not get a mission name; in other words, they could not be baptized. Thus they were prevented from being known by the Christian God, who, if only He knew their names, could prevent their *lembo* (the spirit power in sorcerers) from doing harm. However, in order to avail themselves of as much help as possible from the foreign deity, they urged all the monogamists to become Christians, and the first wives of the polygamists were told to become Christians, for certainly God would look favorably upon them if they gave Him their first wife. Another reason that prompted some men to have their wives become Christians was the belief that adultery with a baptized woman would bring serious illness to the man commiting it. Hence, when the husband must be away, he is sure that there is less likelihood of his wife's becoming involved in extramarital affairs.

Frequently missionaries insist that opposition to the preaching of the Good News is nothing but stubborn religious perversion, the result of Satan's immediate intervention. The truth is that in many instances the so-called "Good News" is really not "Good News" to the people, especially not for the leadership of a tribe. In one area of East Africa the missionary has set himself up with a large establishment, to which have flocked a number of people (in some cases the riffraff of the area). For all the people living on this extensive station the missionary is the "judge and the chief." Without realizing exactly what he has done, he has actually put himself in direct competition with the chiefs in surrounding villages, for anyone who has trouble in his own village and is under disciplinary action from the elders can run off to the missionary and find asylum. Because of the expanding village that surrounds the missionary's home, he regards himself as conducting an indigenous mission, for he is at the very center of the "native life." However, he is not there as a prophet, but as a chief, and the message he brings, not by his words but by his actions, is certainly not indigenous. Moreover, the growing opposition as well as the continued resistance of the African leaders to this work reflects not their rejection of the religious content of the message, but their hostility to the social implications, namely, that the missionary is becoming the biggest chief of them all, and in so doing is robbing the various chiefs of their people. This feeling on the part of African leaders is an old one. As far back as 1851, one chief in South Africa is quoted as saying:

> I like very much to live with the teachers [i.e., missionaries], if they would not take my people, give them to the government, for they are my people. . . . Is it God who tells you to do so? I do not like your method of breaking up the kraal. Let the believing Kaffir look to his own country-men, and not go away, but teach others.[10]

Changes in society, especially as they affect social relations, inevitably tend to shift the religious values in behavior. Among the Kakas in the early days adultery was punished by death, and the clan or family concerned was purified by the blood of a sacrificed chicken.[11] When the French took over, adultery became a sin, like many others, with a fixed penalty, including a fine and jail sentence—which meant being kept from heterosexual activity. The adulterer himself was the only one who suffered. It was no longer a matter that concerned the tribe as a whole, and it soon lost its religious implications. Thus sin became "materialized" by the payment of fines, and the religious background of behavior was quite altered.

The fact that effective communication within any social context must inevitably follow the social structure seems quite evident. However, what has happened in a particular instance in the Huichol tribe of Mexico may add certain significant insights. A young man, Román Diaz, who became a Christian a few years ago, has become inter-ested in evangelizing his neighbors. With the instruction of the missionary, he has made himself particularly useful to his own people by learning some simple remedies for easily diagnosed illnesses. He dispenses medicines for such ailments and has developed quite a reputation as a new kind of "medicine man." When people come to him for medicines, he follows the standard routine used by the tradi-tional medicine man, who never treats a patient unless, after conversation of an hour or more, he and his patient have established just how they are related through birth or marriage. The Huichols are a relatively small tribe, with a long tradition of marriage only within their group and great emphasis upon genealogies, so that sooner or later one can establish his relationship to virtually every other member of the tribe. After thus establishing social ties, the new medicine man diagnoses the illness and prescribes the medicines, which he then dispenses. The patients almost always arrange to stay around for a few days to see how they fare and whether they need further treatment. During this period the "Christian medicine man" takes a good deal of time to chat informally with all those who wish to hear. Moreover, much of this instruction he gives in traditional forms of chanting, which have a high theological and didactic content. Little by little he is making a significant impact upon a highly "defensive" group of people. From the point of view of communication his methods are more effective than those of a typical foreign medical doctor, who would set up a clinic and as a specialist leave all the religious instructions to the "theologically trained personnel." For in Huichol culture healing and religion go together, and religious instruction should be given by the medicine man himself if it is to be given credence.

An effective church always incorporates into its structure the valid indigenous forms of social organization. This is not syncretism, but indigenization, the invariable and necessary means of making the Good News relevant in any community. Marie F. Reyburn, in an analysis of one area in Ecuador, South America, outlines a number of social features of the Quechua culture which can be incorporated with profit into an evangelistic witness to the total community:[12] (1) the use of kinship groups (by incorporating the systems of godfathers and godmothers into the Protestant church); (2) the election of heads of families as church leaders (this is the present pattern of Indian life, in which the male heads of families are responsible for various community functions and affairs, including fiestas); (3) the use of more elaborate ceremonies, e.g., in baptism and marriage (since these are at present so important in the Christo-pagan religious system); (4) the sponsorship of liquor-free fiestas (as a legitimate means for social expression and community solidarity); and (5) the development of co-operatives for group enterprises (this is a traditional pattern of Indian community life, and could be effectively carried out by Christian congregation).

People are such an integral part of the social structure in which they live that only in and through this structure can they be reached and live out their faith.

CHAPTER 6

The Dynamics of Communication

> *For we all make many mistakes, and if any one makes no mistakes in what he says he is a perfect man, able to bridle the whole body also. If we put bits into the mouths of horses that they may obey us, we guide their whole bodies. Look at the ships also; though they are so great and are driven by strong winds, they are guided by a very small rudder wherever the will of the pilot directs. So the tongue is a little member and boasts of great things. How great a forest is set ablaze by a small fire! And the tongue is a fire. The tongue is an unrighteous world among our members, staining the whole body, setting on fire the cycle of nature, and set on fire by hell. . . . With it we bless the Lord and Father, and with it we curse men, who are made in the likeness of God.*
> —JAMES 3:2–6, 9

UP TO the present point we have discussed communication in terms of a more or less static set of circumstances. But communication must also be viewed as a force, for information is power. On the strictly interpersonal level, information has a tremendous dynamic, for not only are people powerfully attracted by it (whether it is gossip or new theories of astrophysics); they also insist on spreading news with a surprising velocity. As startling news travels it seems to create a void before its path by virtue of contrast with other information. As it moves into this void, it develops increased momentum and within a short time can spread itself out over an astonishing area.

The potential of any bit of news is governed by three principal factors: (1) the unexpectedness of the announcement (a statement that the sun rose this morning has much less dynamic than the news that the President has had a heart attack); (2) the proximity of the event (a disastrous flood in Japan gets much less news coverage in a home town paper than the drowning of a well-known local business man); and (3) the value of such information to the participants in the communication (the discovery of uranium deposits in northern Canada is not so electrifying to housewives in Muskogee, Oklahoma, as an unprecedented sale of new frocks in the local department store).

The power of information can scarcely be exaggerated, even when it concerns the rise and fall of civilizations. For the most part we usually discuss these major sociopolitical changes in terms of the development of new inventions or the tapping of new natural resources, when a nation is rising in power, and in terms of such catastrophes as war, pestilence, and the failure of natural resources when nations fall. However, one must also recognize the significance of information, in its broadest sense, as a vital factor. Inventions are in themselves essentially matters of information, for it is not the material substance that goes into a machine, but information about how to make and operate it which is really important. A system of political and legal institutions, such as Rome bequeathed to the ancient world, was primarily information. The dynamic of Christianity was likewise centered in a new kind of communication, even as the resurgence in China today is primarily sparked by a new set of concepts which have been communicated to the people. On the other hand, when societies distintegrate or collapse, it is not always because physical resources have given out; it may be because the people suffer the intellectual boredom of no more "worlds to conquer" or the social fatigue that comes from a monotonous and humdrum existence. Many primitive societies that exist in a state of almost complete equilibrium reflect a relatively low level of development because there are few challenges of new information from the outside, and, on the inside, there are no Joneses for anyone to keep up with, since there is no one Jones who has much more information than any other Jones in the tribe.

When new information comes to a group of people, it tends to trigger two strong emotions: (1) desire and (2) fear. The first is the more creative and generative of the two responses, for it prompts people to try to imitate, emulate, and adapt new ideas or objects to their own use. The second emotion is more intense, and for a period of time it is far stronger and more dramatic than the first. It can produce catastrophic results, including suicidal devotion to the social group.

Nativistic Movements

Some of the most instructive examples of the power of information are to be found in the study of the so-called "nativistic movements" among primitive peoples. They demonstrate not only the power of information, but also the ways in which this power affects the community and is channeled, diverted, and at last largely dissipated. The specific nature and characteristics of any nativistic movement depend very largely upon the local circumstances, but the main types seem to be responses to the intensity of the frustration and pressures which beset a people. These various stages and types may be described as (1) general breakdown of the socioreligious structure; (2) intense socioeconomic pressures; (3) frustration of desires; and (4) disillusionment and boredom.

In many parts of Africa the people have experienced in varying degrees a socioreligious breakdown of the older patterns of life. Christianity, in the multiple agencies of church, school, and medicine, has eroded away much of the distinctly religious aspect of the traditional life, and the intense urbanization and dislocation of people for purposes of work (whether in mines, plantations, or factories) have destroyed many of the older social norms. As a result Africans have felt compelled to try to reorganize life around new concepts and values. Three principal emphases have been adopted: (1) millenarian hopes for a new day, (2) healing by magical means, and (3) witchcraft.

The particular ways in which these themes have been woven together by different groups have produced some bizarre results. The different movements—there are more than 2,000 different independent Christian and pseudo-Christian groups in South Africa, not to mention those which are never officially registered with the government—are perhaps best classified as Zionist and Ethiopian, following L. P. Mair.[1] The Zionist movements are those typified by emphasis on healing by native medicines, the use of old-style diviners, the local "prophet," and the detection of witches by elaborate ordeals. These Zionist groups emphasize the past and appeal primarily to the rural people. The Ethiopian type of movement concentrates on internal political organization and follows the "chief type" of structure. It makes great promises of material goods to the people and builds its strength largely in the cities, where the people are more politically minded. The Zionist movement can be characterized as a valiant attempt to find reinforcements from the past in order to stem the tide of the future; while the Ethiopian type of movement is aimed at rallying the people around a new political standard (since the traditional village chiefs have no power in the cities) and to make use of new techniques and modern means of coping with deteriorating circumstances. In these movements there is often a distinctly new syncretistic religious element, in which an African is proclaimed a prophet for the Negro world, paralleling Moses for the Jews, Christ for the Europeans, and Mohammed for the Arabs.

When life becomes utterly unbearable because of intense socioeconomic pressures, people may "explode" in a series of violent reactions against the powers that be. Such an explosion occurred in the late nineteenth century in the United States, when the Indians of the West had been pushed off their land, had seen the wild game almost exterminated, and were facing starvation. At this time the so-called Ghost Dance movement began. It promised the Indian people the return of the ghosts of their ancestors as allies in the forthcoming fight to rid the country of the white man. The people were promised miraculous immunity to the white man's bullets and the ultimate triumph of their cause under circumstances which would bring back the aboriginal way of life—this time better than ever, for it would be free from death, disease, and misery. There was a certain moral character to this movement, for many of the leaders insisted that the Indians were suffering privations because they had departed from the teachings of their fathers and had been corrupted by the white man's ways, and especially by his liquor. This movement was doomed from the beginning, but in desperation the people invoked the supernatural resources which for them were the only possible way of escape. They did not seek to acquire the white man's possessions or power. They wanted only to restore the old way. However, despite the evident folly of such an undertaking, and even some of the disastrous defeats at the beginning, thousands of Indians became completely caught up in the Ghost Dance movement, so powerful was this new set of concepts and promises made in a time of despair.

Many nativistic movements are not the result of a complete breakdown requiring a general reorientation, or of an actual state of threatened annihilation, but reflect the people's desire for new things, advantages, and prestige. The Cargo Cults in Melanesia, beginning as far back as 1892 and continuing in varying forms almost to the present time (the most famous outbreak was the Vailala madness in 1919), reflected the people's intense envy of the white man's possessions. Since magic coercion has been a dominant element in Melanesian religion, it is not strange that the people conceived the answer to the problem of acquiring the white man's immense material advantages to be the arrival of a promised ship, filled with all sorts of miraculous cargo for the people, even machine guns with which the white people could be killed or driven away. Such a cargo would produce a kind of millennium for the people; they would not have to work any more, but merely enjoy their magically obtained wealth. In some of these Cargo Cult movements, Christianity was expressly rejected, but in others certain Christian features were incorporated. The hysterical seizures of the people (often regarded as madness) when they received messages from the spirits—messages which repeatedly reassured them of the coming cargo—were a strictly indigenous form of religious expression.

When there is physical deprivation, people try to kill their oppressors (as in the Ghost Dance movement in the United States); when there is psychological deprivation, people choose one of two ways out: (1) a stimulant, such as the Cargo Cults, which offers millennial hopes of success, or (2) an opiate, by which people can "escape from it all." The peyote cult in the United States spread as more or less of a religious opiate. As a relief from the cultural stagnation and boredom of complete psychological deprivation—at a time when the old patterns of life had passed away and there was no chance of reviving them—many Indians found solace in the chewing of the peyote bean, which comes from a small cactus grown in northern Mexico. This drug induced amazing visions, with bright kaleidoscopic visions of color, and a general sense of euphoria. Many Indians interpreted the peyote as being the Holy Spirit, and for them peyote became a focal element in the "Native American Church"; but the other paraphernalia of cowhide, rattle, and thunderbird were strictly indigenous, and the staff, with some suggestion of adaptation of the cross, became a fully composite symbol. Some of these symbols provided Indians with a veneer of prestigeful associations, while the other features seemed to provide, at least for a time, some of the *raison d'être* which people must have in order to exist. Other Indians, who were not interested in the peyote cult, drifted often into habitual alcoholism as the best escape from psychological deprivation. However, this alcoholic escape was not religiously organized and institutionalized as it was among many Indians in Latin America.

Despite the enormous burst of social energy displayed in these nativistic movements, these developments are almost always very short lived, for (1) the goals are largely negative, since the people attempt to turn back history, and (2) the rewards simply do not compensate for the enormous expenditures of energy. Hence, the movements peter out very quickly.

Indigenous Christian Movements

In comparison with so-called nativistic movements, we may ask ourselves whether indigenous Christian movements are actually different, and if so, why. In answering these questions, the development among the Tzeltals in southern Mexico provides a useful basis for discussion. Prior to the religious awakening of the last ten years, any attempt at cultural improvement among the Tzeltals was completely ineffective because of the widespread use of black magic. People were afraid to improve their lot appreciably for fear that jealous neighbors would cast a spell on them. The *brujo*, a combination of medicine man and sorcerer (which was uppermost depending upon his particular assignment at the time), constituted an antisocial menace who dominated the socioreligious life, largely for his own benefit and by means of debilitating fear. At the same time, the material resources of the people were dissipated largely through drunken fiestas, conducted under the auspices of the Christo-pagan religious system. As a result, the people were desperately poor, fearful of change, and incapable of making any appreciable alterations in their system; for, in addition to the internal tensions, there were always the outside pressures of the *mestizo* population, which owned the coffee land in the area and depended very largely on a cheap supply of labor. And the laborers could often be gotten even cheaper if plied with liquor and placed under obligation through debts.

Into this situation came missionaries with new information which proved to be a completely liberating force. One of the first things people learned was that black magic did not have the power attributed to it, for those who became believers were seen to be liberated from its force. They also found that the new kinds of medicines being distributed by the missionary and her nurse companion were much more beneficial than the concoctions of the *brujo*. Moreover, the medicines were always given in a religious context, for there was always prayer for the individual patient. In the third place, this Good News of reconciliation with God and confessing of sins to Him also meant confessing one's faults and injuries against others, including the asking of forgiveness. The result was the reconciliation of family groups and the wiping out of long-standing grievances which had paralyzed social interaction. Furthermore, this new faith was made to serve certain crucial needs through Christian festivals for the clearing of the land and the harvesting of crops. Moreover, there was a liberating force in education, for the people soon began to learn to read and as a result could not only read the Bible, but could also protect their rights in contracts and land agreements. All this development stimulated the building of schools for the children with local financial resources; for now the people had more money than ever before, since they worked harder and no longer dissipated their earnings in economically useless ways, but saved and spent more wisely.

An important reason for this accomplishment was that the communication of the message had been (1) in the people's own language (previous attempts in evangelization of the area had been tried through Spanish and interpreters); (2) through the use of indigenous media, such as the preparation of a series of ten hymns which contained the basic elements of Christian teaching (people who wanted to become Christians would ask the Christians to teach them to sing); and (3) explanations of Biblical truths were communicated to the people in cultural contexts which were meaningful (e.g., the explanation of how people are saved by the "blood of Jesus Christ" was explained on the analogy of Tzeltal practices of using blood in indigenous healing ceremonies).

In this development, which has resulted in a rapidly growing Tzeltal church of more than 5,000 members within a period of about ten years (though the initial learning of the language by the missionary and the groundwork took additional time), the basic features are:

(1) new content for certain old institutions, e.g., clearing and harvesting festivals; (2) a new orientation toward the totality of life, with complete allegiance to this radical change in values; and (3) the undoubted working of the Spirit of God in this program, for despite all the sociological circumstances propitious to some change, this radical displacement of the old in favor of the new could not have taken place as a result of merely human factors or natural forces.

Circumstances Favorable to the Development of Indigenous Christian Movements

It is obvious that certain circumstances are far more favorable than others to the development of Christian response to the message of the Good News in Christ. The favorable factors are usually: (1) a society in process of change (a society which is more or less in equilibrium is much more difficult to change and harder to direct than one already experiencing some change, of whatever kind); (2) new social groupings (before stratification of a society sets in, the people are much more likely to respond to outside information); (3) the recognition of unmet needs, whether for health, social security, or economic welfare; and (4) the novelty of the challenge (it is very difficult to challenge a group which regards the proposed solution as "old stuff." Information has its greatest power when it is novel and fresh).

Though these factors, as stated in general terms, hold for various types of societies, one must recognize that in a certain sense all societies are in process of change, even though the change may be slight. Moreover, while in some parts of a social structure conditions may not be favorable, in other segments of the society one may find precisely the conditions that are most propitious. In this phase of our analysis, however, it is important to remember the differences between the urban heterogeneous society, for which different rates of change on different levels may well be true, and the homogeneous folk society, which is more likely to be favorable or unfavorable as a whole, and not in terms of class segments. In some of the more primitive societies, certain groups which may be nearer to the outside world, and therefore under more socioeconomic pressure, may be more favorable to the Good News. On the other hand, they are sometimes the very ones who think that they have been exposed to this solution before, and having rejected it once, they see no point in accepting it now.

The history of change in any society is never a steady upward progress, but usually reflects several stages in a process which Anthony Wallace calls "revitalization."[2] Wallace speaks of five principal steps: (1) steady state, (2) period of individual stress, (3) period of cultural distortion, (4) revitalization, and (5) new steady state. When the problems are especially acute and the reactions severe, these types of changes can also be described in terms of energy expenditure and may be diagrammed as follows:

In this diagram the first steady state, with just enough energy expenditure to keep things running more or less smoothly, is followed by one of severe challenge, such as occurred in the case of the Indians of the Western United States during the last century. This challenge culminated in heroic, though futile, efforts at survival. It is at the peak of this first "hill" of energy expenditure that one gets the nativistic movements, especially of the more violent type. After this stage there is usually a period of defeat and disillusionment, involving a good deal of cultural distortion and displacement. At the bottom of this valley one finds the bizarre cults and escapist sects, including also alcoholism, with or without religious sanctions. After this period of disillusionment, the social group, provided it is still intact, usually begins a period of revitalization or readjustment to the pressures, and in so doing finds this time some positive, rather than negative, solutions. At last, a new plateau is reached and life levels off again.

Sometimes this response pattern can be accomplished within a single generation, but not infrequently it takes three generations; for the first generation ends with frustration, the second generation spends its time largely in disillusionment, and the third makes a new adjustment. This progression has certainly been the story with several of the Indian groups in the United States. An effective Christian approach to such groups can be made most successfully when the society is on the upgrade, whether toward an initial challenge, or later, in the process of revitalization, after some measure of defeat. When on the downgrade, the society as a whole has usually lost much of its sense of corporate responsibility. At that stage, people are more likely to respond as individuals than as social groups.

Factors Which Provide the Initial Impulse for Christian Movements
   Having viewed some of the basic characteristics of the development and decline of some indigenous movements, it is important to note briefly some of the specific factors which seem to provide the initial impulse, or which may be said to "trigger" Christian movements. One often discovers that the initial dynamic of a Christian movement is reflected in a release from fear. The vast majority of Haitian coverts to Protestant Christianity—most voodooists also regard themselves as good Roman Catholics, and hence no conversion process is thought possible or relevant—indicate that one of the important motivations for becoming a "believer" is release from the fears of black magic. Voodoo practitioners first conceded that their medicines had no power over the Protestant missionaries, then admitted that they could not affect the Haitian believer. This admission, and often complaint, proved to be an important reason for many people to desert voodooism. Those who have not personally experienced such a release from fear can scarcely appreciate what it means for a man to find himself suddenly released from the prison of his own constant worries. One man, for example, as a boy had been given a small bottle of red fluid. At the request of his father, a medicine man had prepared this "soul bottle" for the boy, and had told him that as long as the liquid remained in the bottle, i.e., as long as the bottle was unbroken or the liquid did not escape from the carefully sealed opening (it had been daubed with wax and tied with string and covered with cloth), the boy would live. But once the liquid was gone, the boy would die. For years he had treasured this "soul bottle," not only as the symbol of his life, but as the very condition of his existence. But at last he had discovered that his soul was not in a bottle but in the hands of God, who was not bent on terrifying him but who wanted to show him His love. The experience of this man, and thousands of others like him, explains something of the dynamic quality in the Haitian movement toward Protestant Christianity.
   The dynamic "push" in some indigenous Christian movements is provided by a sense of history. People realize that they are "somebody"—not just people, but chosen by God, with a purpose for their

existence and a place in history. It is significant that the Old Testament passage most quoted in the New Testament is Psalms 110:1, "The LORD said unto my Lord, Sit thou at my right hand, until I make thine enemies thy footstool." For the Christians of the first century this verse meant not only the divine validation of their Lord and Master, but the fact that in the end he would triumph over all enemies, and that they, as his followers, would realize their divine destiny. Often people initially respond to the Good News because it provides new goals—a new kind of kingdom on earth, in which the will of God is pre-eminent. In still other situations it seems that the very growth of a movement is in itself a dynamic force, for the increased numbers of people in any organization do not necessarily mean merely arithmetical increase of strength; in many instances groups exhibit a kind of growth in geometric proportion, for as they grow they increase their dynamic strength by the square of their numerical increase. In other words, doubling the size means quadrupling the power, for people respond to others not as mere additions, but as re-inforcements of the initial drive.

Internal Problems in the Growth of Christian Movements

In the growth of Christian movements there are always a host of internal problems. They usually center about three basic difficulties: (1) the tendency to think that everything must be done at once or according to some strict sequence; (2) the usurping of control by foreigners; and (3) the diverting of a movement toward peripheral or unworthy goals. When confronted with a dramatic response to the gospel, there has often been a tendency for missionaries to think that everything must be taught to the people all at once, and that without thorough instruction no one should be permitted to "advance" to church membership. There is, of course, some sound reasoning in such caution, for in some situations the church has been packed by people whose motives were suspect and whose understanding was faulty. On the other hand, an even more tragic mistake is to try to do everything at once, or to insist that people who do not understand much of the content of the message must pass along by certain prescribed stages (like the order in Masonry) in order to be fully accredited believers, even though their loyalties have been won to Christ. As McGavran has pointed out so well,[3] a distinction must be made between discipling and teaching. One must make every effort to "process" the new converts as quickly as possible, while the fires of their new loyalties are burning brightly and their enthusiasm is sufficient to see them through some of the inevitable radical changes and adjustments. It is quite true that in most people's movements illiteracy is high and Biblical knowledge is low. Nevertheless, such groups are unusually stable, rooted in the indigenous culture—a natural bridge for communication to others—and have remarkable possibilities for growth, if within the first generation there has been a dynamic and vigorous thrust in the direction of the church. It is this crucial first impulse which must be carefully guarded and properly employed if the fullest results are to be realized.

In many circumstances it is almost inevitable that missionaries should feel that they are the ones best able to take over the leadership of people's movements. They feel that that is what they were trained for and the reason for their being in the field. On the other hand, it is significant that a high percentage of mass movements toward Christianity have actually been sparked by people who were once removed from the mission station context, usually persons thoroughly bicultural or completely accepted in the local situation. For example, in the Meo area of Laos, among the Tobas of northern Argentina, and in the Harris movement in West Africa, the immediate drive was sparked not by the missionaries, but by indigenous leadership. It may be argued that even though the people themselves are best able to make the initial communication, they are not sufficiently prepared for the follow-up. In a sense this is true; but at the same time, if the movement is "decapitated" by removing the indigenous leadership from its position of dynamic thrust, it may come to a halt. Apparently one reason for the steady advance of the spiritual revival which has been spreading for some thirty years in East Africa (including areas of Uganda, Kenya, Tanganyika, Ruanda-Urundi, and Congo), is the fact that missionaries who shared some of the initial sparking of the movement have been careful not to control it. Some contend that certain aspects of this development have been undesirable. Nevertheless, it is probably one of the longest, most sustained movements on the mission field.

Another inevitable problem is the tendency to divert a people's movement to some peripheral or unworthy goal. Sometimes such a goal takes the form of a crusade against some particular indigenous custom, so that the Good News about Jesus Christ turns out to be, "bad news about monogamy." Sometimes hindrances are put in the way by concentration on such side issues as *lobola*, the paying of the bride-price, which many missionaries no longer regard as antithetical to Christianity. In still other instances, missionaries have introduced denominational disputes, which may have had relevance a century ago in certain areas of the United States, but are completely irrelevant to the life of the Filipinos in Panay, the Congolese in northeast Congo, and the Chontals of Tabasco. Our pet doctrines and theological "peeves" are always too small to be a proper goal in a work of the Spirit of God.

External Opposition to the Growth of Christian Movements

The results of communication of the Christian faith in any area are normally followed by one of five patterns of reaction: (1) almost complete rejection, (2) indifference, (3) slow but steady acceptance by a small minority, (4) rapid acceptance by a fast growing group, and (5) acceptance by one group and strong resistance or fanatical opposition by another. In terms of our immediate concern with certain problems of communication dynamics as related to external opposition, we are primarily concerned with the fifth, or last type. Though in many instances the social structure of the society is such that a dissenting minority is permitted to grow without opposition, there is usually a reaction in the majority group, and often it is violent. The opposition, however, usually goes through three phases: (1) strong violent persecution, often including the killing of new believers and the destruction of property; (2) toleration of the remaining believers after the first flush of persecution has died down, but general ostracism and exclusion of them from social functions; and (3) admission of the minority to a limited number of functions, with gradual acceptance and reincorporation into the society.

In the first stage, the extent of violence is more or less directly proportionate to the real or imagined insecurity of the people and the extent to which they prize their homogeneity. In general, such attitudes are much stronger in face-to-face societies than in others. The toleration which follows in the second stage is similar to the way in which a society treats lepers. They are not utterly expelled, but they are shunned, avoided, and—for all practical purposes—disowned. However, if there are no outside influences to whip up recurrences of persecution, a majority in any community usually outgrow their hostile attitudes, for, after all, these people have previously been "members of the family." In the last stage there is a tendency to reabsorb such persons into the social group. In Mexico the Protestants in a number of small towns have suffered bitter persecution at various times, but in a number of instances they have been reincorporated. In one village the Roman Catholic majority, which had suffered from a succession of irresponsible local treasurers who made off with the town funds, especially during fiesta time, decided to elect a Protestant treasurer of the town, largely because they knew that he never drank and that he had a reputation for being reliable. He accepted the post, and after the usual fiesta celebrations, the city fathers discovered, much to their amazement, that all the bills were paid and none of the money was missing. As a result, this treasurer was later elected mayor of the town.

Of course, it is possible for persecution to be so long and severe as virtually to eliminate the minority cause, as happened in Spain and Belgium during the Inquisition. However, when the opposition is not able to destroy the minority, but is sufficiently intense to force the new believers together into a strong social structure, persecution can advance the communication of the message, particularly if at the same time the minority cause wins the sympathy of people in general. For example, the persecution of the church in Madagascar during the nineteenth century, and the strong opposition to the Evangelical community in Ethiopia during the Second World War and in Colombia, South America, during a recent political upheaval, resulted in a consolidation and advance of the Christian movement.

The "Cooling Off" of Christian Movements

Once a Christian movement has reached its peak of expansion, instead of maintaining a high plateau of spiritual life and activity it normally tends to "cool off." Not that the people return to the same level of religious response as before the "revival" or "movement"; but they may well become "lukewarm" about the new faith. There is nothing essentially strange about this reaction; it is typical of all human movements, religious or otherwise. They all follow, in one way or another, the second law of thermodynamics, namely, that temperature tends to fall. This second law, often spoken of as the law of "entropy," is supplementary to the first law, generally called the law of conservation of energy.

In any human movement entropy sets in for a number of reasons. In the first place, there is a tendency toward the dissipation of energy. Each man goes his own way, and thus without some organization to effect common goals the whole movement seems to collapse, almost like a burst bubble. To prevent this rapid entropy or dissipation of energy, people always seek to organize in order to give the movement direction and to make use of combined strength. All this is very well, but it must be remembered that it also takes energy to keep an organization running. Many good movements have been killed by overorganization. Too much organization robs a movement of the energy necessary for a continued upward surge, and may discourage new bursts of energy from unexpected sources, since the very channeling of energy tends to prevent individuals from starting out on their own. In Latin America some significant Evangelical Indian movements have been ruined by an organization so complex that it consumed most of the energy available. Many co-operative church movements which have expended most of their energy in making the wheels go round have come to a similar end. Long-range planning, valuable and efficient as it often is, can also contribute greatly to entropy, for in the very process of mapping out a future course one must predict just how and where certain events will take place. Unless, therefore, one builds into a system a great deal of flexibility and mobility in response to new needs, one will end with a program which for all practical purposes dictates where and how the Spirit of God must work for the next five to ten years.

Another source of entropy, or cause for "cooling off," is the fact that the original information loses its power because it becomes old and commonplace. As noted in Chapter 4, it loses its dynamic because news is converted into behavior, and behavior into habit. The habit can be very efficient, but it can also become quite irrelevant —mere custom. Similarly, *faith* tends to become *creed*, and *creed* ends up as mere *recitation*. There is no doubt that ritual has its value, for it acts to conserve the "energy" of the original communication. But at the same time that it becomes ritual, it also tends to become habit, and as such has less dynamic or impact. One extreme of ritual entropy is the Latin Mass, which originally carried a good deal of information; but it is now pure mystery, with an entirely different kind of information, the appeal of which lies in its habitual emotional stimulus and not in its relevance to the issues of human behavior. On the other hand, Pentecostal outbursts of emotion, including violent dancing, screaming, speaking in tongues, and hysteria are quite ritualized, despite their apparent informality. Actually, the timing of such events and the persons who will participate are relatively predictable once a particular congregation and its manner of worship are known. The fact that Pentecostal congregrations seem to know quite well when they are all to quit praying aloud is evidence of the ritualized forms. It is also true that the Pentecostal outbursts, though they have great "information" (in their technical sense) when they first occur in any congregation or community, soon lose their dynamic. It is for this reason that Pentecostal churches normally bring in one outside evangelist after another, for only by the introduction of new "information" and "energy" can a high pitch of emotional tension be sustained.

Information may not merely grow old; it may also lose its distinctiveness by syncretism. That is to say, as information concerning some new belief spreads out, it tends (1) to collect cognate or related ideas and (2) to be accommodated to the ideas with which it is in competition. Its spread may be facilitated by making it similar to ideas already current, but at the same time the lessening of its distinctiveness also cuts down its dynamic. This is what has happened in the spread of Roman Catholicism among the Indian populations of Latin America. At present there is in many regions a complete syncretism which some of the best elements in Roman Catholicism (e.g., the Maryknoll Fathers) have completely repudiated and are working against. In the same way, Unitarianism began as a "Christian church," but its orientation became less and less Christian (for if Christ is not the Second Person of the Trinity, he is not the focal point of faith). Finally, the Unitarians have dropped the designation of "Christian church," for their ideological base has been redefined.

In some instances entropy increases rapidly because the original goals of the movement prove to be entirely too limited. At times they may even be strictly negative. This has been the case with certain aspects of ultra-Fundamentalism, for the tendency to contend with the brethren, rather than "contending for the faith," has caused some of the previous strong supporters of the conservative position to dissociate themselves from the movement. No matter how worthy may be his motives, a person cannot wage a conflict successfully and with the full support of others unless the ultimate goals are more than conflict. Only the mentally ill can thrive on destruction; normal people are never content unless they are building and creating, for we are made in the image of God, not of Satan.

Another factor often involved in this "cooling off" is that of failure to anticipate the rapid cultural change which may follow the movement, bringing the people into previously unthought of contact with the outside world. This was the case in one movement in Mexico which began in a very isolated area and spread rapidly with all kinds of religious fervor and promise. After a few years this movement became organized within the patterns of a denominational church, and those who formerly felt the responsibility for going out to evangelize now settled down and relaxed, feeling that the duly elected officers of the church should care for this responsibility. But in addition to this kind of "cooling off," the community was suddenly plunged into contact with the outside world. The oil industry decided that this area was a likely place for drilling; they opened a highway into the area and brought in machinery, outside personnel, etc. This was inevitably accompanied by people who came in to capitalize on the oil camp by prostitution and other vices. It was about this time that several of the most promising people of the local church drifted away and completely repudiated the faith which they had been so zealously propagating just a few years before. Apparently, since no one had anticipated this contact with the evils of civilization, the church life had been developed in such a way as to relate to the peasant life of the people in their mountain fastness, and no provision had been made to forewarn and prepare them for an encounter with the world outside. As one of the remaining faithful said later, "we had heard about the evils of the world, but when the oil men came they saw the world close up." They fell away because they were unprepared for it.

Probably in a good many of the isolated communities where missionary work is being done, there is a tendency to treat people as though they are always to continue being isolated; and although they may not suffer a sudden contact with the outside world such as the above, they are nevertheless going to inevitably be brought into contact with outside influences for which the younger generation is not being adequately prepared through the church.

Perhaps the quickest way for a movement to "cool off" is for the people to discover that the goal has disappeared or that it has been reached. Without a goal there is no longer a reason for existence. The March of Dimes movement almost came to such an end. After the development of the Salk vaccine and the apparent triumph over poliomyelitis, the leaders found that they had to add the conquest of other diseases to their goal, and especially such diseases as would appeal to mothers, who had constituted the principal money raisers. America has seen the gradual diminution or demise of a number of fraternal orders which a century ago served the purpose of providing certain lower-middle and upper-lower class people with status-conferring institutions. But the service club has taken over the positive functions of these groups, and now the competition from television and the spread into suburbia have doomed many of these groups, whose goals could not be reformulated in terms of changing circumstances.

One aspect of entropy is especially significant, namely, the tendency for certain persons, who for one reason or another "backslide" or repudiate their stand with the minority, to go to great lengths to prove their reidentification with the "old crowd." Such persons often plunge into a much worse behavior than they were ever guilty of before, since they believe that only in this way will they be readmitted into the old group. Moreover, by these deeds they "decontaminate" themselves from religious influences. On the other hand, the new convert to Christianity is usually extremely circumspect about his behavior, often to the point of being "too good" or "too holy," for he thinks such behavior constitutes a kind of "purification" from, as well as "expiation for," his past way of life.

However, when a *leader* within a minority religious movement returns to his former group and "falls so far," it is inevitable that there will be social and religious repercussions. Even though he may not carry others with him, a rapid cooling off of enthusiasm will occur. For this reason many close-knit minority groups, especially secret societies in Africa, insist that upon initiation a new member commit a great sin, often murder or incest, so that he cannot in the future afford ever to deny by word or deed his affiliation with the group. The same type of behavior is often demanded of street gangs in American cities. Such a practice is reflected also in the open confessions and public denunciation trials in Communist countries; for the traumatic effect of such an experience is to make the victim sever completely any ideological identification he may have had in the past with those who are now denounced. These practices are designed for the very purpose of preventing entropy and insuring the continued support of the movement.

A final factor in the entropy of religious movements is the effect of those who are not included within the movement. Of course, intense persecution can wipe out a minority group, but a certain amount of persecution can, as noted above, actually prevent entropy. However, when a particular segment of society is simply outside the movement, for one reason or another, it has an effect upon the "temperature" inside, even though there is no special opposition. In Africa, one factor that produces a great deal of entropy in the Christian movement is the tendency to concentrate on the education of men and to leave women more or less on the outside. Since, in African life, as elsewhere, children receive their most important value concepts from their mothers at a very early age, the education and instruction of women, who will "indoctrinate" their children, should have very high priority. In Japan a great deal of attention has been paid by missionaries to the higher education of Japanese young people. But in Japanese society as a whole it is assumed that young people are likely to be quite "radical" during adolescence, and the fact that many thousands of them become Christians during their school days is not usually regarded by their Buddhist parents with particular alarm. It is regarded as only part of the "Westernization process." However, once these young people are married and assume adult responsibilities, they are supposed to give up adolescent excesses, whether these are membership in a Christian church or adherence to a radical socialist party. Thus to concentrate heavily upon one segment of the society, while neglecting the structure as a whole, means that the enthusiasm of that one segment may cool off rapidly when it returns to the larger social setting.

The Reduction of Entropy to a Minimum

If it is the natural tendency for religious movements to die out or to cool off, is there really anything that can be done to keep them alive? Of course, if one wishes to speed up the cooling off process, it is always possible to do so by embalming the movement in ritual, burying it in ceremonies, and piling on the grave the burden of an impossibly top-heavy organization. Dependence upon visual instead of verbal symbols can soon shift the focus of attention from behavior to emotion. Furthermore, in the process of heavy ritualizing of religion there is always the accompanying feature of substituting ritual for real behavior. These techniques are in fact guaranteed to make short work of any budding religious movement.

However, the question of whether one can do anything constructive to preserve the vital elements in a movement from disintegrating under the dead weight of entropy has real validity. Seriously speaking, there are two principal alternative approaches: (1) tying a movement to some other movement or program which has greater cultural validity, and (2) revitalizing the program by new information.

In following the first course of action one does what many institutions have done. For example, Shintoism, which even in prewar Japan was religiously "debunked," though still tottering on its mythological legs, was successfully revived by being identified with nationalism. Similarly, Islam, which as a religious system has been suffering a long decline, has been revived as a symbol of Arab unity. Even the initial enthusiasm for the Virgin of Fatima was never very great until she became a symbol of the Roman Church's holy war against Communism. A number of other movements, some Protestant, have experienced a new lease on life after they became champions of anti-Communist opinions and policies.

Though harnessing one's faltering program to the rising star of another movement is one way of keeping it alive, one must recognize that the original movement cannot under such circumstances stay in its own orbit. It is inevitably deflected from its earlier course so that its original *raison d'être* can scarcely be recognized. (In many instances, of course, this transformation may be justifiable.)

On the other hand, if one wishes to provide a movement with a continuing momentum as a means of increasing its drive and extending its influence, there are two essential techniques to be employed: (1) new information must be constantly supplied to the movement, and (2) new applications of this information must be found. The significance of the Reformation was not the Ninety-five Theses nailed to the door of the Castle Church in Wittenberg, Germany, in 1517, but the constant and growing volume of sound thought and intelligent scholarship that characterized the growing influence of this intellectual and religious emancipation. In Luther's act, the Reformation had only its beginning. The volume of "information" has continued to grow and to be constantly revitalized by added insights.

Some people have been seriously concerned for the Protestant faith in these days, when competing ideologies seem to have so much attraction and the message of the church seems in contrast to be trite and irrelevant. But there is an important source of real hope, for a veritable revolution in Biblical thinking is going on. In many quarters men and women are becoming aware, as never before in a century, of the implications of the radical truth of the Bible and the unique character of the Christian faith. The testing of our faith in the crucible of world conflict is producing a tough-mindedness able to face reality and at the same time a determination to proclaim faith in a way that holds real promise, for it is a new source of information, badly needed in our sophisticated, bored Western world.

New information is not the whole story, however. There must be new applications of this truth to life. At present men are discovering that, though psychiatry may diagnose the trouble and bring it to the surface, it is only the power of God which can truly transform personality. ("Ye must be born again.") Similarly, the relevance of the layman's witness is a factor unparalleled in the predominantly professional ministry through the centuries. The meaning of Christ, not merely as a way to heaven, but as a way to life—in fact the only way to an abundant, full life—is gradually dawning upon men and women. In these circumstances the church is not just a steeple pointing men to heaven, but a fellowship in which people learn how to live.

However, there is in any revitalization one further factor which is not a technique, but a supernatural outpouring of the power of God upon receptive hearts. In the ultimate analysis, despite all the social, political, or economic factors which may enter into the dynamic aspects of a Christian movement, the power is of God, or the movement is not Christian. Nevertheless, God works through these human agencies which reflect and channelize human needs. That He does so should not be surprising: for the same God who created man in His image is very unlikely to abandon the use of the very processes which He has, as it were, built into His creation. Furthermore, at every point in the dynamic development of any Christian witness, there is one crucial and basic prerequisite—"Pray therefore the Lord of the harvest to send out laborers into His harvest (Matthew 9:38).

CHAPTER 7

Psychological Relationships in Communication

> Then Job answered:
> "I have heard many such things;
>   miserable comforters are you all.
> Shall windy words have an end?
>   Or what provokes you that you answer?
> I also could speak as you do,
>   if you were in my place;
> I could join words together against you,
>   and shake my head at you.
> I could strengthen you with my mouth,
>   and the solace of my lips would assuage
>   your pain.   —Job 16:1-5

SINCE communication consists not only of a message, but occurs *between* participants,[1] there are inevitably a number of psychological factors in communication which must be understood if one is to comprehend the true nature of the communicative event. Up to the present point in our treatment of communication we may have given the impression that people are really not people, but only counters in the process of communication. The truth is quite to the contrary. The participants in communication are completely human, with their typical array of feelings toward language, the circumstances of communication, and those who share in the communication. However, it is only after having discussed communication in its wider cultural setting that we are now in a position to appreciate the psychological factors in the individual's role.

The Psychological Attitudes of the Source
toward the Symbolic System of the Message

One of the most obvious problems in determining the psychological factors in communication is to try to understand the attitudes of the source of any message toward the very medium (principally language) which he must use in communicating.[2] For one thing, people differ greatly in their capacities to verbalize, even in their own mother tongue, and there is an even greater problem when they try to communicate in a foreign language. Some people seem hopelessly unable to learn a foreign language and often in consequence are accused of being stupid, mentally lazy, or poorly instructed. The truth is that in almost all instances where reasonably intelligent persons have tried to learn a foreign language, and yet have failed to learn it satisfactorily, serious psychological problems could be discovered in their individual backgrounds. In certain cases these difficulties have been found to reflect a difficult childhood experience with problems of language prestige. Thus, for example, the individual may have grown up on the "wrong side of the tracks" and have had to change his original dialect of English to one with greater prestige value. This repudiation of the language of the home in favor of another, in which he feels intensely the necessity for never making a mistake (so as not to betray his origin), has often left such an imprint upon some individuals that in later life they cannot emotionally bring themselves to make mistakes in language, even in foreign tongues.

There are also many children of immigrant parents who have tried "to forget their parents' language" and have overtly denied being able to speak or understand it. Some of these persons have found it very difficult to adjust emotionally to speaking a foreign language, for to do so seems to imply unconsciously an identification with something that has been repudiated at an earlier stage, and thus to represent a regressive emotional step.

There are others who learn to "communicate" in a foreign language, in the sense that they get across their meaning, but who consistently butcher the pronunciation and mutilate the grammatical forms, even when they may know better. Such persons may suffer from a number of psychological problems. They may, for example, be individuals who insist primarily on one-way communication, or they may not be sensitive to the out-group, though these same persons may be very acutely aware of criticism from the in-group. In fact, lack of sensitivity to the out-group is for many persons almost directly proportionate to sensitivity to the in-group. In other words, people who do not "care a rap" about what "foreigners think" are usually very alert to what their own compatriots feel about them. The reverse is also often true, for those who may be more or less nonconformists in their own culture may be very sensitive to the out-group. Nonconformism in itself normally implies rejection of certain in-group values, and since one of the strong in-group values is internal sensitivity, in contrast to external unawareness, the nonconformist often reverses the situation.

There are still other persons who never seem to learn a foreign language well, despite proper exposure and inherent capacity, simply because they are dramatic, romantic souls who never have time for the details of life. For such people, keeping the genders and the sequences of tenses correct is too much like having to tidy up one's room every morning when there is the great outdoors to be explored and a thrilling new day to be "lived up."

On the other hand, one's psychological attitudes toward language may go much deeper than the problems involved in learning to speak it correctly. They may involve one's total perspective of the language mechanism and exhibit a "retreatism" and "escapist" tendency from the struggle of effective communication. Some missionaries try to purify the indigenous language of its irregular forms and insist on borrowing words or making up terms on foreign models, instead of describing a concept in indigenous terms or readjusting the area of meaning of a native term by qualifying modifiers. They may also strictly avoid using words with pagan connotations, as if the words themselves were leprous or unclean. These attitudes do not reflect a desire to improve a language so much as an escape from the struggle of communication and a retreat from personal involvement.

The Psychological Attitudes of the Receptor
toward the Symbolic System of the Message

One would assume that all people were equally favorable toward their own language as a medium of communication, but such an attitude does not always exist, at least not on the surface. Some people who are socially insecure may, when faced with pressure from a more prestigeful language, completely disguise their real feelings or alter their normal type of reaction. At least overtly, they may insist that they prefer the foreign language, which they do not understand adequately, to their own mother tongue, which they know very well. On the other hand, if the sociopolitical system should change suddenly, such persons, who once were proud of their knowledge of a foreign tongue and contemptuous of their own, may feel compelled to reverse themselves.

On the other hand, since many people are oppressed by those speaking more prestigeful languages, they tend to react unfavorably to messages in foreign languages and to prefer their own. They may, however, find it impossible to discuss certain concepts in their own language, while at the same time some topics can be discussed only in their mother tongue. This limitation usually depends entirely upon the nature of the subject and the contexts in which such concepts have been learned. Christian Hopis, for example, almost all of whom are bilingual in varying degrees, habitually discuss Christianity in English, though they can speak about some of its concepts in Hopi. They are, however, generally quite incapable of discussing Hopi religion in English. As long as a conversation centers about Christian ideas and backgrounds, these people usually find it much easier to communicate in the foreign idiom, for virtually all they have learned about Christianity has come to them essentially through English. Even when interpreters are used, the interpretations involve English thought forms, not Hopi ones. For the Hopi religion, however, the English language is simply impossible to use, for there has been no practice in communicating Hopi religious ideas in English. As far as the Hopi Christian is concerned, therefore, there are two religious worlds—Christian and Hopi. Few Hopis have ever attempted to bring them together, and no missionary has ever sufficiently grasped the structure of Hopi religion to help them to do so.

Psychological Relations between Source and Receptor

In a communication in which the source is uncertain, one of the first questions is, "Who said it?" Roger Brown[3] reports an interesting experiment in which a statement equivalent to "Revolution is a good thing" was given to students, but the source was given as Jefferson in some instances and as Lenin in others. The reactions of students to this statement were found to depend very largely upon their attitude toward the presumed source.

The actual process of communication involves not only mutual adjustment (discussed in Chapter 3), but also the important factor of identification. This term is convenient to use, but not so easy to define. In fact, *identification* is by necessity a very complex concept, for it involves the totality of interhuman relationships. As a result, it is a good deal easier to say what it is not than what it is. For one thing, it certainly is not imitation, a process that usually involves cheap paternalism or superficial ingratiation, and not real empathy. When, for example, a youth worker thinks that he must have a crewcut to identify himself with adolescents, or a father that he has to act like a boy in order to be a pal to his son, he is only imitating, not identifying. A person in a foreign cultural situation must avoid any sentimental or romantic attempt, whether conscious or unconscious, to "go native." A person who attempts identification in this way is no more competent to judge situations realistically and to participate in them effectively than one who has lost his memory is able to understand what is going on around him. Identification means, not being someone else, but being more than oneself.

The reactions to false identification on the mission field are as harsh as those we ourselves feel in a similar situation. In the Cameroun, some very well-intentioned and devout Roman Catholic missionaries attempted to get close to the people by living under circumstances which were as nearly identical as possible to those under which the indigenous people lived. However, the Africans did not particularly appreciate the heroic efforts of these Europeans to come down to their relatively primitive standards. Their reaction was essentially, "If these Europeans know how to live better than we do, why don't they? We would, if we could!" The essential difficulty with the false identification found in imitation is that it creates contempt, the most important barrier to mutual understanding.

One reason why we succumb so easily to false identification is that it is so important a part of the continual propaganda that bombards our literate world. Such techniques as "name calling" (damning by association), "transfer" and "testimonials" (which drag in glamorous personalities who are supposed to convince us that we should think and do as they do), "plain folks" (in which the propagandist falsely gets "folksy"), and "bandwagon" (in the sense of "Everyone is doing it") are all based on the theme of supposed identification.[4]

Our task, however, is not to propagandize people into the kingdom of heaven, but so to identify ourselves with them that we may effectively communicate "the Way." This identification can be achieved only by realistic participation with people in their lives, not by working for people, but with them. Furthermore, this participation must not be restricted to the nonsymbolic aspects of life, e.g., providing food, shelter, medicines, or even secular education. Governments can do all these things just as well, if not better, than missions. The Christian's task is to participate with people on the symbolic level, whether of ideas or of activities. Unfortunately, we may assume that participation means merely common activities directed and sponsored by us. This problem is well illustrated by what happened to a missionary in West Africa who carefully instructed the school boys how to play American football. After their instruction the boys all went romping off through the brush, to return an hour later demanding pay—for to them football was not play but work. On the other hand, a missionary who had taken the time to go out and play one of the indigenous group games with the students and teachers at one of the mission schools was specially thanked the next day by the teachers, for, they said, "You are the first one who ever played with us." In a sense, play is a more symbolic activity than work, and it is closer to the area of human interpersonal communication. William Smalley has effectively stated the basic problem in terms of "neighborliness or proximity,"[5] for physical association is no guarantee of psychological identification.

A careful distinction must be made between outer and inner identification. The fact that one lives in a poor hovel, has a beaten-up old car, and refuses to have a refrigerator because it is likely to "separate" one from the people near by, is nothing more than external identification. Of course, the possession of a lovely house, big car, powerful radio, motion-picture camera, hi-fi set, electric-light plant, and other paraphernalia that so many missionaries take for granted can constitute a barrier to identification if these things keep one from people and serve as symbols of one's inner isolation or lack of identification. In themselves, however, things are only things—it is only when people attach values to them that they acquire meaning and serve to thwart effective communication.

In one area of Latin America some very devout, sincere, Protestant missionaries have purposely denied themselves all but the very minimum of outward things in order that they may more readily reach the Indians. But though they live physically very close to the people, there is little or no identification on the level of social or religious culture. These missionaries never have guests in their homes and are almost never invited to the homes of others. They are completely unaware of the social structure of the villages in which some of them have lived for well over ten years, and they still do not understand the network of communication that reflects this structure. In religious matters these missionaries have learned about a few of the "superstitions" of the people, but they do not take these religious beliefs seriously and deal with them as real issues. For them they are merely "stupid, silly customs." Moreover, they have not learned what really makes the societies tick—the drives, goals, objectives, and purpose of the people. They live like the people, but they cannot think like them; and until they do there is no real communication.

Inner identification does not mean it is necessary to adopt the value system of those one seeks to communicate with; rather, that it must be taken seriously. The one who achieves inner identification must be aware of people's ideas, understand their viewpoints, and be genuinely sympathetic with their struggle for self-expression, even though he may not agree with its forms. He may not, for example, wish to countenance for a moment the low standards of sex morality, but he must recognize the fundamental values in life which give rise to such standards and at the same time realize that the indigenous people may have almost equal cause for misjudging him. For example, in many parts of the so-called primitive world, what we consider sexual immorality is not regarded as particularly bad, especially if adultery is not involved, but "blowing one's top" is thought to be completely despicable—clear evidence of lack of self-control and good manners. Our society, on the other hand, views such emotional tantrums more or less as a normal psychological catharsis.

Degrees of Identification in Terms of Levels of Communication

One error that has plagued the emphasis upon identification is the assumption that if one is to communicate with other people there must be full and complete identification. Obviously this theory is not true, and this fact has led some to question just why or how identification is so important. The answer to this problem is to be found in the correlation of degrees of identification with the various levels of communication.

The first, and lowest, level of communication is one in which the message has no significant effect on behavior and the substance of the message is essentially self-validating. For example, if someone says that two and two make four or that there is a newsstand just around the corner, no one is particularly concerned that the source should psychologically identify himself with the receptor. A person can verify for himself that two and two make four and with a little effort can prove whether the informant is right about the newsstand. Hence, from the receptor's point of view the type of person who acts as the source of such information is largely irrelevant.

In the second stage of communication, there is a message which, though it has no permanent effect on a man's total value system, does affect significantly his immediate behavior. For example, if a man says that a flood is sweeping down on the town because a dam has broken, the receptors want to make sure that the source identifies himself with his own message—namely, that he also is making preparations to leave town. Otherwise, they may conclude that the man is demented or that he intends to ransack and loot the houses if he can hustle off the people in time. Similarly, if a man insists that a particular dog has rabies, those who listen will inevitably discern whether his behavior toward the dog gives evidence that he really has identified with his own message. In this second level of communication, unless the source identifies himself with the message, the effect upon the receptor is largely nullified.

On the third level of communication, the message not only concerns a large segment of a person's behavior, but also his whole value system. If, for example, someone insists that a man should abandon his carefree way of life, settle down, marry, and raise a family; or if he tries to convince another that he should repent of his sins, become a Christian, and lead an entirely different type of life—it is important that as the source of such a message, he has more to offer than merely being a married man himself, or than showing by his life that he is himself a Christian. In addition to identification with his message, he must also demonstrate an identification with the receptor; for the receptor must be convinced that the source understands his, the receptor's, particular background and has respect for his views, even though he may not agree with them. To give weight to the message, the source should in some way have something of the same background as the receptor. This means that "he must be all things to all men, in order that he may win some" (1 Corinthians 9:19–22).

There is, however, still a further and deeper level of communication, namely, one in which the message has been so effectively communicated that the receptor feels the same type of communicative urge as that experienced by the source. The receptor then becomes a source of further communication of the message. This level involves "entrusting to faithful men who will be able to teach others also" (2 Timothy 2:2). For this level of communication it is necessary that the receptor be identified in turn with the source. In this last stage of communication the identification becomes complete.

Cultural Barriers to Identification

There are other impediments to identification than those resulting from false concepts about the nature of identification and from cultural snobbery and personal "stuffiness," both of which reflect personal and cultural insecurity. These other barriers, cultural in nature, are part of the social structure of societies and cultures. They are of two types, depending upon whether they involve two distinct cultures or different subcultures within a single society.

The foreign missionary becomes identified with another culture only in a limited way, at best, for he cannot and must not deny his own cultural heritage. Moreover, though he may become bilingual, he almost never becomes bicultural, for his very background precludes full identification and participation in the lives of others. He may be, and usually is, a very welcome source of new information—and to serve in this way is essentially his function. Moreover, he may experience a relatively high degree of involvement; but in the last analysis, when the game is being played in its most intense moments, he is on the sidelines, and never more than advisory to the coach or captain of the team. From the viewpoint of dynamic cultural change, he is a "friend of the court" and not one of the litigants. In other words, in the ultimate analysis he is always dispensable, for he is never wholly identified—not so much in terms of his own feelings in the matter, but by the people themselves.

Within a single society people do pass from one subculture or class to another, but the change is almost always in a single direction. Or, stated in other terms, the cultural circumstances do not constitute insurmountable barriers to certain types of "social passing" but may do so to others. For example, people often pass from a face-to-face society into an urban society, but the reverse course is more difficult.

In other words, the "hayseed" can usually be more readily accepted in the city than the city dweller can be accepted in the country, because any face-to-face society is more sensitive to the backgrounds of people and more critical of different behavior than is the urban society. In the large city, where there are always many different patterns of behavior, deviations from the norm do not attract anything like the same attention they do in smaller communities.

Similarly, people pass from minority groups into majority ones more easily than is the case in reversed situations. A person of Christian and Missionary Alliance background is much more readily received into a Presbyterian church than is true of the reverse,[6] and a member of the Plymouth Brethren group can join a Methodist church and be accepted fully into the fellowship much more easily than a Methodist can identify himself with the Plymouth Brethren. The basic reason is that minority groups are almost always suspicious of infiltration, resistant to outside pressures, and hesitant about "foreign elements." Their very minority status has taught them not only to be cautious but also to be insistent upon a close fellowship, for their lack of size is compensated for by the intensity of their "belongingness." However, when we speak of minority and majority groups, we do not refer merely to size, but also to ethos. The Southern Baptists, for example, are a much larger group than the American Baptists (fully five to one), but it is much easier for a Southern Baptist preacher to be accepted in the north among American Baptists than is true of the reverse course, for the Southern Baptists, regardless of their size, retain something of their minority ethos from post Civil War days. One of their great strengths is this "family loyalty," which has been preserved despite their recent rapid growth.

In addition to "social passing" from face-to-face to urban and from minority to majority groupings, it is also easier for one of a lower-class status to be fully accepted in an upper-class status than the reverse, despite the apparent contradiction implied. If a person proves his right to higher status in American life, he is usually granted it, except in certain very exclusive groups, where, as the saying goes, "You must have said *tomato* with an *ah* for three generations." However, a person who tries to identify himself with a lower group, particularly if he evidently has capacities for higher status, continues almost indefinitely under a cloud of suspicion. The people simply cannot understand this type of behavior, since it reverses all the norms of social climbing. They suspect that he may have been disowned by his own social group for some heinous behavior, that he may be hiding from the law, or that he is suffering from some mental unbalance. Vicarious identification is never free from misinterpretation, any more now than it was in the case of Jesus Christ.

Basic Ingredients in Effective Identification

As a prerequisite to any type of identification, one must recognize first that he is identifying with specific persons, not with a generalization or a type. A missionary in Thailand does not "identify with the Thai," but with particular Thai individuals, who may be of quite different types: educated residents of Bangkok, pedicab drivers who live on the streets, rural farmers in the vast rice fields, and mountain villagers, who often specialize in raising opium.

Furthermore, despite one's desire for complete identification, the very process of obtaining partial identification is possible only if one recognizes the inherent limitations. Otherwise one will spend his time in fruitless questioning of others' motives and endless self-accusation for not having succeeded in this ever so close, but ever so distant goal.

William Reyburn has well illustrated the ultimate impossibility of complete identification in his account of living and working among Quechua Indians in Ecuador. The Indians insisted on addressing him as *patroncito* (the equivalent of "boss," but with an ameliorative ending showing favorable appreciation).[7] Reyburn objected that he was no *patrón*, for he had no land and was no *hacendado*, with Indians working for him. In fact his house was more poorly furnished than any of theirs. But his friend insisted, "But you wear shoes." Reyburn then began to wear Indian sandals, but his friend still addressed him as *patroncito*. At last, after trying to show that he should not be called *patroncito*, for he had calloused hands from hard work, Reyburn asked still again, "Why do you insist on calling me *patroncito*?" To which his Indian friend replied, "Because you were not born of an Indian mother." In the ultimate analysis our identification can only be partial. However, if our communication is to be effective, our identification should be as extensive as possible.

If we are to effect even a reasonable degree of identification, it is necessary that we first fully recognize our own motivations. Our interests in identification must not be some subtle projection of our

unsatisfied desire to dominate, nor must they represent any unconscious attempt to escape from our own cultural milieu. We must not
dodge reality by trying to find some strange, exotic niche, or think that
we can compensate for our hidden failures by engineering the lives of
others. Sometimes, in our eagerness to escape from ourselves, we try
to pry into the affairs of other people, either to satisfy our morbid
curiosity or to congratulate ourselves upon the fact that we are really
"not as other men are." But all this will not do. We shall soon get
stopped dead in our tracks by people who can see through our sham.
We must therefore "know ourselves" before we can expect to know
others or to communicate with them.

The next requirement for identification is to know others. To do
so, one very effective tool is a familiarity with the field of anthropology
and the techniques whereby customs and cultures different from our
own can be understood.[8] We can never expect to communicate with
a person unless we know something about how he looks upon the
world and why he responds to it as he does. For example, when a
missionary in northern Congo suggested that, in order to clear the
church rolls of persons who had long since moved away, or with
whom the church had completely lost touch, the membership cards
should simply be destroyed, the elders were up in arms. It was all
right to erase the names from the rolls, but the cards containing the
names should never be destroyed, for that was like destroying a man
in effigy. The importance of the name in this culture is very great.
For example, a woman called her son by the name of the missionary,
and from then on, in speaking to the missionary's wife, she always
spoke of her son as "your husband." At first the missionary's wife
could not understand such a remark as "Your husband likes to sleep
under the bed," until she realized that the woman was not speaking
of the missionary but of her young child. Of course, there is no actual
confusion about the facts in the African's mind, but there is a kind
of presumed symbiotic relationship between people of the same name.
One cannot communicate with such people without knowing their
traditional patterns of usage and their views of the world.

Identification means also participation in the lives of people, not
as benefactors but as colaborers. Moreover, this participation should
be neither forced nor rigged, but a genuine interpersonal experience.
Such participation should not be purchased at the price of "financing
the deal" nor granted merely because the people have pity for our

frustrations. It must be genuinely desired by all, in order to be effective for any.

Another requirement is that we be willing to expose ourselves to being known. To know others is not enough, if we are ourselves unwilling to be known. The former can be only smug paternalism and unbecoming curiosity, unless we are equally willing to have others know us. We must be willing to admit, for example, our exaggerated emphasis on the virtue of punctuality, which so much of the rest of the world regards with wonder and unabashed contempt. We may also just as well confess our preoccupation with things, in contrast to concern for people, for we are in many respects a gadget-oriented society, concerned about people primarily in terms of what the people in question think about us. We are also addicted to one kind of megalomania—we insist that everything must get bigger. Quantitative growth seems often to push qualitative performance into the background. It is not easy for us to confess these attitudes, but we usually have them, and the sooner people know us, for better or for worse, the greater can be our identification.

Finally, however, the indispensable ingredient in identification is a genuine love for people. This love must not be a sentimental romanticizing about a certain group of people in general, but a profound appreciation of certain individuals in particular. We must genuinely enjoy their presence and experience a growing sense of mutual indispensability. Only in this way can we really identify, for we become like those we love.

CHAPTER *8*

Communication and the Total Cultural Context

"The sower sows the word. And these are the ones along the path, where the word is sown; when they hear, Satan immediately comes and takes away the word which is sown in them. And these in like manner are the ones sown upon rocky ground, who, when they hear the word, immediately receive it with joy; and they have no root in themselves, but endure for a while; then, when tribulation or persecution arises on account of the word, immediately they fall away. And others are the ones sown among thorns; they are those who hear the word, but the cares of the world, and the delight in riches, and the desire for other things, enter in and choke the word, and it proves unfruitful. But those that were sown upon the good soil are the ones who hear the word and accept it and bear fruit, thirtyfold and sixtyfold and a hundredfold." —MARK 4:14-20

HAVING examined the various phases of communication and the cultural contexts in which communication must take place, we now return to the central theme of how communication can best be effected within the total cultural framework. Our questions concern principally two elements: (1) the formal features of method and mechanisms of communication, including the circumstances, setting, techniques, media, channels, and roles of the participants, and (2) the content of the communication, including problems of relevant adaptations, indigenization, and syncretism.

The Circumstances of Communication

One of our most serious blind spots is our failure to appreciate the circumstances under which communication should take place. In even such a simple matter as the distance that the source and receptor should stand apart in conversation we may find ourselves badly misunderstood and misunderstanding. In the Mediterranean world and in Latin America a speaker normally stands very close to a person to whom he wishes to communicate. If we Americans are the receptors, it is very likely that we will tend to back away, for we normally maintain about two to three feet of distance between ourselves and any source of communication. The result is that the other speaker advances somewhat closer and again we retreat. We unconsciously interpret this advance as being overbearing, and our interlocutor in turn concludes that we are not interested or are trying to put him off. Similarly, when we speak, we tend to give the impression of standoffishness or even of hostility, because we maintain such an "unusual" distance. The same type of problem is particularly acute in offices, for more often than not, when an American arranges chairs in his office, the Latin feels that he has to pull his chair up closer, and the American behind the desk then immediately becomes defensive.

Missionaries to some of the Indian tribes in the United States have thought that loudspeakers would be a good way of reaching the people, for not only would such a method seem novel and hence attract attention, but the volume would be sufficient that the people could hear throughout the entire village, even without leaving their houses. Nothing, however, could be better calculated to offend and mislead such people. In the first place, American Indians tend to regard religion not only as a "commodity" of very high value, and hence not to be commercialized by loudspeakers, but also as something intensely personal which can usually be understood only by means of initiation. The use of the loudspeaker tends to destroy the sanctity of religion, and the offense of booming the message into one's home, especially when it is not wanted, seems the height of inconsiderateness, if not of insolence.

In general, we think of religious communication as taking place more suitably within a church structure, and for that reason missionaries sometimes build churches even before there are any converts. In many cases, however, the communication of Christianity inside a distinctive type of building, especially before a sizable congregation has been formed, has proved a liability. In a recent Meo Christian movement in Laos, it was found that as long as the "services" were held in the chief's home, the attendance was large and the interest keen. But once churches had been built and people had to enter them in order to receive the message, there was a distinct falling off of interest and participation. For one thing, entering a church is regarded as almost tantamount to identifying oneself with a movement, before one even knows much about it. This problem becomes even more complex when the churches in question are of foreign architecture.

Not only do our ideas of religious communication tend to center about a church building, but they are also definitely ritualized as to time. Services are usually held Sunday morning, possibly in the evening as well; Wednesday night is set aside for prayer meeting; Thursday night for choir practice, with the scouts, pioneer girls, youth night, men's night, and the women's guild spliced in. But there is nothing especially sacred about such a schedule even among ourselves. In one chapel in downtown London there are no services at all on Sunday, but the church is open every noon for well-attended chapel services. Some churches have no men's night, for the men have no night to get together, but they have a 6:30 o'clock breakfast for prayer and inspiration once a week before they go off to their work in the city. Women's meetings are often held in the mornings, and church services are held early Sunday morning and at 4 or 5 o'clock for afternoon vespers. Some Christian groups on college campuses meet as late as 10 o'clock in the evenings for devotions or for lectures, which go on till 11 o'clock, and then discussion breaks up at midnight. In Ephesus, Paul apparently hired the hall of a teacher, Tyrannus, during the siesta hours (from 11 A.M. till about 4 in the afternoon), at which time he had a better chance of reaching those who stopped work during the middle of the day and could drop in to hear what this Jew was talking about, a matter that seemed to have captured the attention of so many people.

Not only must our times of meeting be subject to special modification if communication is to be affective; the very occasions we commemorate by religious gatherings are often quite diverse. The Chols of southern Mexico make quite an affair of the consecration of a new home. They have taken over an indigenous rite and have thoroughly Christianized it, thus providing a most important functional substitute. Moreover, they have introduced a very interesting element into the matter of watching over the sick. The customary practice has been for all the relatives to join together around the bed of the sick patient, and to have the medicine man chant on and on through the night until the patient either shows definite signs of improvement or dies. The Christians also meet together when people are critically ill. They have hymns and prayer, and then, while many of the relatives stay on, they continue to play phonograph records of Scripture readings during the entire night. By morning all the people can recite the passages from memory.

Probably the greatest injustice we do the Christian message is to isolate it culturally to certain places and times. We seem very loath to talk about our faith even in our homes. We skirt such subjects with a kind of noncommittal evasiveness which perplexes people of different cultures, e.g., Hindus, Buddhists, and Muslims, who are in the habit of engaging in lengthy discussions of religion in their homes and at dinner parties. But in America religion is the one subject which seems quite taboo as dinner talk—better describe a gruesome operation than to bring up the subject of the uniqueness of Jesus Christ. No one wants to bear the onus of being a religious fanatic, and as a result he bears the burden of being religiously dumb.

Communication Techniques and Media

The sermon has become so focal a point of Protestant religious communication that we tend to equate the two, but it is questionable just how much communication the average sermon actually effects. In some instances the themes are so threadbare and the content so predictable that the "information" is almost nil. Too often the Sunday morning service becomes the ideal time for the second Sunday morning nap or for uninterrupted planning of the afternoon's activities or the week's work. There is a great deal of truth in the comment of the little boy who, in answer to a question about how he liked the first church service he had ever attended, said, "The music was all right, but the commercial was pretty long." It is scarcely a cause for wonder that people stay away from the church, when they have never been convinced that going would benefit them. Of course, there are churches that are full because people have a fixed habit of attending them, but in others one normally finds that where the church is filled one is likely to find effective communication, involving not only the sermon, but the worship of the people.

The sermon is only one means of communication—and often not the most effective. Bartolomé de las Casas, the famous Spanish Roman Catholic missionary to the Indians of Latin America, was perhaps most effective when he taught the doctrines of Christianity to the Indians through training four young men to sing to the people the story of Jesus Christ and salvation. Certainly one of the most impressive communications it has ever been my privilege to see and hear was an anthem in the Baptist church in Vanga, Belgian Congo, where, just before the choir arose to sing, a man came forward in the church and placed a large basin of kerosene on the pulpit and set a match to it. As the flames leaped up, the choir began to sing an anthem written by the African director:

> The city that forgot God
> Gomorrah, Gomorrah
> The city that forgot God.

Over and over and louder and louder this theme rang out, until suddenly the choir stopped singing, and in the distance some choir members who had slipped out of the choir began to wail, scream, and cry somewhere in the background. Then, as the lamentation in the distance died away, the choir took up the theme again, "The city that forgot God, Gomorrah, Gomorrah." More and more quietly they sang, until at last we could not quite tell when the music ceased. It was an unforgettable communication.

Unfortunately, our religious music, especially as it has been crudely adapted to other cultures, is often pathetically inadequate. There is the story of the taxi driver in India who was asked by a man just when the services in a certain Christian church could be over, to which the taxi man replied, "I don't know, but there are always four noises, and there have already been two."

Not only music, but dance as well may be a means of communication. In the Presbyterian church service in Batouri in the Cameroun a few years ago two women put on a dance at Christmas time to dramatize the annunciation to the Virgin. The woman who was dancing the part of Mary came forward from the congregation, dancing in a graceful, but hesitant manner. Just then the angel danced in from the outside, with a most excited rhythm. As the two danced on the platform the angel communicated the message verbally and Mary responded, following the Biblical narrative. At last the angel danced off again with the same excited, ecstatic dance. During the time that the angel was communicating the divine announcement, Mary's entire rhythmic movements were slowly but steadily adapted to those of the angel, until, when Mary finally danced back into the congregation, she was dancing in the same exalted manner that characterized the dance of the angel who had brought the thrilling message from heaven. This was significant communication, employing one of the most effective indigenous media.

Even in our own society we have found drama a highly important means of religious communication and expression, but within our churches drama is on the periphery of our concepts of communication. The reason is that though we as a society are strongly motivated to be onlookers of drama—we are thoroughly addicted theatergoers and television watchers—we are not particularly participators in drama, as, for example, people are in Africa, where some of the commonest events give rise to vivid, spontaneous acting.

Many of the Indians of Latin America are gifted folk dramatists, and the Kuripakos, on the Amazonian border of Colombia, have found an effective way of communicating to visiting Indians their acceptance of the gospel message. To do so a group of Indians cluster around a medicine man who, surrounded with all his paraphernalia— rattles, wands, sticks, and drums—chants over a small fire, while the people look on in amazement and wonder. Then a man comes out of the forest; in his hands he carries a little book from which he reads the story of Jesus. He goes slowly round and round the little huddle of pagan worshipers, continuing to read until at last some begin to listen, and finally one and then another rise, leave the medicine man, and begin to follow the reader of this wonderful book. After a dozen or more have joined behind the reader, they all break out into singing. Quickly more and more leave the medicine man, until he is finally left entirely alone. At last he also joins, and then the circle closes in on the smoldering fire and the people throw onto the fire the heathen paraphernalia. As the flames leap up, they sing to the power of Jesus' Name. This type of spontaneous drama tells more in a few minutes than a sermon could communicate in hours. Moreover, it is more than a mere enactment of a story—it is the reliving of an experience and the reaffirmation of a conviction. The importance of this type of communication is that it involves complete identification, not merely with words, but with actions. It is the closest approximation to the living reality that symbolism can ever have.

One of our enthusiasms as exponents of the Western world is mass media. We seem to think that the wider the audience, the more valuable the message. If our commodities were only soup, soap, and soda pop, this might be true, but the message of the gospel is a way to a new life and not a way to health through someone's "little liver pills." Each man lives in a somewhat different world, despite our standardizations. Moreover, this new life is not a simple set of rules, but a radically new orientation. The trouble is that with mass communication we must make the message more and more generalized in order to make it fit more and more people, until at last it is often abstracted out of all contact with concrete reality. We seem to adopt the principle of saying less and less to more and more. Somehow we think that we are achieving more if, like motion pictures and television, we pitch our mass appeals to the lowest common denominator. Norbert Wiener has described this process in American mass communication as "the ever thinning stream of total bulk of communication."[1]

What makes even less sense is the tendency for popular Christian radio programs in the United States to spend considerable sums of money getting such messages translated, or in some instances poorly adapted, to foreign language audiences. The results are pathetically meager in terms of the expenditures involved. What is needed is the creative development of local programs at home and abroad which can communicate not merely through words, but also through effective music, drama, and indigenous art. Not that mass media are unimportant in confirming the views of those who are faithful listeners and in "softening up" an audience to further inquiry, but the message of life must be carried primarily by life if it is to be interpretable in the context of people's lives. The radio can prompt a man to do what he already would like to do anyway or it can help him to decide upon one of two alternatives he already has in mind. However, mass media are not so well designed to elicit creative responses to new challenges, for they are too impersonal, too detached, and too easy to turn off.

The Roles of the Participants

No effective communication can possibly take place unless the participants stand in relevant, understandable relations to one another. The source must have a valid role within the context or his words will be relatively meaningless. It is for this reason, for example, that the Bible societies have consistently employed the principle of selling the Scriptures. This practice is followed not because of the profit involved in the sale—in fact it would often be cheaper to give New Testaments away and easier to raise money from the American public if appeals were made on that basis. However, there is a purpose in selling, namely, to provide the seller with a legitimate role and a valid reason for communicating a message about this all-important book. The colporteur can thus travel about as a book salesman (and there are always many in all literate societies), he can present his wares and try to explain to people in the house or marketplace why they should buy this book. Moreover, he thus has an opportunity to give his own witness to the value of the book for him. If, on the other hand, he were giving books away, his motivations would be instantly suspect and people would wonder who was supporting this kind of propaganda.

The validity of this approach is interestingly confirmed by an experienced colporteur who on a number of occasions, on asking people to buy a Bible, received the reply that they already had one. Invariably, he asked them how often they read it, or how much they liked it, for his role as a salesman permitted him to make such inquiries quite naturally. Whenever he learned that the people did not read the Scriptures or had not done so for a long time, he inquired about how they procured such a book. Without fail, the answer was that someone gave them a copy. There are, of course, many circumstances in which the giving of Scriptures is desirable, e.g., to prisoners of war, inmates of institutions, people in hospitals, personal friends, etc., but when such gifts are made, and also when the Scriptures are sold, the effectiveness of the communication is usually in direct proportion to the validity of the role of those who serve as "sources."

At the same time, one must recognize the principle of communicating to receptors who are in a position to respond. If the village is likely only to respond as a unit, this is the unit which must be confronted; or, if people can respond only as families, the challenge must be to families. Not that people are to be rejected who break away individually from the normal social patterns and wish to register their convictions. But in general the receptors should be so challenged as to make it possible for the decision-making unit in the society to recognize the full implications of their corporate responsibility.

The Contents of the Message

More often than not, we become so concerned with certain features of the formal transmission of the message that we confuse form and content. If, as for example among the Huichol Indians of Mexico, it is rare that any passage of Scripture is ever twice quoted in exactly the same way (in fact, Huichol stylistic requirements almost prohibit the word-for-word repetition of anything), there is a tendency for missionaries to think that the message has not been adequately communicated. We sometimes forget even the canons of communication which prevailed in the time of Christ, in which word-for-word transcription of messages was not regarded as culturally relevant, and quotations from the Old Testament were more often than not made from memory—sometimes from the Hebrew Old Testament, sometimes from the Greek translation, the Septuagint, and in other instances as a blend of the two.

On other occasions we are so alarmed by the differences of the media that we presume that the content cannot possibly be communicated. In the Portales Interdenominational Church in Mexico City there is a first-rate ranchero orchestra, of sufficient quality to be able to play in any of the élite hotels of the city. The rhythm and brilliance of this orchestra is a far cry from the majestic, solemn tones of the organ in the Church of St. John the Divine in New York City, but this orchestra in Mexico City communicates its message to many more people than does the organ in New York City. Moreover, a high percentage of the "hymns" sung by this congregation are based on typically Mexican music, which has for most Mexicans nothing of the tedious drag that for them characterizes much British and American hymnody. But this use of new forms is no more shocking than what Charles Wesley did for Methodist churches, when he framed the popular tunes of his day in rich harmonies and wrote inspiring words to match.

Having emancipated ourselves from false attachment to formal differences, we can perhaps examine more carefully some of the more significant problems of adaptation of content. What is actually involved here is not the altering of the essential content of the Biblical message, but the encasing of this message in a culturally relevant verbal form. Our real objective, then, is not a change of content (which is, as we shall see, the essence of syncretism), but rather a fitting of the same content into such culturally meaningful forms as will be fit vehicles for the communication of the message. In doing so one can never take over an entire religious system as such and simply pour into it a different content. To do so would do violence either to the indigenous system or to the Christian faith. What is done is to select significant features of the people's world view (especially as regards religious practices) and provide meaningful interpretations of the Christian content through the use of these indigenous symbolic forms.

Among the Tobas in Argentina, one of the dominant themes is "sharing," for this is a symbol and mechanism of Toba life. This seminomadic group of Indians maintains a relatively cohesive social structure because every Toba feels constrained to share with all his clan and neighbors almost everything that he has. Thus his world view is very different from that of the average Protestant missionary, who has a strongly individualistic orientation toward life, in which providing for one's own family, saving for a rainy day, and improving oneself have high priority values. However, the message which was effective for these Tobas was not one based on the concept of individual responsibility before God, but one of sharing. God was described as sharing His Son with mankind, and His Son as sharing his life with mankind, not only by dying for them, but also by sharing with them his Spirit. All people then who share in this common gift of God give evidence that they belong to the tribe of God; they are all His children, and as such they must share with one another in this new fellowship of the faith. In addition to this element in the proclamation of Christianity to the Tobas, there was the fact that in the early indigenous way of life, only the shaman, or medicine man, could have ecstatic religious experiences. However, the Pentecostals who brought the gospel to the Tobas promised the people that everyone who became a Christian would experience this ecstatic state, as proof that he had received the Holy Spirit. On the basis of this presentation of the content of the gospel in terms of certain aspects of Toba cultural forms, within a short time more than twenty congregations of believers were formed.

Among the Quechuas of Ecuador a presentation of the message of the gospel in terms of sharing would be quite meaningless, for there are no cultural forms which would provide a vehicle for communicating such a concept. On the other hand, the Ecuadorian Quechua people do have a view of the religious world which provides some relevant bases for communication. In the pre-Colombian culture the Inca was the head of a very rigidly structured society. Under him were various leaders responsible for several hundred thousand people each, and gradually the social structure was subdivided into groups of 10,000, 1,000, 100, and finally 10 families, each with its own governing officer and community leadership. Communication, which was highly organized in the Inca empire and statistically controlled by the use of quipus (different types of strings in which various kinds of knots indicated numerical amounts), passed along this structured society, from the top down and from the smallest unit up to the Inca. (There was a remarkable two-way flow of information for a totalitarian, though beneficent, society.) When the Spanish conquerors took over the country by the relatively simple means of deceitful betrayal of the Inca and his immediate associates, they left the social structure more or less intact, but superimposed upon it their own governmental and religious authority. Thus, in the place of earlier spirits and gods who were supposed to be protectors of the various regions and groupings of people, the Quechuas accepted, often with mere rechristening, the protection of the saints, whether family, regional, or national. The view of present-day Ecuadorian Quechuas is that, even as in secular affairs one must petition each succeeding level of government officials through the mediation of the immediately lower level, so in religion one must implore the family saint to intercede with the village saint, who in turn prevails on the saint of the region, and then finally by several steps Mary is entreated, and she intercedes with Christ and God. Each step is regarded as a *palanca*, or "lever." Within this rather complex and extensive system the proclamation of the gospel comes as a relevant explanation of how God has actually communicated with men—not through a series of saints, each with less and less spirit power, but pre-eminently and decisively through His own Son, who is the one and only *palanca* between men and God. Moreover, by reconciling men to God he has made it possible for them to speak directly to

God; for whereas before men were fearful of God's wrath against their sins, they know now that in Christ He has forgiven men. He therefore wants people to behave like His children, who never hesitate to approach their human fathers for what they need and therefore should never cease to speak to their heavenly Father about the deepest concerns of their lives.

In some instances the manner in which the Good News of Jesus Christ is presented appears to be so different from the manner we are accustomed to that we tend to question whether it can possibly square with the Scriptural message or with legitimate human motivations. Among the Chols in southern Mexico[2] the focus of communication has nothing to do with sin as such, for the people are neither worried about their sins, nor do they look upon sins as primarily a religious matter. Moreover, there is no fear of going to hell, for people think that everyone must go there for a while anyway, and the ultimate effects are supposed to be good. Since God, Mary, and Jesus Christ are all regarded as being generally benevolent, they believe there is no need to pay much attention to them. What does concern the people is the fact that the devil, who heads up the domain of the spirits, has almost complete and sadistic control over the world of men. He must be appeased, or else he will steal a part of a man's spirit and lock it away in a cave. Unless adequate propitiation is made the man is then sure to die. In their view the whole earth belongs to the devil, and hence, to fall on it, or to cultivate it without proper propitiation or compensation to the devil, is extremely dangerous. Moreover, the world is filled with spirits which may maim, kill, and destroy: the spirit of frogs causes bloated stomachs, the spirit of wasps inflicts boils, and the spirit of the earth mole produces toothaches. In such a world, what can God do, who stays so far away and seems so completely detached from man's existence? The Good News is that God sent His Son into the world to tell men that God is not off in some place far distant, but that He loved them and wanted to give them His Holy Spirit, if only they would be reconciled to Him. This Spirit of God is infinitely more powerful than any and all the other spirits. Moreover, the possession of this Spirit is made possible by the death of Jesus Christ, who gave his blood that he might give men life. The Chols understand this concept, for they have traditionally believed that only by the sacrifice of the blood of some animal may they acquire the spirit of the animal and through this means ward off evil. But God wants to give men His Spirit, through which they can truly experience life in all its fullness.

The new Chol Christian naturally does not understand all the implications of this message at first, any more than we comprehend the different conceptual forms in which the Good News comes to us, but this cultural pattern of Chol life provides a means of insight and understanding by which the Spirit of God may perform His "saving work of grace." The result of this message, plus its fuller exposition as people so grow in experience that they can appreciate its larger implications and richer historical context, has been a movement of more than 5,000 Chol Christians.

The test of effective communication is, of course, the response. But this does not imply a purely pragmatic view, in the sense that if a communication works in the lives of a number of people, it must of necessity be true and adequate. This is not the case, for obviously people respond to error as well as to truth. The response is not a test of truth, but a test of communicative effectiveness. The difficulty is that in the case of so much communication there can be no response because the communication is utterly meaningless. The man who translates literally "gird up the loins of your mind" (1 Peter 1:13) as "put a belt around the hips of your thoughts" is not providing any basis for response, for the message is itself meaningless and so is incapable of eliciting an intelligent answer.

We must, however, be prepared to realize that the response to a message may be negative as well as positive; for the grace of God provides for rejection as well as acceptance. Man is no marionette dangling on the invisible strings of divine capriciousness. He is a moral agent, whose decisions are real even though they may be wrong. Anyone communicating the Christian message must make certain that rejection of it is based upon a comprehension of the message, and not upon its incredible or irrelevant formulation. Missionaries among one of the Indian groups in the Southwest have failed in many instances to provide even an adequate basis for rejection. For one thing, in speaking of Christianity they have never used the indigenous word for religion which the people themselves employ to describe their own and other Indian religious systems. For these Indians, the white man does not even have a religion, only a series of beliefs equivalent to a philosophy. For baptism, missionaries had used the phrase "to brand with water," but to the Indians this meant "ownership" rather than initiation into a new religious faith. If they had only used the Indian term for initiation, in the sense of "to initiate with water," they could have entered into meaningful "conversations" with these people. Moreover, in the word for "holy" they employed a term meaning "undefiled" or "unblemished," but in the language there is an excellent term for "holy," which is almost exactly parallel to the Greek term *hagios*. The use of this word would likewise have provided a basis for effective communication in a context in which some intelligent response, whether positive or negative, would have been possible. Irrelevant communications which have sidestepped the real religious issues have produced more or less indifference, which is far more detrimental to the lives of the people and the ministry of the church than is direct and open opposition. All too often people have attributed rejection of the Christian message to human perversity or Satanic influence, when in many cases it was due to sheer irrelevancy of the communication.

Indigenization vs. Syncretism

In making communicative adaptations our fear is that we shall lose the content of the message in the process of adapting it to the receptors. A concern for this difficulty is a very valid one, for it is easy to permit the message to be twisted out of recognition by using forms which do not fit it. In the second century A.D. one of the very early experimenters in this field, Justin Martyr, in his famous dialogue with Trypho, presents a view that Greek philosophy in a sense constituted the *Logos*, or "Word" of God, in a pre-Christian form. Justin's zeal and "apologetic" defense of the Christian faith is to be admired, but Justin was not engaging in making the message indigenous so much as in Hellenizing the source. He was not content to use the categories of Greek philosophy, in which he was well trained, as a means of communicating the radical uniqueness of the Christian faith. For him this extra-Biblical wisdom was likewise a source or revelation. It must be said, however, that Justin was essentially cautious in his use of this approach, much more so than many others who have followed in his wake.

Not that we must look upon all extra-Biblical sources as being false, suspect, or lacking in profound and true insights, for they reveal much about the nature of the world and of man and offer important ways of looking upon the relationships of the infinite to the finite. But they do not reveal God, in the sense of the God and Father of our Lord Jesus Christ.

Indigenization consists essentially in the full employment of local indigenous forms of communication, methods of transmission, and communicators, as these means can be prepared and trained. Syncretism, on the other hand, involves an accommodation of content, a synthesis of beliefs, and an amalgamation of world views, in such a way as to provide some common basis for constructing a "new system" or a "new approach."

We recognize that in any communication, even when there has been no attempt at indigenization, there is a tendency toward syncretism. In the early church there was a widespread ancestor cult worship, as witnessed by so many tomb inscriptions requesting the prayers of the dead for the living. This cult led eventually to the modern phenomenon of "saint worship." Even as devout a woman as Monica, the mother of St. Augustine, used to carry food and drink to the graves of the dead. However, despite the fact that there is a tendency to syncretism in all situations, the avoidance of indigenization of the message is no solution. In fact, where there is no indigenization of the message, syncretism is usually greatest, for without indigenization there is no meaningful confrontation of religious systems and no intelligent "Yes" or "No" to the claims of Jesus Christ.

That adaptations occur or that indigenization of communication is necessary should not strike us as either strange or new. Even the anthropomorphic language of Scripture reflects this same basic requirement of indigenization of thought forms in order that, within the limitation of a cultural horizon, men may still understand God, who must be explained in human terms (i.e., by words such as *arms, hands, eyes, throne, loving, repenting,* and *seeking*) if we are to understand Him at all. Moreover, when the writers of the New Testament undertook their task of communicating in verbal forms the uniqueness of Jesus Christ, and the resultant outpouring of God's Spirit in the transformation of human lives and the formation of a new fellowship of believers, they found it necessary to use the very words and thought patterns of their day as indispensable means of communicating what had happened. Millar Burrows summarizes this development and points up its contemporary implications with striking effectiveness.[3]

In his first letter to the Corinthians, Paul says of his own missionary work that to the Jews he became as a Jew, to those outside the law, he became as one outside the law; he became "all things to all men" in order to win some of them (9:20–22).

This was both inevitable and necessary. If the Apostles who spread the gospel through the Roman Empire had tried to devise new forms of expression for the new things they had to say, they would not have conveyed any meaning at all. They would have been like those new converts whose joy was so ecstatic that it found utterance in unintelligible "speaking in tongues." It used to be supposed that the Greek in which the New Testament was written, which is quite different from the language of the classical Greek authors, was a special new language created by Providence for the proclamation of the gospel. The discovery of many contemporary documents, written on papyrus, has shown that the Greek of the New Testament was the language used at that time throughout the Greco-Roman world in correspondence, business and other everyday affairs. The gospel was preached to people in their own language.

Throughout the history of the church all significant advances have likewise been made only when the church has followed this same pattern and communicated its message in the living language of the people. Not that throughout the centuries certain adaptations have not appeared. Such adaptations have been an inevitable development as the gospel has met with different historical periods and confronted diverse cultures. Interpretations of passages concerning women wearing veils, footwashing, braiding of hair, and women speaking in church have all undergone successive modifications in various times and places. But the genius of the Christian faith is not to establish a fixed system of behavior, but to be able to sanctify to the glory of God any and all forms of human relationships. This process may involve in one instance a harvest ceremony in Ceylon and in another a Christian co-operative community among the Mezquital Otomis of Mexico, but regardless of the forms, wherever the content is the message of God's redeeming love through Jesus Christ and wherever in response to this message men and women live redemptive lives in their own communities, we can be certain that here is the communication of the Good News.

There are always many aspects of indigenous Christian movements which may impress us as strange, incorrect, or even as unworthy of our formulation of the gospel message, but we must look beneath the surface of the forms to see the reality of the transformation.

Only then can we appreciate fully the significance of the communication.

Among the Otomi of the Mezquital region of Mexico a very significant program has been carried out under the leadership of an unusual Indian named Venancio Hernandez. This group suffered severe persecution from hostile neighbors in the region of Ixmiquilpan, and finally arranged to purchase for their use a barren hill, near the international highway. There they built modest homes—quite in contrast to those a government agency had built earlier for some Otomi families, which were so elaborate that the Indians lived in hovels near by and used the houses for barns to protect their animals. This Christian community offered sanctuary to any person who was persecuted because of his new faith or who wanted to learn about the "new way" by living among the people. There are actually no formal instructions given to such new residents. As Venancio Hernandez explains it, "We just want them to come and live with us, work with us, and worship with us. In this way they can best understand what a redeemed life means." There is remarkable wisdom in this approach, for the community has attempted to work out the implications of "the redeemed life" in all its aspects. In the first place, there is emphasis upon the "redemption of our bodies," which for these people means divine healing. Many of the people are entirely too poor to afford regular doctors, and moreover, they are convinced that as they earnestly pray for healing of themselves and their neighbors, God will answer. One cannot deny that there have been some remarkable instances of otherwise inexplicable cures. They also lay great stress on "the redemption of our hands," by which they mean the co-operative economic efforts of the people (a dominant feature of traditional Indian community life), whether in road building, in which they have amazed Mexican engineers, construction of new churches (having made ready all the materials, they can complete a chapel within a day, and before any opposition can organize), home industries in the central village, or in the pooling of economic resources for the betterment of the Christian community. There is also emphasis on "the redemption of our minds," meaning that older people are instructed in reading and that the young people are sent to school, in contrast with so many villages in the Mezquital. Lastly, the emphasis is upon "the redemption of our souls," by which they describe the transforming power of God to give men "eternal life," beginning now. The community is essentially a "theocracy," led by a group of the most dedicated members of the church, but always with a view to finding God's will for the community. In doing so the people spend a great deal of time in prayer and fasting. The leaders, in particular, spend long days and nights in prayer, often up in the hills away from the community. Of course, there are problems involving undirected enthusiasm, ecstatic involvement, and a tendency to exclusivism as regards other Christian groups, but the power of this movement, which now includes some 2,000 members, not only in the central village but in more than twenty other communities, is the manner in which these people have sought to find a total answer to their total problems. For them it has been "all or nothing," and as a result they have discovered the joy of utter commitment.

CHAPTER 9

Scripture Translation and Revision As Techniques of Communication

> And all the people gathered as one man into the square before the Water Gate; and they told Ezra the scribe to bring the book of the law of Moses which the Lord had given to Israel. And Ezra the priest brought the law before the assembly, both men and women and all who could hear with understanding, on the first day of the seventh month. And he read from it facing the square before the Water Gate from early morning until midday; . . . and the ears of all the people were attentive to the book of the law. . . . Also, Jeshua, Bani, Sherebiah, Jamin, Akkub, Shabbethai, Hodiah, Maaseiah, Kelita, Azariah, Jozabad, Hanan, Pelaiah, the Levites, helped the people to understand the law. . . . And they read from the book, from the law of God, clearly; and they gave the sense, so that the people understood the reading.—NEHEMIAH 8:1-3, 7-8

IN DISCUSSING the difficulties encountered by the British Committee in their new revision of the Bible, Professor T. H. Robinson remarked, "The most fascinating thing about translating is that it is so impossible." Although absolute communication is impossible, nevertheless, translators of the Scriptures have contrived in one way or another to communicate with remarkable effectiveness. A brief analysis of what they have done and how they have done it may help point the way to fundamental principles which are valid not only for translation and revision, but also for the broader problems of communication, on whatever level and with any type of symbolic system.

Any Bible translator, and especially one who is working in a situation where the receptor language and culture are markedly different from that of the source language, is confronted with two principal types of difficulties: (1) the cultural discrepancies, and (2) the linguistic diversities. There may, for example, be no wolves in the region where the translator is working. What then does he do? In some places he can use the equivalent of "jackal" or "hyena," both of which are related to the canine family, as a substitute for "wolf" in figurative language. But since in certain other parts of the world the normal cultural equivalent is the leopard, a number of translators read, "I send you out as sheep among leopards" (Matthew 10:16) and "they come as hungry leopards disguised in the pelts of sheep" (Matthew 7:15).

These cultural differences are not, however, as great a problem as the diversities of language structure, whether formal or semantic. A language such as Puebla Aztec, for example, does not have a passive voice. This means that all passives must become actives, and hence "Judge not, that you be not judged. For with the judgment you pronounce, you will be judged," must be rendered as "Do not judge others, in order that God will not judge you; for in whatever way you pronounce judgment on others, God will in the same way pronounce judgment on you." Similarly, a language may not employ a singular form with generic meaning. Hence, "Love thy neighbor" would invoke the question, "Which neighbor?" In many languages one must use a plural if the more general concept is to be communicated. Accordingly, the translation must read, "Love your neighbors."

At times it is the semantic structure of the language which causes problems of equivalence; for example, though we as English speakers talk about the emotional focus of the personality as the "heart," this is by no means a universal situation. In fact, the Chujs of Guatemala speak of the "abdomen," the Marshallese speak of the "throat," and in some contexts the Totonacs of Mexico may speak of the "spleen." In a number of languages of Africa, including several of the so-called "Sudanic" languages of the northern Congo, one must substitute the "liver" in this expression. Hence, certain familiar passages must be rendered in quite different ways, e.g., "Let not your liver be troubled" (John 14:1), "So you have sorrow now, but I will see you again and your livers will rejoice" (John 16:22), "These people honor me with their mouths, but their livers are far from me" (Matthew 12:34).

One basic reason for these difficulties is that corresponding symbols in two languages may have quite different "functions." Stated somewhat more accurately, we may say that the referent-functions of corresponding symbols may be equivalent, but the conception-functions may be quite different. In some areas of the Philippines, for example, to wag the head from side to side means "Yes" rather than "No." The same symbolic action, both in gesture and as described in language, has quite a different meaning from that in English. In 2 Corinthians 6:11 the Greek idiom, *to stoma hêmôn aneôgen pros humas*, is often rendered literally in English as "Our mouth is open to you"; but if this phrase is translated word for word into some of the languages of West Africa, it commonly means that the person in question is raving mad.

On the other hand, quite different linguistic symbols, in the sense that they have diverse referent-functions, can have relatively equivalent conception-functions. In English we say "hold your tongue" when we want a person to be silent; but in Gourma, a language of West Africa, he is told to "hold your gall bladder."

Diverse Types of Translations

In translating there is an almost infinitely graded scale from excessively literal, word-for-word renderings to the most paraphrastic free parallels. In the past it has been customary to refer to a relatively close or literal rendering as a translation and a very free equivalent as a paraphrase, but there are certainly no agreed upon criteria for making such distinctions. Moreover, what we have is not a strict distinction of types, but a polar series, running from the most rigid type of correspondence, which we may call a "gloss" translation,[1] to a very free reproduction of the original, which we may call an "equivalence" translation. The purpose of a gloss translation is to reflect as much as possible of the linguistic and cultural form of the source language. In terms of our diagram in Chapter 3, this would mean attempting to communicate as much as possible of ⚠ (the form of the language) and ⚠ (the form of the culture). For this type of translation the old interlinear "ponies" plus a literal gloss at the side were excellent. On the other hand, most people seem to prefer, not a gloss translation, but one which is more nearly an equivalence, in terms of the linguistic and cultural circumstances in which they live. They are not so much concerned with the formal resemblance as with the dynamic equivalence. In other words, they want to be able to interpret the relevance of the message within the context of their own lives, without having to consider or be distracted by the formal structures of the original communicative setting.

Equivalence, however, is not a simple matter. Essentially it involves three different, though closely related, factors: (1) stylistics, which includes the formal structural relationships, (2) the referential meanings of symbols, and (3) the conceptual meanings of symbols. No translation can employ any one of these factors exclusively, but it may give greater proportionate weight to one in contrast with the others.

The Scottish renderings of the Psalms, as sung or chanted in the Presbyterian Church of Scotland, are equivalence translations, giving priority to the stylistic factors of the poetical form of the receptor language. The following example illustrates what happens to the familiar first Psalm:

1   That man hath perfect blessedness
      who walketh not astray
In counsel of ungodly men,
      nor stands in sinners' way,
Nor sitteth in the scorner's chair:
2   But placeth his delight
Upon God's law, and meditates
      on his law day and night.

3   He shall be like a tree that grows
      near planted by a river
Which in his season yields his fruit,
      and his leaf fadeth never:
And all he doth shall prosper well.
4   The wicked are not so:
But like they are unto the chaff,
      which wind drives to and fro.

5   In judgment therefore shall not stand
      such as ungodly are;
Nor in th' assembly of the just
      shall wicked men appear.

6   For why? the way of godly men
        unto the Lord is known:
    Whereas the way of wicked men
        shall quite be overthrown.

Again, a translator may give priority to the referential meanings of symbols, with the conceptual and stylistic functions subordinated in that order. Weymouth[2] and Rieu[3] have produced highly significant translations of this type. The following selection from Rieu's rendering of John 5:1–11 is illustrative of his cautious but effective handling of equivalences.

There followed the Jewish Festival, and Jesus travelled up to Jerusalem.
    By the sheep-gate in that city there is a pool with five arcades, which in Aramaic is called Bethzatha. A number of disabled people, blind, lame, and withered, used to lie in these arcades; and there was a man there who had suffered from his trouble for thirty-eight years.
    Jesus, seeing him lying there and knowing that he had been ill for a long time, said to him: "Have you the will to become well again?"
    "Sir," said the sick man, "I have no one to put me in the pool when the water is ruffled, and while I am on the way someone else gets in before me."
    Jesus said: "Rise, pick up your stretcher and walk." And immediately the man was cured, picked up his stretcher and walked.
    It was a sabbath day, and the Jews said to the man who had been cured: "This is the Sabbath and you ought not to be carrying your stretcher."
    He replied: "It was the man who cured me. He *told* me to pick it up and walk."

J. B. Phillips in his translation of the New Testament has given priority to the conceptual function of symbolism, subordinating in many instances both referential meaning and stylistics. He has succeeded in producing an equivalent translation which, though it often departs from the so-called "wording of the original," nevertheless communicates the equivalent concepts in a brilliant manner. A typical example of Phillips' treatment of the Epistles follows:

In my opinion whatever we may have to go through now is less than nothing compared with the magnificent future God has planned for us. The whole creation is on tiptoe to see the wonderful sight of the sons of God coming into their own. The world of creation cannot as yet see reality, not because it chooses to ʰe blind, but because in God's purpose it has been so limited—yet it has been given hope. And the hope is that in the end the whole of created life will be rescued from the tyranny of change and decay, and have its share in the magnificent liberty which can only belong to the children of God!

It is plain to anyone with eyes to see that at the present time all created life groans in a sort of universal travail. And it is plain, too, that we who have a foretaste of the Spirit are in a state of painful tension, while we wait for that redemption of our bodies which will mean that at last we have realized our full sonship in him.—ROMANS 8:18–23

Translation As the Closest Natural Equivalent

From the viewpoint of the Bible translator the most satisfactory definition of translation seems to be "the closest natural equivalent, first in meaning and secondly in style."[4] Unless a translation aims at some degree of equivalence it is largely useless, for it cannot be understood. On the other hand, it must not be just any kind of equivalence; rather, it must be one which is the "closest" and which at the same time is still in a natural form of expression. No translation should betray by its very form its foreign origin,[5] though it is inevitable that the unfamiliar content, including strange settings and concepts, almost inevitably stamps a translation as not indigenous.

In general one must give priority to meaning, whether referential or conceptual, rather than to form. Otherwise, the results will be a distortion of the original, not a reflection. What is ultimately sought in translating can thus perhaps best be summarized by saying that a truly bilingual (and "bicultural") person, in comparing the receptor language text with one in the source language, should be able to say, "That is just the way we would say it." Such an ideal will inevitably mean making a number of formal differences in the message in order that the concepts may be equivalent. In Nilotic Shilluk, for example, the only way one can talk about God's forgiveness is literally, "God spit on the ground in front of us." This idiom arises from the practice of plaintiffs and defendants having to spit on the ground in front of each other when finally a case had been tried and punishments have been meted out and fines paid. The spitting (which has an entirely different cultural value from what it has with us) symbolizes that the case is terminated, that all is forgiven, and that the accusations cannot come into court again. The literal referent-function of this

Shilluk expression is quite different from the conception-function, but the latter is what counts, for the referent-function does not dominate the communicative value to the point of requiring that the expression be understood literally. It is a figure of speech and is recognized as such.

Problems of Equivalence

The fact that languages differ is obvious. But how these differences in languages are to be classified and treated is not easy to decide. One fruitful approach is to analyze the differences by means of comparing the data of the source language with those of the receptor language. This method offers a natural and practical way of approaching the task of decoding the source text and encoding it into the receptor language.

In comparing two languages one almost always finds several types of nonconformities. That is to say, there are data in the source language which, in terms of the receptor language, are (1) nonexistent, (2) obscure, (3) ambiguous, (4) implicit, or (5) explicit, and which in the receptor-language translation must be either (a) obligatorily included or (b) optionally omitted. The intersections of these classes of material provide us with some fundamental principles about how to produce as high a degree of equivalence as possible.[6]

1. *Nonexistent in the source language but obligatory in the receptor language.* In the Villa Alta dialect of Zapotec it is obligatory to indicate in the verb whether an action takes place for the first time or is a repetition of an event. In the expression, "and leaving Nazareth he went and dwelt in Capernaum" (Matthew 4:13), the translator must decide whether Jesus had ever been in Capernaum before. There are no specific Biblical data on this point. One can only surmise from the general circumstances of Jesus' life that he probably would have been in Capernaum before, possibly on a trip back and forth from Jerusalem, or perhaps on business or for pleasure. At any rate, the translator cannot avoid the issue, despite the lack of specific Biblical evidence; for in this dialect of Zapotec it is impossible to be neutral on the subject—the verb forms must specify one or the other circumstance.

2. *Obscure in the source language, but obligatory in the receptor language.* In a number of the languages of Southeast Asia one encounters elaborate systems of honorifics, including not only gram-

matical forms but also selections of words. The choice of forms and
vocabulary is dependent upon the manner in which a person's status
is interpreted, often in terms of higher, equal to, or lower than that
of the speaker. One must then decide just how Jesus would be addressed by the Pharisees or religious leaders of his day. Transposed
into the cultural context of Southeast Asia, would they recognize him
as a rabbi and hence grant him a corresponding honorific status, or
would they speak down to him because of his youth and presumptuous ideas? On the other hand, how would he address them? Would
he use dignified forms, while at the same time denouncing their
hypocrisy? There is no sure way of knowing what to do, for the cultural situations are so disparate and the Scripture evidence so obscure
as to make certainty impossible. The situation is further complicated
by the fact that contemporary readers in these cultures tend to judge
the situation quite out of its original context; in some languages they
have insisted that Jesus, because of his divine status, must be addressed with honorifics, irrespective of the local circumstances in
which the recorded communications took place. The translator,
moreover, cannot avoid the problem, regardless of the obscurity of
the evidence, for the receptor languages in question make such distinctions obligatory.

3. *Ambiguous in the source language but obligatory in the receptor
language.* Ambiguity differs from obscurity in that, though the evidence for obscurity is impossible of accurate interpretation, in ambiguity there are at least two, possibly more, almost equally good
alternatives. In a language that requires a distinction between inclusive and exclusive first person plural (the difference between "we"
meaning "I and those to whom I am speaking" and "we" indicating "I
and my associates, but excluding those to whom I am speaking"), the
fourth chapter of John is a difficult one. When, for example, the
Samaritan woman says, "Are you greater than our father Jacob, who
gave us this well?" is she using the inclusive or exclusive "our"? In
other words, does she include Jesus as likewise the offspring of Jacob
and hence one who would be in the lineage of recipients of the well?
Or would she be inclined, because of the typical ethnic jealousy and
animosity that prevailed between Jews and Samaritans, to speak of
Jacob as being exclusively the father of the Samaritans who bequeathed the well to them rather than to the Jews? One can pro-
pound almost equally good reasons for one or another viewpoint. But

again, when the receptor-language forms obligatorily call for either the inclusive or exclusive first person plural, it is necessary to make a choice, despite the fact that the original by no means provides a certain clue to the proper alternative.

In many instances the Biblical Greek text is ambiguous, even in terms of its own categories, and thus is also ambiguous in terms of the receptor language. Only rarely under such circumstances can the ambiguity be satisfactorily preserved. In John 1:9 there is a famous ambiguity, for the phrase "coming into the world" may modify either the "light" or "every man," and no mere comma in English can resolve the difficulty or preserve the ambiguity. Either it is "the light coming into the world lightens every man" or "the light enlightens every man as he comes into the world." Though earlier translations tended to follow the latter interpretation, most present-day exegetes favor the former.

4. *Implicit in the source language but obligatory in the receptor language.* Hebrews 7:3 speaks of Melchizedek as being "without father or mother or genealogy," and having neither "beginning of days nor end of life." Such a statement has been taken by some people to imply a theophany; for as far as the explicit content of the statement is concerned, it would appear that Melchizedek was an utterly unusual type of person who came directly down from heaven. On the other hand, the context is such as to indicate implicitly that the person discussed is not a supernatural individual, but rather that there is no record of his father, mother, lineage, birth, or death, and that despite these facts he could serve as a high priest to God and could minister to Abraham. Since in some languages it is impossible to be implicit about this matter of the "record" unless one wishes to communicate an entirely false "message," it is essential to take what is implicit in this passage and make it explicit in another language. Accordingly, a number of translations into foreign languages read, "there is no record of his father or mother or family line, and it is not known when he was born or when he died." Such expressions as "there is no record" and "it is not known" would appear to be additions to the text; but in a sense they are not, for they are only taking what was perfectly evident (though implicit) in the original and making it explicit in the translation.

5. *Explicit in the source language but requiring a different treatment in the receptor language.* There is almost no limit to the variety

of adaptations which must be made in adjusting explicit statements
in the source language to corresponding expressions in the receptor
language. On the lowest level of modification are certain grammatical
alterations. In Acts 1:24, for example, in the Greek the duality of
the men who were being considered as candidates to take Judas'
place is expressed by means of a numeral modified by a pronominal
adjective (literally, "these the two"); but in Hopi the duality of men
is expressed by adding a dual suffix to the noun "men."

Another level of alteration involves such changes as: (1) the re-
casting of active expressions into passive ones, where certain languages
require passive equivalents (e.g., "he returned to Capernaum," Mark
2:1, becomes "Capernaum was returned to by him" in Shilluk, in
Africa); and (2) the shifting from nominal to verbal constructions,
where "John preached the baptism of repentance unto the forgiveness
of sins" becomes in many languages "John preached that people
should repent and be baptized so that the evil deeds which they had
done would be forgiven." Still a further level of alteration occurs in
the adaptation of semantic structure, where "mercy" may be translated as "his abdomen weeps for him" (Conob, spoken in Guatemala), "he looks upon their misery" (Kpelle, spoken in Liberia), and
"to feel with the poor" (Mazatec, spoken in Mexico).

Where the receptor language has no obligatory requirements for
the rendering of particular types of expressions in the source language, the problems of translation are greatly diminished. Nonexistent information in the source language is of course irrelevant to
the problem, for if such data need not be supplied, one should not
add them to the receptor-language text. Obscurities or ambiguities in
the source text may often be left obscure or ambiguous in the receptor
language. Of course, there is no special virtue in a translation which
is not clear in meaning, nevertheless, where the original is obscure or
ambiguous, the translator should not undertake to improve upon it.
The translator's task is not to edit the original, but to reproduce it
in terms of the closest natural equivalent, including the transmission
of the obscurities and ambiguities when this can be done. However,
the exact reproduction of obscurities and ambiguities is very difficult,
and rarely is it accomplished successfully.

When there is implicit information in the original text, and it is
optional whether it be left implicit or made explicit in the receptor
language, it is often legitimate to make it explicit in translation. The

reason for doing so is that, whereas the reader of the original text had a good deal of background knowledge on which to draw, and therefore in a sense the channel of communication, namely, the message, was not so heavily loaded with "information," quite the opposite situation may exist for present-day readers in culturally diverse situations. For a person totally unfamiliar with the original setting, it is often necessary to build into the text a certain degree of redundancy, usually by filling out implicit data by explicit statements, so that the two texts may actually be equivalent in the amount of "information" they carry. For example, in many translations into so-called primitive languages it is standard practice to use classifiers with various proper names or unknown borrowed terms. Instead, then, of merely the word *Jordan, Jerusalem,* or *Galilee,* the translator employs, at least in their first occurrence, such phrases as "river Jordan," "city Jerusalem," and "province Galilee." Similarly, for unknown borrowed terms, he may use certain descriptive classifiers, e.g., "precious stone ruby," "expensive cloth linen," and "large wild animal called bear."

The result of these adaptations is that the text in the receptor language is almost always longer than the original. It is significant that Adoniram Judson's translation of the Bible, probably the best "missionary translation" in any Oriental language, is about 25 per cent longer than any of the subsequent revisions. Certainly part of the reason for its success was the fact that Judson was willing to build into it a certain amount of "redundancy" in order that it might be an effective vehicle of communication.

Revisions of the Scriptures

The production of translations in so-called "new languages" may be thought of in terms of spatial extension of the message. But there is also a temporal dimension in this process of communication, namely, the constant revision of the Scriptures in any one language. There is a tendency for Americans to think that in English we have only the King James Version (also called the Authorized Version) of 1611, the Revised Version of 1901, and finally the Revised Standard Version, plus the crop of recent translations by Goodspeed, Moffatt, Phillips, Rieu, Charles Williams, Kingsley-Williams, and Verkuyl. The truth of the matter is that a number of translations preceded the King James, including the work of Wycliffe, Tyndale, Coverdale, the Geneva Bible, and the Bishops' Bible. But after the King James

Version was published in 1611, the translation and revision of the Bible into English did not stop. In fact, between the King James text and the Revised Standard Version, of which the New Testament was published first in 1946, there have been more than 500 translations and revisions of Bibles, New Testaments, and individual books into English, not to mention scores of scholarly translations which have been "buried" in commentaries on the text.

One may quite rightly ask why so many revisions are required. Are our traditional translations so erroneous as to require such a host of changes? Do so many revisions merely add up to the fact that we cannot be certain about what the Scriptures mean? Are such translations and revisions merely a form of subtle attack upon the traditional tenets of our faith? The answers to these questions are fourfold, including: (1) better knowledge of the original texts, (2) more accurate understanding of the meanings of the Biblical passages, (3) changes which have occurred in the English language through the years, and (4) a revised concept of communication, and hence of translation.

A surprising amount of new information about the text of the Bible has been acquired within the last few years. The story of the discovery of the Qumran manuscripts has excited thousands of people. Some persons have even been led to think that, buried in these caves along the Dead Sea, was evidence that Christianity was derived from a monastic, militant community of Essenes, intently looking for the coming of the Messiah. A more sober study of these documents, however, has shown that in no way do they diminish the uniqueness of the ministry and significance of Jesus Christ; but they have surely provided us with highly important background data by which we may better judge the significance of Jesus within the framework of his own culture and times.[7] These findings have also given us important light on some of the obscurities in the Hebrew text of the Old Testament. In our present Scriptures, for example, there is an awkward discrepancy between Exodus 1:5 and Acts 7:14. In the Masoretic Hebrew text (which is the standard Hebrew text of the Old Testament, and substantially the only one known to us before the Qumran discoveries), Exodus 1:5 states that the family of Jacob which went into Egypt numbered seventy persons. In Acts 7:14 we read that Jacob's kindred numbered seventy-five. It has always been of interest that the Septuagint Greek translation of the Old Testament, which was finished at least a hundred years before Jesus Christ, and which constituted the "Bible" for most of the early Christians, reads "seventy-five" at this point in Exodus 1:5. It is therefore significant that in a Qumran manuscript which includes this passage in Exodus, the reading is "seventy-five," not "seventy" as in the Masoretic tradition.

In Deuteronomy 32:8 the Revised Standard Version followed a conjectural reading which gave "according to the number of the sons of God," rather than the more traditional Masoretic rendering, "according to the number of the sons of Israel." Again it is of importance that in a Qumran fragment this use of "sons of God" is confirmed.

For Amos 9:11 the Damascus Document and the Florilegium, both found at Qumran, read, "and I will raise up the booth of David," instead of "in that day I will . . ." as in the Masoretic Hebrew text and in the Septuagint. What makes this little variant so significant is that in Acts 15:16, where this passage from Amos is quoted, the Greek follows the wording of the Qumran material, not the texts preserved to us in the Masoretic or the Septuagint tradition.

Though the discovery of the Qumran manuscripts is a fascinating tale in itself, the publication of recently discovered New Testament manuscripts, especially those in the Bodmer library of Geneva, are no less significant, and perhaps, if we knew their history, no less spectacular. One of the most important manuscripts in this collection is a second-century papyrus containing the first fourteen chapters of John, almost entirely preserved. This earliest extensive witness to the text of John has some very important readings. For example, in John 1:18, where traditional texts have read, "only begotten Son who is in the bosom of the Father," a few ancient witnesses read, "only begotten God who is in the bosom of the Father."[8] Some scholars had passed off this reading as being perhaps the result of some overzealous scribe trying to introduce a further proof of the deity of Jesus Christ. However, the occurrence of "only God" in this second-century papyrus is highly significant evidence of what the author of this Gospel may have written.

In John 7:52 there is a curious expression translated usually as, "no prophet arises from Galilee"; but a number of prophets had come from Galilee, and no Old Testament prophecy specifically excluded the possibility of Galilean prophets. Because of this fact,

Owen some years ago suggested that one single letter might be missing from this verse, for the occurrence of the Greek definite article
would completely change the meaning. The text would then read,
"The prophet [in the sense of 'the Messiah'] shall not arise from
Galilee." This very reading is found in the Bodmer papyrus, which
thus serves to clear up a previous obscurity in the text.

Certain preferred readings of the better Greek manuscripts may at
times appear disturbing, especially to our unthinking acceptance of
certain favorite passages of Scripture. This was my personal experience
with Romans 8:28, for I had regarded the form, "all things work
together for good to them that love God, to them who are called
according to his purpose" (King James Version), as being quite the
last word about divine assurance. However, when I discovered that
the best Greek manuscripts have quite a different reading, namely,
"in all things God works for good with those who love him . . ." I
was disturbed, for it seemed that this verse had been irreparably dam-
aged. Then I began to realize that, rather than this verse having
suffered a loss of meaning, it was in its revised form completely true.
One cannot say that all circumstances automatically work together
for good to the Christian, for we are not the recipients of this sort of
benign and impersonal beneficence. On the other hand, it is quite
true that in all the circumstances of life God is there at the very
center of events and working for the accomplishment of His glory
and our eternal good.

One of the basic reasons for revision of the Scriptures is that these
better-attested forms of the Hebrew and Greek texts should be made
available. Some theologically conservative people have resisted such
changes because they have mistakenly assumed that such alterations
in the Bible would somehow destroy their faith. However, the Protestant heritage and the source of evangelical faith have never rested on
the history of ecclesiastical tradition or of scribal mistakes. Those
who most insist upon the inspiration of the Scriptures by the Holy
Spirit should be in the very forefront of those eager to evaluate and
accept the well-attested results of contemporary textual scholarship.

Not only can it be said that revisions are required because we have
better information about the form of the Biblical message; it is true
also that revisions are necessary because we have a better understanding of how the message of the Scriptures should be interpreted in the
light of the total cultural context. On the level of grammatical usage,

contemporary scholarship can clear up a number of difficult points. In John 20:17 traditional translations represent Jesus as saying, "Do not touch me, for I have not yet ascended to my Father." Such a statement seems very standoffish and "out of character" for our Lord. Furthermore, in Matthew 28:9 we are told that on their return from the tomb, the women met Jesus and "clasped his feet." Some preachers have tried to reconcile these statements by claiming that, after speaking to Mary, Jesus went immediately to heaven to report to His Father and then returned, all within the space of a few minutes. But such explanations are entirely unnecessary, for we now know that the particular form of the verb used in John 20:17 means, not "do not touch," but "do not continue to hold onto."

Extensive lexical studies of the Bible have continued to reveal highly important insights that give Scripture passages quite new meanings. The Greek term *ataktôs*, rendered "disorderly" in older English translations, fits very poorly in the third chapter of 2 Thessalonians, where the context is about the necessity of a man working or "he should not eat." It has now been found that *ataktôs*, despite its so-called etymological meaning, correct in classical times, had by New Testament times acquired the significance of "living in idleness," or "refusing to work for a living." This word now makes sense. Another very suggestive insight is the meaning of *aparchê*, as used in Romans 8:23.[9] In certain contexts this word has been found to mean "a birth certificate of a free person." Rather than the Spirit being merely the first installment of God's redemptive plan (equivalent to Paul's use of *arrabôn*), the Spirit may be regarded as our certification of sonship, a meaning which seems to fit the context admirably.

In addition to better knowledge of the texts of the Scriptures and their meaning within the cultural setting in which they were used, we must also reckon with changes within any living language. Such words as *prevent* (in the sense of "to go ahead of"), *meat* (for "food"), *purge* (for "prune"), *conversation* (for "manner of life"), *charity* (for "love"), *mansions* (for "rooms"), and *artillery* (for "bow and arrows") have all changed in meaning through the years. The same types of changes are found in all living languages. Recently, for example, a revision of the Spanish Bible was undertaken, primarily with the purpose of eliminating usages which have become archaic in the last three hundred years.

Of course, it is quite possible to teach people an archaic form of language. Furthermore, people often take considerable pleasure in religious language which they do not understand. For many of the obscurities in meaning and the dissimilarities from everyday usage of archaic language enhance the mystical value of the words and phrases. Such tendencies can be found not only in so highly developed a system as the Roman Catholic Church, where the most sacred ceremonies are conducted in a language for the most part quite unknown to the laity; they are found also in scores of primitive tribes, where local medicine men enhance the occult nature of their practices by using strange and archaic forms of speech. On the other hand, the Bible can be the Book of life only when it is translated into life by those who comprehend its transforming message. Its force lies not in the magic of its words but in the power of its message.

Undoubtedly another factor that contributes to the types of revisions of the Scriptures now being made is the new concept of communication and its relation to translation. In fact, a translation which does not communicate its message is, in the more accurate sense of the word, not a translation. It is merely a string of correspondences without an equivalent set of meanings which permit the receptor to respond to the message in substantially the same way that the earlier receptors responded to the original message. This emphasis upon dynamic, rather than formal, equivalence has meant that revisers no longer view their task as limited to the finding of some set of linguistic labels by which the reader may study out the meaning in terms of the original cultural setting; rather, they see their task as directed toward the discovery of symbols which will permit an equivalent type of response within the new cultural context.

It is significant that, throughout the history of the church, the extent of translation and revision has always been directly proportionate to the church's spiritual vitality and dynamic growth. A church that is producing important translations and revisions is aware of its mission in the world and keenly conscious of the need for greater comprehension of the message.

In periods of transition there are always many devout people who strongly resist any revision of the Scriptures. This resistance is not surprising. Those who have attained a certain understanding of the Christian faith through a particular medium of communication see no reason why others cannot do the same. Moreover, they have many hallowed memories associated with a particular translation or revision of the Scriptures. Any change seems to destroy the basis of their faith, for their religious experience is often focused upon a particular system of exegesis rather than upon the reality of a living Lord.

It is quite understandable, therefore, that, when first published, the King James Version was bitterly denounced. In fact, a scholar named Hugh Broughton was noted for his violent attacks upon the King James Version. Others denounced it for all kinds of presumed errors. One accusation was that the translation had been distorted to suit the translators' personal views and to cater to King James' predilection for witchcraft. The Pilgrim fathers would not permit the King James Version to be carried in the *Mayflower*. They clung tenaciously to the Geneva Bible, published some sixty years before. In fact, it was fully seventy-five years before the King James Version can be said to have "won out," and only then in some considerable measure because of royal sanction and a monopoly by the King's printers.

At the present time, when we are again in a period of transition, some people seriously wonder which of several reasonably accurate translations of the Scriptures they should use. The only valid answer is "the one which communicates the truth most effectively to the constituency in question." For many this will continue to be the King James Version, especially for public worship, since the majestic phrases and long association provide a rich heritage for the communication of the message. For many other persons, who have not the same long familiarity with the King James Version, some of the more contemporary translations are undoubtedly more meaningful, for they communicate their message directly and forcibly, unencumbered by seventeenth-century grammatical forms and vocabulary. The important consideration is that we not find ourselves so engaged in controversy about the form of the message that we fail to comprehend its content.

CHAPTER 10

The Theological Basis of Communication

> In the beginning was the Word, and the
> Word was with God, and the Word was God.
> He was in the beginning with God; all things
> were made through him, and without him was
> not anything made that was made. In him was
> life, and the life was the light of men. . . .
> And the Word became flesh and dwelt among
> us, full of grace and truth; we have beheld his
> glory, glory as of the only Son from the Father.
> —JOHN 1:1–4, 14

ONE of the essential difficulties in determining a theological basis for communication is the necessity of disengaging Christian truth from the cultural forces in which it has been embedded throughout history.[1] The whole movement of the expansion of the church, and more recently of the distinctly "missionary outreach," has been intrinsically bound together with secular phases of culture. A careful discrimination between the two, in order to determine a fundamental theological basis for the processes of communication (in contrast with the content), is therefore almost impossible.

In Roman Catholicism the missionary zeal that prompted the early missionaries to "Christianize" the subjects of Spain's conquests was undoubtedly sincere. However, the operative coalition of secular and sacred powers certainly failed to achieve the communication of the Good News of the new life in Christ Jesus. Similarly, the close alliance between colonial governments and Protestant agencies has resulted in many instances in grave misunderstanding of the fine, consecrated work of educational missionaries. One significant fact emerges in this connection in Africa. When, for example, Africans riot in countries in which the government is nominally Roman Catholic, Protestant institutions and personnel are almost always conspicuously avoided or protected by the rioters, as being in some way related to the African point of view. In the same way, in areas in which British colonial power has operated, there is generally quite a widespread sympathy among the Africans for Roman Catholic missionaries, who—by being different from the ruling group—seem to the Africans to be identified with their point of view.

However, missions have often been in direct conflict with their own governmental or commercial interests. Early missionaries to India were in constant battle with the East India Company, and in the South Pacific the American Board missionaries found that the owners of whaling vessels looked with a jaundiced eye on any attempt to convert the "natives."

Despite the problems involved in trying to isolate from one another the secular and the sacred impulses, motivations, and processes of communication, we must attempt to do so if we are to understand properly the theological basis of such communication. This process of discrimination must include an attempt to see how, through two thousand years, this problem has been a focal point of serious tensions.

History of the Tension between the Church and Culture
A significant early statement about the church is to be found in the famous Epistle to Diognetus possibly of the second century:[2]

For Christians are not distinguished from the rest of mankind in country or speech or customs. For they do not live somewhere in cities of their own or use some distinctive language or practice a peculiar manner of life. They have no learning discovered by the thought and reflection of inquisitive men, nor are they the authors of any human doctrine, like some men. Though they live in Greek and barbarian cities, as each man's lot is cast, and follow the local customs in dress and food and the rest of their living, their own way of life which they display is wonderful and admittedly strange. They live in their native lands, but like foreigners. They take part in everything like citizens and endure everything like aliens. Every foreign country is their native land and every native land a foreign country.

A superficial reading of this passage would seem to indicate that everything had worked out nicely—that there were no problems. But a second examination will show that there was a tension even at this stage. Christians were to be in the world but not of it. They were enmeshed in the activities of culture, but they possessed quite a different system of values. They participated in the accomplishment of certain purposes, but their ultimate goals were distinct and different.

A comprehensive and significant analysis of the tensions which have characterized the church in its various segments throughout history is offered by Richard Niebuhr,[3] who distinguishes three major positions of the church: (1) "Christ against culture," (2) "Christ of culture," and (3) "Christ above culture," in which the last position is subdivided into three classes: (a) the synthesists, who look upon Christianity as the fulfillment and restorer of human values, (b) the dualists, who contend that man is subject to two moralities and must live in this tension, and (c) the conversionists, who believe that God comes to man within his culture in order to transform man and through him the culture.

The theme of "Christ against culture" is well reflected in 1 John: "Do not love the world or the things in the world. If any one loves the world, love for the Father is not in him. For all that is in the world, the lust of the flesh and the lust of the eyes and the pride of life, is not of the Father but is of the world" (2:15–16). "We know that we are of God, and the whole world is in the power of the evil one" (5:19). Certainly the early church seemed primarily against the *cosmos*, "the civilized world," and many of the early Christians would have nothing to do with the world. They saw its passing in the apocalyptic message of the Book of the Revelation, and many sought an ascetic escape from it. Modern parallel answers are found in Quakerism, the Mennonite movement, and in certain phases of the Jehovah's Witnesses movement.

The "Christ of culture" was widely proclaimed by the Gnostics, who tried to make the forms of Christianity acceptable to certain elements of Greek philosophical outlook. Abélard followed in the Middle Ages, and modern parallels are to be found in those who attempt reconciliations between traditional Christianity and evolution and who view psychoanalysis as a key to the understanding of Jesus Christ. The Church and Christ combine in the Roman Catholic view of society, as ideally viewed under the rulership of the Roman

Church. Certain Protestant views of the emerging brotherhood of man under the guidance of the Christian spirit have a similar orientation.

Throughout the centuries the Christian movement has seen a continual tension, whether in the form of a synthesis, advocated by Justin Martyr and Clement of Alexandria, who saw a relationship between Stoic love and Christian love, or in the position of Thomas Aquinas, who rejected the world but made the church the fosterer of the true culture. The difficulty with this latter viewpoint is that the culture tends to be absolutized while the Infinite is reduced to mere finiteness and the true dynamic of the Christian faith is lost.

The dualists have held to a kind of double loyalty. They have insisted on the separation of church and state, but have left man to continue in both. This position is that of Roger Williams, and in many significant respects also that of Luther. As Niebuhr puts it, man is regarded by the dualists as an amphibian living in two realms.[4] The conversionists look to the creative redemptive power of God and to the history of dramatic interaction between God and man. In the end there is the final victory of the Son of God, for unto him "every knee shall bow whether in heaven or on earth." This doctrine of reconciliation, conversion, and transformation is represented in the positions in Calvin and Wesley.

It is inevitable that in all these attempts to solve the problem of the church and culture, there has been a commingling of behavior, motivations, and beliefs, for man is not so easily compartmentalized that he can act out his life by playing two roles on the same stage and during the same scene. Inwardly, at least, he is not "of this world," but outwardly he must be "in this world" if he is to communicate effectively to it and with it. The church has therefore always reflected the cultural context in which it has had its life. The pious, strict attitudes of the early church in Jerusalem were vastly different from the sophisticated worldliness that characterized the church in Corinth. Members of the Jerusalem church, who were narrow in their cultural outlook, and who insisted on keeping many aspects of the law with a zealous provincial suspicion of the spread of their faith, would have been utterly shocked to have visited the Corinthian church, which indulged in gluttonous feasts to celebrate the *agape*, and whose loose morals shocked not only the much-traveled Paul but evidently had even caused embarrassing gossip in the pagan community. It has been equally hard for some Anglicans from England to adjust themselves to the exultant informality of many Anglican services in East Africa, and some Presbyterians from the United States seem quite unable to accommodate themselves to the emotional outbursts of related Presbyterian churches in the Cameroun. How much more difficult is it then for a quiet Quaker from Indiana to feel at home with the dancing hysteria of some Pentecostal services in Chile, or for a shouting Landmark Baptist from Arkansas to regard the ritual forms of a High Church service in England as anything other than pure idolatry and heathenism.

Of course, some developments in historic Christianity have gone beyond the limits of Christian faith and have incorporated so much that is fundamentally pagan that we cannot with honesty regard the resultant syncretistic forms as Christian. In the Christo-paganism typical of many areas of Mexico and other Latin American countries, there is very little left of the Christian message. God may be feared, because He sends pestilence, famine, and earthquake, but He is not the One to whom a person prays. In fact, He is not the only god, for He shares His domain with a female deity, the Virgin, the "Mother of God" and the source of life. Furthermore, the saints and all the deities are dependent on the people for sacrifice and offerings. Moreover, the Indians' fascination with death and the symbols of death has nothing to do with any idea of the resurrection. In fact, in the elaborate Passion Week ceremonies conducted each year in Antigua, Guatemala, the high point is the crucifixion which takes place on Friday. The resurrection is only a kind of dreary aftermath and anticlimax, after many of the people have left. Men will pay large sums of money to march in the parade and help carry the sarcophagus out to the tomb, but they will not even stay to witness the drama of the resurrection. The truly Good News has been relegated to a footnote on the last page, and as a result the newness of life has been swallowed up in the mystery of death. The reasons are not hard to find, for, as Freud has demonstrated, man seeks death more than life, despite his overt insistence to the contrary, for death can blot out his immeasurable failures, while the prospects of a new way of life seem to make quite unsupportable demands upon his already flagging spirit and gnawing conscience.

In contrast to the pagan content of other Christian groups, Protestants are inclined to be quite smug about the purity of their own faith, their Bible-centered doctrines, and their reproduction of the first-century church. But there is no reason for pride. Too many Protestants are also intensely race-conscious, despite the plain teaching of the Bible (Acts 17:26), and we certainly make distinctions in class, despite James' admonitions (1:9, 2:1–7). Often we have a thoroughly materialized and "socialized" view of success, so that a church is rated by the size of its budget and a minister by the number of his social contacts and his country-club connection. Despite all our efforts, the "world is too much with us" for us to be too critical of others, for the beam in our own eyes blinds us to our own problems of cultural relevance and communicative effectiveness.

Two Contrasting Approaches to Communication

The theological basis of communication procedures may be described perhaps most meaningfully in terms of two contrasting types, though we recognize that there are infinite gradations of actual practice between these two poles. The one may be called the "common ground" approach and the other "the point of contact" orientation.[5]

One of the most frequently cited examples of an early "common ground" approach is the letter of Pope Gregory the Great to Mellitus and Augustine, working in England toward the end of the sixth century:

When Almighty God shall bring you to the most reverend Bishop Augustine, our brother, tell him that I have, upon mature deliberation on the affairs of the English, determined upon, viz., that the temples of the idols in that nation ought not to be destroyed; let holy water be made and sprinkled in the said temples, let altars be erected, and relics placed. For if those temples are well built, it is requisite that they be converted from the worship of devils to the service of the true God; that the nation, seeing that their temples are not destroyed, may remove error from their hearts, and knowing and adoring the true God, may the more familiarly resort to the places to which they have been accustomed. And because they have been used to slaughter many oxen in the sacrifices to devils, some solemnity must be exchanged for them on this account, as that on the day of the dedication, or the nativities of the holy martyrs, whose relics are there deposited, they may build themselves huts of the boughs of trees, about those churches which have been turned to the use from temples, and celebrate the solemnity with religious feasting, and no more offer beasts to the devil, but kill cattle to the praise of God in their feasting, and return thanks to the Giver of all things for their sustenance;

to the end that, whilst some gratifications are outwardly permitted them, they may the more easily consent to the inward consolations of the grace of God. For there is no doubt that it is impossible to efface everything at once from their obdurate minds, because he who endeavours to ascend to the highest place, rises by degrees or steps and not by leaps. Thus the Lord made Himself known to the people of Israel in Egypt; and yet he allowed them to use the sacrifices which they were wont to offer to the devil in His own worship so as to command them in His sacrifice to kill beasts to the end that, changing their hearts, they might lay aside one part of the sacrifice, whilst they retained another; that whilst they offered the same beasts which they were wont to offer, they should offer them to God and not to idols; and thus they would no longer be the same sacrifices. Thus it behooves your affection to communicate to our aforesaid brother, that he, being there present, may consider how he is to order all things. God preserve you in safety, most beloved son.

This letter and the view it represents have had so significant an influence on the development of Christianity in northern Europe and in later phases of the expansion of the church that it merits our consideration as one of the approaches to the concept of "common ground." It must be said, however, that the Roman Catholic Church has not always employed the approach recommended here; for in Mexico there was almost total destruction of the pagan temples and objects of worship, and in China, when the famous Jesuit missionary Ricci suggested at the end of the sixteenth century that some form of ancestor cult be included in the Roman Catholic approach to the Chinese, the Pope refused to grant such a request.

At the same time, this letter of Pope Gregory and the later development of the same point of view in Jesuit missions certainly indicate quite clearly the fundamental viewpoint of finding some common ground as a basis for religious understanding. The English of the sixth century were not to be deprived of their temples, their festival occasions, or their sacrifices; but these rites were to be conducted on presumably a different basis by the use of different names and through the ministrations of holy water and the addition of relics. What Pope Gregory undoubtedly wanted was a different basic set of beliefs with essentially the same cultural forms. What he got was a continuation of the same cultural forms and beliefs, with only a different nomenclature, for there was no significant change in the religious concepts of the English people until several centuries later.

Whereas the "common ground" employed by Roman Catholicism has often been in matters of ritual and symbol, such as retention of the pagan symbols of the sun and the moon (as in Mexico), or the burning of incense to the rising sun (as in Guatemala), or the use of the moon symbol of Astarte (in Lebanon), in Protestantism the "common ground" has usually been conceptual in nature. This difference between the Roman Catholic and Protestant approaches is understandable, since the Roman orientation to religious reality is predominantly through visual symbols and the Protestant orientation is almost exclusively through belief. While some Roman Catholics would take over pagan symbols, many Protestants would almost as eagerly adopt pagan beliefs, at least in a provisional form and on an elementary level. For example, some missionaries have regarded pagan sets of beliefs and practices as constituting the "Old Testament" of the indigenous society. They have contended that in these viewpoints one can find "common ground" for the establishment of a Christian orientation as the fulfillment of these distorted, but basically true, aspirations. On a more sophisticated level, some Protestants have tried to see the Buddhist view of the total unreality of the material world as a parallel to the Christian's other-worldliness, and the longing of the Buddhist for absorption into Nirvana as corresponding to the Christian mysticism and longing for identification with the Infinite. One must not deny the resemblances, but the agreement is more superficial than real. The Buddhist will readily agree with the theme, "The world passes away and the lust of it," but he would never accept the following clause, "but he who does the will of God abides for ever" (1 John 2:17). The Christian and the Buddhist may agree that this world is evil, but the Christian is convinced that it must be redeemed by the power of God and that it is worth transforming, for God made it. The Buddhist insists that there can be no salvation in the midst of material involvement, but only an escape from the phenomenal, which holds the soul down. The flight must be a total freedom from the material, an escape into the otherness of nothingness.

In contrast with this position of trying to find "common ground," we may rather search for "a point of contact," in order to communicate effectively. This does not mean that the parallelisms should be emphasized in order to ease the transitions, through minimizing differences and maximizing similarities. Rather, the parallelisms are emphasized in order to provide one with an intelligible basis for communication, without involving any initial field of agreement. Thus in certain aspects of Buddhism we recognize a number of similarities to Christianity, not as common bases of belief, but as elements that make communication possible.

We insist upon a "point of contact" approach rather than a "common ground" orientation because it is impossible to take any element of belief out of its context and still have the same belief. Religions are systems, and the individual beliefs have meaning only in terms of the system to which they belong. It is the same as with language, in which, as noted in Chapter 4, no two words in any two languages have the same meaning. Thus no two beliefs in any two systems, despite their superficial similarities, present a basis for "common ground." They are only points of contact, on the basis of which we may communicate the distinctiveness of the Christian faith.

In Islam, for example, there is a belief that God reveals His truth to mankind. Christians also have a belief in revelation, and thus there is a point of contact, but the two concepts of revelation are quite different. In Islam, God sends His truth, but never comes. For Islam this would mean imposing limits on His sovereignty. But in Christianity to come is precisely what God did. In fact, the belief in the absolute total sovereignty of God should not preclude His doing precisely what the Muslim says God cannot do. Between Islam and Christianity there is thus no common ground in the doctrines of revelation. There is, however, a similarity of cultural function which provides a point of contact for effective communication.

Similarly, in Islam there is the tradition of the crucifixion, but at the last moment God snatched Jesus from the cross to rescue him— the symbol of victory for the prophets and servants of the true God. But Christianity shows the way of the suffering servant, the redemption of life by vicarious atonement, the reconciling love of the Father. The historical event of the crucifixion provides, not a common ground, but a point of contact, or, as we may also say, "a point of departure" for intelligent communication.

This point of contact may, however, be a matter of ritual, rather than of belief. As in the case of Tzeltal land-clearing and harvesting ceremonies (p. 143), the point of contact is the deep concern of the people for the soil and their emotional attachment to it as the basis of their life. (For many of the Mayan peoples, the myth of the creation of man is that, after unsuccessful attempts to make man out of the dust of the ground, God finally created him out of ears of corn.) In the Tzeltal situation, however, the pagan ceremonies were not merely given new names—as though there were some common symbolic element in the two rites—but, by building on a point of contact in the Tzeltal culture, a distinctly Christian ceremony was inaugurated which provided a functional substitute.

Christ and Culture

Nowhere in the Gospels is Christ reported as having specifically dealt with the problem of culture as such. Nevertheless, the fact that all he did and said was related to the immediate context of people's lives makes his orientation toward culture of supreme importance for the Christian. On the one hand, we can say that Christ's view of his own divinely appointed message was one of contact and continuity. Thus the proclamation of the kingdom of heaven was a promised fulfillment of the historic aspirations of the Jewish people to whom this message was directed. In other words, it was addressed to a community of faith, to the people of Israel, as the answer to the promise made by God to the fathers. At the same time there was an element of continuity in the revelation, for this was not only the cultural fulfillment for a people, but a divine unfolding of the plan and purpose of God as revealed first to the prophets. Thus the proclamation was anchored in the Old Testament revelation, to which Jesus constantly referred, and which the church later recognized as having been fulfilled in him.

On the other hand, in Jesus Christ there is a break with the past, a discontinuity with the culture. His followers were to be in the world, but "not of it" (John 17:14). His own "kingdom was not of this world" (John 18:36), and in the temptations (Matthew 4:1–11) Jesus rejected all the worldly apparatus of contemporary culture and secular leadership. Men were admonished to repent—to be done with the traditional ways of life, and to be baptized into a new fellowship. By Jesus' own example the traditional ritualistic forms were shockingly violated as being in conflict with the real purposes of God (see p. 29).

Moreover, in Christ there is a discontinuity with the revelation of the Old Testament, despite his statement that not one jot or tittle of the law should go unfulfilled (Matthew 5:18). In this same context he declared repeatedly, "It has been said, but I say to you . . ." (Matthew 5:22, 28, 32, 34, 39, and 44). The revelation of the Old Testament has now been superseded by one who is fulfilling it. He shifts the perspective from the "God of Abraham, Isaac and Jacob" to "our Father." Finally, he summarizes the entire Law and the Prophets into two requirements which untie religion from its immediate cultural involvement, for Jesus states, "You shall love the Lord your God with all your heart, and with all your soul, and with all your mind. This is the great and first commandment. And the second is like it, You shall love your neighbor as yourself. On these two commandments depend all the law and the prophets" (Matthew 22:37–40, and compare Romans 13:9–10, and Galatians 5:14). These two supercultural pronouncements are rooted in the depths of human consciousness, for love is the most profound and transforming experience of life; they are rooted also in the context of human culture, for men are not admonished to love love, but to love their neighbors.

In these two summary commands Jesus announced his break with the traditional cultural forms in order to proclaim a new supercultural way of life. The order of the two commandments is significant, for behavior must be first and foremost oriented toward God. Correct behavior is not true behavior until it is God-centered, for God is its ultimate base. Moreover, this very love of God—not mere submission to His will—is in itself only a reflection of His Grace, for "we love because He first loved us" (1 John 4:19). Furthermore, by insisting on the love of God rather than mere obedience to God, Jesus raised the whole level of existence from the formal and the material to the symbolic and the spiritual. The criterion of righteousness was no longer to be correct behavior, but a new heart; not scrupulous adherence to law, but unrestricted commitment to God, as revealed in Jesus Christ.

Fundamental Principles of Interpersonal Relations

Jesus laid down two essential principles for interpersonal relations, two standards by which all cultural behavior is to be judged. These are equity and love. The first principle, that of equity, is recognized in one way or another by all societies, for in all cultures those who stand in certain relations of mutual responsibility to one another are also related by laws or customs of equity. Of course, the way in which equity is formulated differs from tribe to tribe and culture to culture, but it is fundamental and basic to all social concepts. This does not mean that all societies have an equalitarian view of humanity —not at all. What is meant is that between one person and another there are always some rules of mutual assistance or avoidance which reflect the indigenous viewpoint of equity. One can even find a very crude but effective concept of equity in Laos, where it has traditionally been the practice in witch trials to force the accuser (the medicine man) and the accused (the alleged witch) to sit together in a pot of oil as it is heated over a fire. The first one to jump out is clubbed to death. Despite the many cultural forms which tend to disguise equity, there is fundamentally a profound regard for the maxim of "an eye for an eye and a tooth for a tooth," or, as expressed in folk wisdom, "what is good for the goose is good for the gander."

The equity which Jesus Christ announced is not, however, the cold and often brutal equity of "an eye for an eye" but the warm and human quality of love, expressed in the equalitarian formula of "loving one's neighbor as one loves oneself" (Leviticus 19:18). This statement comes from the Old Testament, but as an Old Testament passage it had been applied to the exclusive community of Judaism. For Jesus, a man's neighbor was anyone in need. This made equity something not limited to a single race or religious group, but the right and obligation of all mankind. In fact, this love was to be extended to enemies (Matthew 5:44) as well as friends, and for this there is no Old Testament parallel. Jesus even extends the concept of equity to forgiveness, when he declares, "For if you forgive men their trespasses, your heavenly Father also will forgive you; but if you do not forgive men their trespasses, neither will your Father forgive your trespasses" (Matthew 6:14–15).

The second social principle enunciated by Jesus was "love" as the basic ingredient in all divine and human relationships. There is, however, no contradiction between the principles of equity and love, for the love which Christ commanded is not a sentimental attachment, but a profound appreciation of the worth and value of people as God sees them. Moreover, this love is the only transforming power in the world. Force may bring about conformity, but only love can transform the heart. Moreover, even in the name of love the church must not use force, whether by the expedient of legislative dictates, so that the kingdom is created artificially, or by the means of "bribes," such as education, prestige, or acceptance into the white man's society,

which are too often dangled before the potential convert as rewards
for identification with the church. A man who is forced or bribed will
in the end inevitably turn against whatever power has so subtly in-
sulted his integrity. The way of love is not fast, but it is sure, for it is
the plan of God.

Application of the Principles of Equity and
Love to Problems of Cultural Change

In the practical application of the principles of equity and love to
the everyday problems of cultural change, there are three alternatives
which must be faced with respect to any institution: (1) let it remain
as a valid institution, (2) alter its form and content as may be
required to eliminate error and give it Christian significance, and
(3) employ a functional substitute in the case of institutions which
are irreparably evil, though functionally relevant.

Not everything associated with a pagan culture is pagan. Within
the structure of such societies there are many valuable features which
can and should be retained, e.g., the tea ceremony in Japan; indigenous music in India; native clothing in the South Pacific (there is no
correlation between lack of clothing and immorality, though within
all societies there are ways of dressing in certain sexually provocative
manners; hence the problem is not the total amount of clothing, but
the extent to which it conforms to an accepted norm of decency);
patterns of hospitality in Africa; and housing among the Indians in
Amazonia. It is now recognized that the *lobola* or "bride-price" arrangement in African society is not altogether wrong, as so many
missionaries at first thought. It is and was undoubtedly abused, but
in the interests of greater stability in marriage and a greater sense
of responsibility to children, it should not have been ruthlessly
denounced.

In many instances the cultural forms are essentially satisfactory,
but they may need certain changes of content. In a Meo wedding in
Laos[6] the Christian community has continued with the traditional
arrangements for the bride-price, the reciprocal feasts by the families,
and the exchange of neckbands. The only alteration has been the
blessing by the pastor, taking the place of the earlier prayers to the
spirits.

Pope Gregory the Great was quite right in believing that the pagan
temples need not be destroyed, for it is far better to place a new

altar in an old temple than to build a new church over an ancient pagan altar, as has happened so many times in Latin America. The difficulty with Gregory's advice to Augustine was that the consecration of the temple was not effected by communicating to the people the real conceptual distinctions between Christianity and paganism; rather, it was done by means of holy water and relics, which, in the religion of the English of that time, was nothing more or less than magic. Such magic they could understand, for it was not essentially different, except in its forms, from the magic they themselves practiced. Hence, neither in the instruction nor in the visual symbols employed did the people perceive any essential difference from the religion they had followed for many centuries.

When an institution, which may have a perfectly valid function in a society, is so corrupted in its form that it is irreparable, the only alternative is to set up a functional substitute. In the Greco-Roman world which Christians first faced, the mystery religions played an important part in relating men to the mysteries of life and to a sense of participation and belonging in the spiritual world, for the gods had died and men felt a deep concern and need for some religious reality. Into this situation the Christians brought baptism as a functional substitute for the initiation rites of the mystery cults. They did not try to revamp the ceremonies of the mystery religions. It could not have been done without either destroying the significance of the mysteries or losing the meaning of the Christian faith. They did, however, make considerable use of the vocabulary of mystery religions, as is evidenced in Paul's writings: e.g., *mystery, author and finisher* (of the faith), in the sense of those who guide the initiate through the ceremonies, and *perfect* (in the sense of initiated). In certain branches of the church, the ceremony of confirmation has become a functional substitute for puberty initiation rites.

In American church life the principle of functional substitute can be seen time and time again. The usual procedure, of course, is simply to denounce what one differs with and by negative commands to try to eliminate it, especially from the youth, who are more inclined to experiment with alternative types of behavior. Such denunciations have concerned dancing, bobbing of hair, Sunday baseball, the wearing of slacks, movies, card playing, and drinking. However, the churches which have only said "No! No!" without providing functional substitutes, have either lost their young people to the world or, if they have kept them, their young people have become so far removed from the world that they live abnormal, artificial lives, fortified only by pride in their essentially negative behavior.

However, in our emphasis upon the behavioral aspects of the end results of communication we may tend to forget the essence of the communication itself. For the early church, the announcement of the Good News was essentially threefold: (1) Jesus is the fulfillment of God's plan of salvation, (2) therefore repent and be baptized, and (3) witness as a member of the new community of God. The ways in which this message was proclaimed are very diverse. For example, compare Peter's sermon at Pentecost (Acts 2:14–39) with Paul's statement to the Areopagus (Acts 17:22–31) and his later defense before Agrippa (Acts 26:2–23). The essential elements of the *Kerygma* are there, but in each case the communication builds upon the receptors' backgrounds and is adapted to the particular situation and circumstance. This means that in other cultural situations the form of the message will also be different. Among the Meo[7] the Christian movement began with a Khmu who witnessed to his own faith, while a medicine man said that this must be what another shaman had prophesied some two years before, namely, that someone would come bringing word about the true God, Fua-Tai. Within a few weeks there were more than a thousand believers, who proceeded to destroy the fetishes of the powerful spirit Tlau; for though they did not cease to believe in Tlau immediately, they nevertheless were sure that the power of Fua-Tai was much greater, for Fau-Tai's son Yesu (Jesus) had the power to release men from the fear of Tlau. Here was immediate abundant proof of the power of God. In the same way, in Colossians 1:16 Paul did not dispute the existence of dominions, principalities, and powers (from the Neoplatonic assemblage of supernatural forces), but declared that regardless of such powers Jesus Christ is over and above them all.

In the ultimate analysis, even as Dr. John van Ess, famous missionary to Islam, used to say, "The real strategy is telling people about Jesus." The one unique message of Christianity is Christ, and the proclamation of his distinctiveness is "the way, the truth and the life" (John 14:6). We thus live within the framework of the world and we witness within the structure of the church, but we either communicate Christ or we communicate nothing that is Good News.

Our communication is primarily sowing the seed, not transplanting churches. It is lighting a spark, not establishing an institution. This does not mean that the communication of the full revelation of God is unconcerned with the church; but the indigenous church we are committed to, whether in central Africa or in central Kansas, is not the church we have structured, but one raised up by the Spirit of God. It is not enough for us merely to "indigenize" our own structures, by trying to insist on the superficial criteria of self-governing, self-supporting, and self-propagating.[8] Many churches have these characteristics but still do not fit within the society where they exist. The development of an indigenous church will always be the living response of people to the life demands of the message. The source of the information, unless he is a full participating member of the society in question, is never more than a catalyst, but as such he is nevertheless an indispensable factor in the divine process.

God's Communication with Man

The basic theological justification of our communicative procedures must rest ultimately on what God has revealed about His own communication with man. In this sense, the original set of diagrams we employed in Chapter 3 is incomplete, for there is no diagrammatic relationship of the source of this Biblical communication to the content and form of the Biblical message. If we are to represent this essential feature, we may modify the original diagram as shown on page 222.

The hyperbolic curve at the top, with infinite extension, represents the infinite attributes of God, including His creative purposes and ultimate plans. This truth, in all its infinite character, has to be communicated within the narrow confines of human language and culture, as represented within the triangle. This can be done only by radical adjustment and the employment of the grid of human experience, as reflected in a particular culture at a particular time.

Our fundamental task is to "relay" this communication in still different forms, but with essentially an equivalent content, so that men in other times and places may be put in touch with the infinite God.

This revelation of God is not by "natural revelation," in the sense that the phenomenal world in and of itself can define God, for this universe disguises Him as well as reveals Him. The very predictability of the processes of the universe is too great (in terms of information

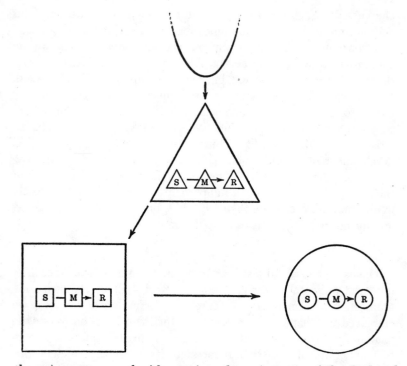

theory) ever to reveal with certainty the uniqueness of the God and
Father of our Lord Jesus Christ. On the other hand, God has not left
Himself without a witness in His universe, for "his eternal power and
deity have been clearly perceived in the things that have been made"
(Romans 1:20). The creation confirms God, but does not define Him.

This means that God's revelation, by word and by act, has come to
man in its decisive form in a single person and in a precise spatio-
temporal setting. Such a revelation involved limitations. For the Old
Testament the truth of God was incarnated in (1) the restrictions
of the historical events affecting the people of God and (2) the
Hebrew thought patterns. In respect to the Son of God, these limitations are spoken of as *kenosis* "emptying" (Philippians 2:6–7), and
of necessity they involved not only the physical limitations of his own
body but the cultural limitations of his own society and culture. This
emphasis upon the humanity of Jesus in no way detracts from his
deity. In fact, in our desire to emphasize the deity of Jesus Christ,
we must not destroy his humanity, or we make his life only a drama,

in which all the lines were memorized in advance. Similarly, to regard him only as human is to destroy completely the meaning of God's revelation of Himself.

It must also be recognized, however, that in the revelation of God within a particular set of cultural circumstances, He also addressed Himself to particular persons with a message which was intended to make sense. The Scriptures are not a collection of cabalistic writings, nor echoes of a Delphic oracle, nor moralizing pronouncements. They are so designed that men and women who hear them will understand them. In Isaiah 7:14 the promise to Ahaz that an *almah* will give birth to a son must make sense, not merely as an indirect reference to some event to take place several hundred years later, but to the specific situation in which the prophet predicts that before the child "shall know to refuse the evil and choose the good" (at the age of moral accountability), Ahaz' two enemies Rezin and Pekah will be overcome. This does not mean, of course, that such a passage is not relevant to the message of the Gospel of Matthew. It is quoted in Matthew 1:23, in complete accordance with the canons of Scripture evidence employed in passages of the New Testament, and its use is fully in keeping with the procedures of communication employed in this historical setting of New Testament times. But the communicative point of view of the Scriptures is not "to mystify the truth" but to reveal it, not to hide verities behind historical accounts, but to face men with the truth in any and all literary forms which they can understand. Unfortunately, the Scriptures have not always been taken in this way. Quite the contrary. The Bible has suffered almost equally at the hands of the typologists and allegorizers who take its plain words to mean something quite different from what was said, and from those who in the name of "demythologizing" have actually only "remythologized" or "re-encoded" the message on quite a different level of abstraction.

A Biblical View of Communication

Though it is impossible for us to do more than merely suggest some of the essential aspects of the Biblical view of communication (an adequate treatment would require a lengthy volume in itself), it is important to outline some of the basic presuppositions about language and communication which underlie the Biblical view. Such an outline follows.

1. *Verbal symbols are only "labels" and are of human origin.* The meaning of the account of Adam giving names to all the cattle, to the fowls of the air, and to every beast of the field (Gen. 2:20) is primarily that language is a human convention and that the words used are essentially labels, not divine epithets.

2. *Verbal symbols, as labels for concepts, have priority over visual symbols in the communicating of truth.* While the pagans saw the mystic objects, the Jews listened to the voice of God. Throughout Scripture there is the constant admonition against idolatrous visual images, but insistence on "Thus saith the Lord!"

3. *Language symbols reflect a meaningful relationship between symbol and behavior.* The Hebrew root *dbr*, most commonly used for "word," means "word," "event," and "thing." There is no attempt made in the Scriptures to distinguish between the symbolic form and the referent for which it stands. The Bible is not concerned with the problem of Greek philosophy, which argued about the relation of the word to the reality behind it, or with the difficulty of modern epistemology, which tries to relate the concept with the reality toward which it points. The focus of the Biblical revelation is the event. God is revealed as one who acts, speaks, and performs miracles, but He does not describe His essence. Even in the account of Christ, we have not a shred of evidence about his physical appearance; only a record of what he did and what he said. From the Biblical point of view, the ultimate reality apprehendable by man is not to be found in isolated qualities, but in behavior relationships expressed by concrete actions in the realm of time. Language is thus a set of symbols to describe behavior, not a mystical code to the eternal essence. In this sense the Biblical view of epistemology is strikingly contemporary, for symbols are being more and more viewed in terms of their functional relationships, rather than on the basis of any hidden conceptual reality.

4. *Communication is power.* There is a strangely modern ring about the fact that the Bible uses language in the sense of power. On the divine level God speaks and it is done, and, even on the human plane, the king commands and his servants perform. But in the human encounter with God there is an even

deeper mystery, for not only does God "speak" to man, but by means of words man intercedes for man with the Almighty.

5. *Divine revelation takes place in the form of a "dialogue."* "Come now, let us reason together, says the Lord" (Isaiah 1:18) is more than a mere figure of speech, for in Scripture God is continually revealed as seeking men out to converse with them, from the story of Eden until the proclamation of the new heavens and the new earth. The entire concept of the covenant of God with men is predicated upon two-way communication, even though it is God who proposes and man who accepts. Of course, in Jesus Christ the "dialogue" of God with man is evident in all of its fullness, but the divine-human conversation is eternal, for the end of man is for fellowship and communion with God Himself, and for this the communication of "dialogue" is an indispensable and focal element.

Implications of the Biblical View of Communication

On the basis of the foregoing brief analysis of the Biblical view of communication and the implications of God's revelation to man, it is evident that two inferences must be drawn: (1) the Biblical revelation is not absolute and (2) all divine revelation is essentially incarnational.

When we say that the Biblical revelation is not absolute, we are only declaring in somewhat different terms what Paul said, "For we see in a mirror dimly" (1 Corinthians 13:12). This use of "absolute" must be clearly understood, however, for it does not mean that the revelation which we have received of God is not true. In fact, God's revelation of Himself is absolutely true; but it is not absolute, in the sense that there is nothing more or that we know everything about God. There are still many mysteries which we as finite persons can never know about the infinite. Our very limitations in time and space (i.e., our cultural backgrounds) and in language (no language is a perfect reflection of reality, but only a mechanism for interpersonal behavior) make such an absolute revelation impossible. On the other hand, this revelation which we have in Christ Jesus is a complete guide for all matters of faith and conduct and it is entirely sufficient, just because it is culturally tied to human categories. It is for this reason that we can understand something of the mystery of God's nature by knowing what He has done and said.

As a corollary of the nonabsolute nature of the communication of God, we must also recognize that we can never attain complete objectivity in our understanding of this revelation. The evidences of Gestalt psychology indicate indisputably the way in which we tend to regroup our perceptions on the basis of our own backgrounds and dispositions. Moreover, we cannot be impartial analysts of truth, viewing it from some distant isolation. We ourselves, regardless of our philosophical or religious views, are unalterably involved in everything that we perceive or think. This recognition of our own inevitable subjectivity and the nonabsolute character of our formulations of faith should not be a cause for discouragement or lack of faith. Rather, we should be led to increased humility as we recognize the boundless measure of God's grace, since the saving faith which is ours does not come from us, nor is it in response to our intellectual powers, but is in proportion as we are willing to accept God's salvation plan. The key to our reconciliation to the will of God is not the intellect, but the heart, for our sin is not error of judgment, but stubbornness of will.

In the second place, all divine communication is essentially incarnational, for it comes not only in words, but in life. Even if a truth is given only in words, it has no real validity until it has been translated into life. Only then does the Word of life become life to the receptor. The words are in a sense nothing in and of themselves. Even as wisdom is emptiness unless lived out in behavior, so the word is void unless related to experience. In the incarnation of God in Jesus Christ, the Word (the expression and revelation of the wisdom of God) became flesh. This same fundamental principle has been followed throughout the history of the church, for God has constantly chosen to use not only words but human beings as well to witness to His grace; not only the message, but the messenger; not only the Bible, but the church.

The incarnational principle of revelation was, of course, most completely exemplified in Jesus Christ, who spoke as no man had even spoken (John 7:46). By means of words and figures of speech which reflected the indigenous culture of his day with utter naturalness, and by means of miracles which gave symbolic evidence of his supernatural relationship with the Father, Jesus communicated in unparalleled ways.

Jesus, however, also communicated by life, in utter identification with men and women. He, like them, knew weariness, hunger, sorrow, grief, keen disappointment, and rejection, even by those who were closest to him. He participated fully in their lives, whether in the joys of a wedding feast or in the foreboding atmosphere of a simple meal, eaten in the shadow of his coming death.

At various times the church has tended to deny the communicational implications of the incarnational truth as found in Jesus Christ. More than once the Bible has been kept from the people and preserved only in the language of an elite few. At the same time, such churches have not been incarnationally involved in the life of the people, but have retreated into a monastic escape from existence; but to escape from spiritual involvement in life is to expose oneself to spiritual death.

The natural result of denying the necessity for witness to the truth, as revealed by God and as recorded and interpreted under the inspiration of the Spirit of God, has been the substitution of other messages, many of which have their complete parallels in ancient times. Like the Sadducees, proud of their worldly sophistication and "ecclesiastical traditions," some men of our times have preached the church rather than the gospel. As with the Pharisees, who were concerned with being accepted by God because of their works, and who substituted their rules for the commandments of God, some today exchange the doctrine of God's forgiveness of sins for mere ethical principles about conduct pleasing to the Eternal. Even the Essenes, those militant exclusivisits, who thought they could please God only by emphasizing their partisan truths, have their counterparts in those who today proclaim separatism, rather than witnessing to the grace of God. There are, at the same time, many modern pagans, who think that God is either a person or force to be used. Therefore some would perform non-Biblical and nonspiritual miracles in His name, with their eyes on the attendance of the throngs. For these Jesus has already said, "And then will I declare to them, 'I never knew you; depart from me, you evildoers'." (Matthew 7:23).

There are others who wish to use God by substituting psychoanalysis for faith, and who think that by the simple exploiting of one's faith, one can tap mysterious powers, even though these are not through Him who is the power of God. Still others support Christianity as a socially valuable myth, and will even send their children to Sunday School and support the ministry of the church because they think that, despite its basic errors, it is socially beneficial. It was in this way that Cicero argued for Roman religion, even after it was dead, and similarly men today maintain an affection for the moral influence of Christianity, even though they deny its supernatural character. Unfortunately, much of the present religious revival in the West results from this kind of pagan pragmatism, which insists that belief in God is good, for it keeps one from worry and has positive psychological advantages. If, therefore, man needs God, he should have Him, with all the necessary paraphernalia to enshrine Him properly, but should never take Him too seriously. Men want only to have a god whom they can manipulate. The last thing that they want is to fall into the hands of the living God, whose "wrath is revealed from heaven against all ungodliness" (Romans 1:18).

There are many reasons for men's having substituted a false message for the true one, but at least part of the answer may be found in the fact that men have been confused about the issue of the authority of revelation. For one thing, they have seemed to think that some doctrine of infallibility confirms the authority of the Bible, rather than realizing that God as the author of the revelation is its real authority. Our faith, then, does not rest in any system of exegesis, but in God, who has chosen to reveal Himself in the imperfections of human language. This record was committed to the church, whose scribes have not infrequently made mistakes in copying it and whose scholars have erred in their interpretations of it. Nevertheless, it was the plan and purpose of God that the message be committed to men, not proclaimed by angels. But despite the injuries that this message has received by the wanton carelessness or misguided enthusiasm of men, this revelation has its source in God and leads men to God.

The Supernatural Character of the Divine Communication

The revelation of God in Jesus Christ and as recorded in the Scriptures is uniquely supernatural, for its source is none other than God Himself. However, God's Spirit communicates with men today, not in the same way as in the full, complete, and final revelation as contained in the Biblical witness, but in the fact that His "Spirit bears witness with our spirit that we are the children of God" (Romans 8:16). Only by the supernatural activity of the Spirit can men possibly experience for themselves the transforming grace of God. This means that all that we have said previously about our communicating the message of life is in a sense only figurative speaking. We ourselves do not communicate this message; we only bear witness to its truth, for it is the Spirit of God that directly communicates and mediates this divine word. The encounter which men have is not merely with an idea, but with God Himself. Hence, the communication in which we are involved is not only supernatural in content (in that it is derived from God); it is also supernatural in process, for the Spirit of God alone makes this message to live within the hearts of men.

This communication of life by life is primarily through the life of the Son, given that men might be reconciled to God. But in a secondary sense, this life is communicated by the life of the church, which is "to complete what is lacking in the afflictions of Christ" (Colossians 1:24) as "epistles read of all men" (2 Corinthians 3:2). We are thus to be partners with God, identified with Him in the ministry of reconciliation (2 Corinthians 5:1, 8), called by God to be identified with men in order that "at the name of Jesus every knee should bow, in heaven and on earth and under the earth, and every tongue confess that Jesus Christ is Lord, to the glory of God the Father" (Philippians 2:10–11).

On one occasion I was talking with one of the great missionary pioneers of Guatemala, who, then in his sixties, was getting ready to make one of his customary walking trips of several weeks out through the mountains in order to visit Indian congregations in the small villages. I asked him why he did not drive his car, in view of his increasingly poor health (he often took sick on such trips) and the new road which had just gone through that region, for he could have driven to many of the places he proposed to visit. His reply was simply, "Oh, I never drive, for the people that I want to reach are not used to someone driving up in a car. What is more, I have never found a man I could not speak to about Jesus Christ, if only we were walking down the same road together."

God wanted to reveal Himself to mankind and He could do so only by sending His Son, who walked up and down the hot dusty paths of ancient Palestine and so lived before his disciples that in the end he could say, "He who has seen me has seen the Father" (John 14:9). This same Jesus calls upon us to walk the steamy trails of the jungle and the bare sidewalks of our cities, witnessing to men and women of God's love for them, that through us they may learn of the love of Christ which alone leads men to God.

Notes

Chapter 1. *An Introduction to Communication*

1. Helen Keller, *The Story of My Life* (New York: Doubleday & Co., Inc., 1902).
2. Norbert Wiener, *The Human Use of Human Beings* (Garden City, N.Y.: Doubleday Anchor Books, 1956), p. 85.

Chapter 2. *Religion and Communication*

1. The very complexity of religious phenomena has given rise to a number of attempts to provide some unifying approach. Perhaps the most significant attempts can be summarized as (1) the dream-to-soul view, espoused by early evolutionists, and especially by Edward B. Tylor, who thought that the phenomena of dreams explained the development of the concept of the soul, and thus of spiritual being, (2) the "devolutionary" concept of a corrupted primitive monotheism, so ardently advocated by Father Wilhelm Schmidt, and many others, including Zwemer, who contended that certain high-God concepts in some primitive societies in existence today are unmistakable evidence of earlier original revelation, (3) religion as social action and interaction as formulated by Emile Durkheim and others, (4) the functional view of religion as utilitarian adjustment to the supernatural, a position which has appealed greatly to a wide range of investigators, from Bronislaw Malinowski to Wilson D. Wallis, and is particularly congenial to many American pragmatists, who tend to find in all kinds of religious activity, from clairvoyance to witch-hunting, some type of positive functioning, and (5) religion as the outworking of psychiatric phenomena, in which people project into the supernatural realm such conflicts

as guilt, dependence, hostility, or emotional attachment. (For relevant bibliographical data see the *Bibliography*.)

Useful as these different views are, they nevertheless do not fully answer the difficulties. They fail to account for such essential matters as (1) the relationship between magic and religion, (2) the extravagant overdevelopment of religion in circumstances where no utilitarian considerations seem to justify it, and (3) the serious dysfunction of religious practices and beliefs which are positively harmful. Moreover, these explanations do not succeed in tying together the widely diverse strands of religious practice in such a way that we can see them in terms of some integrating pattern. Rather, we are left with a view of religion which makes it appear to be an assemblage of many disconnected phenomena, including crystal balls, fire ordeals, peyote worship, secret passwords, puberty rites, death chants, exotic ceremonies, and hideous masks.

An excellent summary of different orientations toward religion is contained in J. Milton Yinger, "The Influence of Anthropology on Sociological Theories of Religion," *American Anthropologist*, 60:487–96 (1958).

2. K. A Busia, "Ancestor Worship," *Practical Anthropology*, 6:26 (1959).

3. At this point it may seem that we are somewhat stretching the use of "communication" to include "transportation" as well. In a sense this is true, but we are not using communication in a way different from its use in theoretical cybernetic discussions. Wiener (*The Human Use of Human Beings*, p. 96), for example, discusses the possibility of theoretical "taping" of the physico-chemical relationships of human anatomical and physiological structure, including one's repertoire of experience, and "communicating" such a structure.

4. Bronislaw Malinowski, *Magic, Science, and Religion* (Garden City, N.Y.: Doubleday & Co., Inc., 1955), p. 41.

5. For a full treatment of many phases of initiation rites, see Mircea Eliade, *Birth and Rebirth* (New York: Harper & Brothers, 1958).

6. We make no attempt here to classify the enormous variety of religious beliefs. This has often been done and in various ways. We are concerned here only with those special elements of belief which are directly and indirectly related to the communicative element in religious practice.

7. For an analysis of "presentational" vs. "discursive" symbolic forms, see Susanne K. Langer, *Philosophy in a New Key* (Cambridge: Harvard University Press, 1942).

8. I am indebted to my colleague, William L. Wonderly, for this sug-

gestion of the analogy of prayer to revelation, though communicatively they take opposite directions.

9. William D. Reyburn, "Kaka Kinship, Sex, and Adultery," *Practical Anthropology*, 5:15 (1958).

CHAPTER 3. *The Structure of Communication*

1. Communications engineers and linguists often use the term "target" to identify this third element in the communication process, but for our purposes "receptor" is more meaningful, since the message does not merely "hit" its goal, but rather has to be "received," or decoded.

2. Clyde Kluckhohn, "Common Humanity and Diverse Cultures," in Daniel Lerner (ed.), *The Human Meaning of the Social Sciences* (New York: Meridian Books, Inc., 1959), p. 247.

3. Robert Redfield, *The Primitive World and Its Transformations* (Ithaca, N.Y.: Cornell University Press, 1953), p. 85.

4. The question can always be raised as to what expression Jesus himself used. It would seem most likely that he used both, but certainly as far as the early church was concerned these phrases appear to have been almost entirely interchangeable, depending upon the participants in the communication.

5. This analysis follows in general outline the illuminating discussion by Mu Tsung-san, Hsü Fu-Kuan, Carson Chang, and T'ang Chün-yi, published in *Practical Anthropology*, 6:84–89 (1959).

6. For a stimulating discussion of basic themes in Latin American society, as they are related to missionary work, see W. Stanley Rycroft, *Religion and Faith in Latin America* (Philadelphia: The Westminster Press, 1958).

7. Lawrence K. Frank, "Psychology and Social Order," in Daniel Lerner (ed.), *The Human Meaning of the Social Sciences* (New York: Meridian Books, Inc., 1959), p. 215.

8. See William A. Smalley, "The World Is Too Much With Us," *Practical Anthropology*, 5:234–36 (1958).

9. This interpretation has been the one most generally accepted by most of the theologically conservative groups, but not necessarily by all. The Swedish Covenant Church, for example, holds to a vicarious atonement, but not a substitutionary one.

CHAPTER 4. *Symbols and Their Meaning*

1. Roger Brown, *Words and Things* (Glencoe, Ill.: The Free Press, 1958), pp. 158–60.
2. It is recognized that writers on semantics use "sign" and "symbol" in somewhat different ways. Charles Morris (*Signs, Language and Behavior* [New York: Prentice-Hall, Inc., 1946]) uses "signs" as a term to include what we here call both signs and symbols. He uses "signals" and "symbols" as two types of signs. Susanne K. Langer (*Philosophy in a New Key*) makes a distinction between "signs" (what Morris calls "signals") and symbols. It is this latter terminology which we are here following, because it agrees somewhat better with popular usage and seems to be a more useful distinction for the average person without special training in the field of semantics. Paul Tillich (see *Theology of Culture* [New York: Oxford University Press, 1959]) employs still a different distinction. For him "signs" include all words and objects in which the referential and conceptual meanings are parallel and immediate. He uses "symbols" only for instances in which there is a secondary conceptual meaning, or in which the referent itself constitutes a symbol of something else, e.g., the cross.
3. Langer, *Philosophy in a New Key*, p. 61.
4. See *ibid.*, pp. 75 ff.
5. Martin Joos, "Semology: A Linguistic Theory of Meaning," *Studies in Linguistics*, 13:53–72 (1958).
6. Langer, *op. cit.*, p. 224.
7. Leonard Bloomfield, *Linguistic Aspects of Science.* Chicago: University of Chicago Press, 1939, p. 37.
8. The following data on the Shipibos were supplied by Mr. James Lauriault in personal correspondence.
9. Undoubtedly another factor in the symbolization of Jesus Christ as an infant was the unconscious identification of the Mass with fertility cult practice and the necessity of reflecting the fact of dying and rising, not in terms of the cross and the empty tomb, but in terms of the dying Christ and the reborn Child; for this places Mary, as the "Mother of God," at the emotional and mystical center of the cult drama.
10. Frank, "Psychology and Social Order," in Lerner (ed.), *The Human Meaning of the Social Sciences*, p. 216.

11. Kluckhohn, "Common Humanity and Diverse Cultures," in Lerner (ed.), *ibid.*, p. 278.

CHAPTER 5. *Communication and Social Structure*

1. David Riesman, *Individualism Reconsidered* (Garden City, N.Y.: Doubleday & Co., Inc., 154), p. 46.
2. Margaret Mead, *Sex and Temperament in Three Primitive Societies* (New York: William Morrow and Co., 1935).
3. Donald A. McGavran, *The Bridges of God* (London: World Dominion Press, 1955), p. 120.
4. *Ibid.*
5. David Riesman, with Nathan Glazer and Reuel Denny, *The Lonely Crowd.* Garden City, N.Y.: Doubleday & Co., Inc., 1950).
6. See also some significant insights on the problem in Will Herberg, "The Christian Witness in an Emerging 'Other-Directed' Culture," *Practical Anthropology*, 5:211–15 (1958).
7. See H. R. Weber, *The Communication of the Gospel to Illiterates* (London: Student Christian Movement Press, 1957).
8. A. Vilakasi, "A Reserve from Within," *African Studies* (1957) reprinted in *Practical Anthropology*, 5:124–38 (1958).
9. William D. Reyburn, "Motivations for Christianity: An African Conversation," *Practical Anthropology*, 5:28–31 (1958).
10. Bertram Hutchinson, "Some Social Consequences of Missionary Activity among South African Bantu," *Practical Anthropology*, 6:69 (1959).
11. William D. Reyburn, "The Spiritual, the Material, and the Western Reaction in Africa," *Practical Anthropology*, 6:80 (1959).
12. Marie F. Reyburn, "Applied Anthropology among the Sierra Quechua of Ecuador," *Practical Anthropology*, 1:21 (1953).

CHAPTER 6. *The Dynamics of Communication*

1. L. P. Mair, "Independent Religious Movements in Three Continents," *Comparative Studies in Society and History*, 1:113–35 (1959).
2. Anthony F. C. Wallace, "Revitalization Movements," *American Anthropologist*, 58:264–75 (1956).
3. McGavran, *The Bridges of God.*

CHAPTER 7. *Psychological Relationships in Communication*

1. See Hendrik Kraemer's treatment of this distinction in *The Communication of the Christian Faith* (Philadelphia: The Westminster Press, 1956).
2. Though some of the psychological problems involved in the use of nonlinguistic media are of intense interest, and some of the problems of communication even within one's mother tongue present some fascinating psychological factors, these are beyond the scope of the present treatment.
3. Roger Brown, *Words and Things*, pp. 320–21.
4. For further discussion of these techniques and certain others, which are not essentially identification, see *ibid.*, pp. 301 ff.
5. William A. Smalley, "Neighborliness or Proximity," *Practical Anthropology*, 4:101–104 (1957).
6. There are, of course, symbols by which the reception of a Presbyterian in the Christian and Missionary Alliance is welcomed, e.g., if he professes conversion and talks and behaves in an acceptable manner.
7. William D. Reyburn, "Identification in the Missionary Task," *Practical Anthropology*, 7:1–15 (1960).
8. An introduction to these problems, especially from the viewpoint of the Christian missionary or minister, can be found in Eugene A. Nida's *Customs and Cultures* (New York: Harper & Brothers, 1954). Another valuable source is a journal frequently referred to in this volume, *Practical Anthropology*, published by a group of anthropologists who are much interested in problems of communication of the Christian faith (Box 307, Tarrytown, N.Y.).

CHAPTER 8. *Communication and the Total Cultural Context*

1. Wiener, *The Human Use of Human Beings*, p. 132.
2. John Beekman, "A Culturally Relevant Witness," *Practical Anthropology*, 4:83–88 (1957).
3. Millar Burrows, *More Light on the Dead Sea Scrolls* (New York: The Viking Press, 1958), p. 53.

CHAPTER 9. *Scripture Translation and Revision As Techniques of Communication*

1. The term "gloss" in this context reflects a usage employed by linguists who speak of a gloss as a literal equivalent of a foreign term. This usage is quite distinct from the manner in which New Testament textual scholars use the word, namely, as a description of some added explanatory notes.
2. Richard F. Weymouth, *The New Testament in Modern Speech* (Boston: The Pilgrim Press, 1943 [fifth edition]).
3. E. V. Rieu, *The Four Gospels* (London: Penguin Books, 1952).
4. Eugene A. Nida, *Bible Translating* (New York: American Bible Society, 1947), pp. 12–13.
5. Hilaire Belloc, *On Translating* (Oxford: Clarendon Press, 1932).
6. The following treatment conforms in general to the handling of these problems in Eugene A. Nida, "Principles of Translation As Exemplified by Bible Translating," in Reuben A. Brower (ed.), *On Translation* (Cambridge: Harvard University Press, 1959), pp. 11–31.
7. See Burrows, *More Light on the Dead Sea Scrolls*.
8. The Greek term *monogenês* actually means "only" or "unique," literally "only one of its kind," and not "only-begotten," for it is derived from Greek *mono-* "only" and *gen-* "kind," and not from *monos* "only" combined with *gennaô* "to beget." For further data on this problem consult F. William Arndt and Wilbur F. Gingrich, *A Greek-English Lexicon of the New Testament* (Chicago: University of Chicago Press, 1957), and Dale Moody, "God's Only Son," *Journal of Biblical Literature*, 72:213–19 (1953).
9. C. Clarke Oke, "A Suggestion with Regard to Romans 8:23," *Interpretation*, October, 1957, pp. 455–460.

CHAPTER 10. *The Theological Basis of Communication*

1. Compare Émile Cailliet, *The Christian Approach to Culture* (New York: Appleton-Century-Crofts, 1940), p. 15.
2. *The Apostolic Fathers*, translated by Edgar J. Goodspeed (New York: Harper & Brothers, 1950).
3. H. Richard Niebuhr, *Christ and Culture* (New York: Harper & Brothers, 1951).

4. *Ibid.*, p. 183.
5. See Hendrik Kraemer, *The Christian Message in a Non-Christian World* (New York: Harper & Brothers, 1938).
6. Linwood Barney, "The Meo—An Incipient Church," *Practical Anthropology*, 4:31–50 (1957).
7. *Ibid.*, p. 45.
8. See William A. Smalley, "Cultural Implications of an Indigenous Church," *Practical Anthropology*, 5:51–65 (1958).

Bibliography

Adeney, David H. *The Unchanging Commission*. Chicago: Inter-Varsity Press, 1955.

Allen, Roland. *Missionary Methods, St. Paul's or Ours?* London: R. Scott, 1912.

————. *Essential Missionary Principles*. Westwood (N.J.): Fleming H. Revell Co., 1913.

————. *The Spontaneous Expansion of the Church and the Causes Which Hinder It*. London: World Dominion Press, 1927, 1949.

Andersen, Wilhelm. *Towards a Theology of Mission: A Study of the Encounter between the Missionary Enterprise and the Church and Its Theology*. London: Student Christian Movement Press, 1955.

Arndt, F. William, and Wilbur F. Gingrich. *A Greek-English Lexicon of the New Testament*. Chicago: University of Chicago Press, 1957.

Baillie, John. *The Belief in Progress*. New York: Charles Scribner's Sons, 1951.

Bally, Ch. *Le Langage et la Vie*. Geneva: Editions Atar, 1913.

Barney, Linwood. "The Meo—An Incipient Church." *Practical Anthropology*, 4:31–50 (1957).

Barth, Karl. *The Doctrine of the Word of God*. Edinburgh: T. and T. Clark, 1936.

Bavinck, J. H. *The Impact of Christianity on the Non-Christian World*. Grand Rapids (Mich.): W. B. Eerdman's Publishing Co., 1948.

Beaver, R. Pierce. *The Christian World Mission: A Reconsideration*. Calcutta: Baptist Mission Press, 1957.

Beekman, John. "A Culturally Relevant Witness." *Practical Anthropology*, 4:83–88 (1957).

Belloc, Hilaire. *On Translating*. Oxford: Clarendon Press, 1931.

Benedict, Ruth. *Patterns of Culture*. New York: Penguin Books, 1946.

Benjamin, A. Cornelius. *The Logical Structure of Science*. London: K. Paul, Trench, Trubner, and Co., 1936.

Berdyaev, Nicolas. *Truth and Revelation*. New York: Harper & Brothers, 1954.

Bevan, Edwyn. *Symbolism and Belief*. New York: The Macmillan Company, 1938.

Bloomfield, Leonard. "A Set of Postulates for the Science of Language." *Language*, 2:153–64 (1926).

———. *Language*. New York: Henry Holt and Company, Inc., 1933.

———. *Linguistic Aspects of Science*. Chicago: University of Chicago Press, 1939.

Boas, Franz. *The Mind of Primitive Man*. New York: The Macmillan Company, 1938.

——— . *Race, Language and Culture*. New York: The Macmillan Company, 1940.

Bouquet, A. C. *The Christian Faith and Non-Christian Religions*. New York: Harper & Brothers, 1958.

Briggs, Harold E. *Language . . . , Man . . . , Society: Readings in Communication*. New York: Rinehart & Co., Inc., 1949.

Brown, Arthur Judson. *The Foreign Missionary: An Incarnation of a World Movement*. Westwood (N.J.): Fleming H. Revell Co., 1950.

Brown, Roger. *Words and Things*. Glencoe (Ill.): The Free Press, 1958.

Brunner, Emil. *Revelation and Reason*. London: Student Christian Movement Press, 1947.

Buber, Martin. *I and Thou*. New York: Charles Scribner's Sons, 1937.

Bultmann, Rudolf. *Primitive Christianity*. New York: Meridian Books, 1957.

Burrows, Millar. *More Light on the Dead Sea Scrolls*. New York: The Viking Press, 1958.

Busia, K. A. "Ancestor Worship." *Practical Anthropology*, 6:23–28 (1959).

Cailliet, Émile. *The Christian Approach to Culture*. Nashville: Abingdon Press, 1953.

Carnap, Rudolf. *The Logical Syntax of Language*. New York: Harcourt, Brace and Co., 1937.

———. *Introduction to Semantics*. Cambridge: Harvard University Press, 1942.

Carver, William O. *Christian Missions in Today's World*. New York: Harper & Brothers, 1942.

Caso, Alfonso. *Indigenismo*. Mexico, D. F.: Instituto Nacional Indigenista, 1958.

Cassirer, Ernst. *Language and Myth*. New York: Harper & Brothers, 1946.

Chase, Stuart. *The Tyranny of Words*. New York: Harcourt, Brace and Co., 1938.

Cherry, Colin. *On Human Communication*. Cambridge (Mass.): Technology Press of the Massachusetts Institute of Technology, 1957.

Cook, Harold R. *An Introduction to the Study of Christian Missions.* Chicago: Moody Press, 1954.

Cragg, Kenneth. *The Call of the Minaret.* New York: Oxford University Press, 1956.

Cullmann, Oscar. *Christ and Time.* Philadelphia: Westminster Press, 1951.

Danielou, Jean. *The Salvation of the Nations.* London: Sheed and Ward, 1949.

Durkheim, Emile. *The Elementary Forms of the Religious Life, A Study in Religious Sociology.* London: G. Allen and Unwin, 1915; New York: The Macmillan Company, 1915.

Eliade, Mircea. *Birth and Rebirth.* New York: Harper & Brothers, 1958.

Farmer, H. H. *Revelation and Religion: Studies in the Theological Interpretation of Religious Types.* London: James Nisbet & Co. Ltd., 1954.

Fleming, Daniel Johnson. *Attitudes toward Other Faiths.* New York: Association Press, 1928.

Forman, Charles W. *A Faith for the Nations.* Philadelphia: Westminster Press, 1957.

Frank, Lawrence K. "Psychology and Social Order" (pp. 214–41) in Daniel Lerner (ed.), *The Human Meaning of the Social Sciences.* New York: Meridian Books, Inc., 1959.

Freytag, Walter. *The Gospel and the Religions.* London: Student Christian Movement Press, 1957.

———. "Changes in the Patterns of Western Missions." *International Review of Missions,* 47:163–180 (1958).

Frick, Heinrich. *The Gospel, Christianity and Other Faiths.* Oxford: Basil Blackwell Ltd., 1938.

Glover, Robert Hall. *The Bible Basis of Missions.* Los Angeles: Bible House of Los Angeles, 1946.

Goodall, Norman (ed.). *Missions Under the Cross.* London: Edinburgh House Press; New York: Friendship Press, 1953.

Goodspeed, Edgar J. (translator). *The Apostolic Fathers.* New York: Harper & Brothers, 1950.

Hayakawa, S. I. *Language in Action.* New York: Harcourt, Brace and Co., 1941.

Herberg, Will. "The Christian Witness in an Emerging 'Other-Directed' Culture," *Practical Anthropology,* 5:211–15 (1958).

Herskovits, Melville J. *Man and His Works.* New York: Alfred A. Knopf, Inc., 1948.

Hocking, William Ernest. *Living Religions and a World Faith.* New York: The Macmillan Company, 1940.

————. *The Coming World Civilization.* New York: Harper & Brothers, 1956.

✶ Howells, W. W. *The Heathens, Primitive Man and His Religions.* Garden City (N.Y.): Doubleday & Co., Inc., 1948.

Hull, Clark L. *Principles of Behavior.* New York: Appleton-Century-Crofts, Inc., 1943.

Hutchinson, Bertram. "Some Social Consequences of Missionary Activity among South African Bantu," *Practical Anthropology,* 6:67–76 (1959).

—Jeremias, Joachim. *Jesus' Promise to the Nations.* Naperville (Ill.): Alec R. Allenson, 1958.

Jespersen, Otto. *The Philosophy of Grammar.* New York: Henry Holt and Co., Inc., 1924.

Joos, Martin. "Semology: A Linguistic Theory of Meaning." *Studies in Linguistics,* 13:53–72 (1958).

Jung, C. G. *The Undiscovered Self.* New York: The New American Library, 1957.

Kantor, J. R. *Psychology and Logic.* Bloomington (Ind.): The Principia Press, 1945.

Keller, Helen. *The Story of My Life.* New York: Doubleday & Co., Inc., 1902.

Kluckhohn, Clyde. *Mirror for Man.* New York: Whittlesey House, 1949.

————. "Common Humanity and Diverse Cultures" (pp. 245–84) in Daniel Lerner (ed.), *The Human Meaning of the Social Sciences.* New York: Meridian Books, 1959.

Köhler, Wolfgang. *Gestalt Psychology.* New York: The New American Library, 1947.

Korzybski, Alfred. *Science and Sanity: An Introduction to Non-Aristotelian Systems and General Semantics.* Lancaster (Penn.): The Science Press, 1933.

✶ Kraemer, Hendrik. *The Christian Message in a Non-Christian World.* New York: Harper & Brothers, 1938.

————. *The Communication of the Christian Faith.* Philadelphia: The Westminster Press, 1956.

————. *Religion and the Christian Faith.* London: Lutterworth Press, 1956.

Langer, Susanne K. *Philosophy in a New Key.* Cambridge: Harvard University Press, 1942.

Latourette, Kenneth Scott. *A History of the Expansion of Christianity.* 7 vols. New York: Harper & Brothers, 1937–45.

Lee, Irving J. *Language Habits in Human Affairs.* New York: Harper & Brothers, 1941.

Lerner, Daniel (ed.). *The Human Meaning of the Social Sciences.* New York: Meridian Books, Inc., 1959.

Lindsell, Harold. *A Christian Philosophy of Missions.* Wheaton (Ill.): van Kampen Press, 1949.

———. *Missionary Principles and Practice.* Westwood (N.J.): Fleming H. Revell, Co., 1955.

Linton, Ralph. *The Cultural Background of Personality.* New York: Appleton-Century-Crofts, 1945.

Littell, Franklin Hamlin. *The Free Church.* Boston: Beacon Press, 1957.

Mair, L. P. "Independent Religious Movements in Three Continents." *Comparative Studies in Society and History,* 1:113–135 (1959).

Malinowski, Bronislaw. *Myth in Primitive Psychology.* New York: W. W. Norton & Co., Inc., 1926.

———. *Argonauts of the Western Pacific.* New York: E. P. Dutton & Co., 1922.

———. *Coral Gardens and Their Magic.* London: G. Allen and Unwin, 1935.

———. *Magic, Science, and Religion.* Garden City (N.Y.): Doubleday & Co., Inc., 1955.

Manikam, Rajah Bhushanam (ed.). *Christianity and the Asian Revolution.* Madras: published for the Friendship Press, New York, 1954.

Manson, William. "The Biblical Doctrine of Mission." *International Review of Missions,* 42:257–65 (1953).

———. "Mission and Eschatology." *International Review of Missions,* 42:390–97 (1953).

Maritain, Jacques. *Approaches to God.* New York: Harper & Brothers, 1954.

Martin, Hugh. *The Kingdom without Frontiers* (rev. ed.). New York: Friendship Press, 1946.

Mead, George H. *Mind, Self and Society.* Chicago: University of Chicago Press, 1934.

Mead, Margaret. *Sex and Temperament in Three Primitive Societies.* New York: William Morrow and Co., 1935.

McGavran, Donald A. *The Bridges of God.* London: World Dominion Press, 1955.

McLeish, Alexander. *Christ's Hope of the Kingdom.* London: World Dominion Press, 1952.

Moody, Dale. "God's Only Son: The Translation of John 3:16 in the Revised Standard Version," *Journal of Biblical Literature,* 72:213–219 (1953).

Morris, Charles. *Six Theories of Mind.* Chicago: University of Chicago Press, 1932.

————. *Signs, Language and Behavior.* New York: Prentice-Hall, Inc., 1946.

Mott, John R. *The Decisive Hour of Christian Missions.* New York: Student Volunteer Movement Press, 1910.

Mu Tsung-san, Hsü Fu-kuan, Carson Chang, and T'ang Chün-yi. "Wisdom which the West Should Learn from the East," *Practical Anthropology,* 6:84–89 (1959).

Neill, Stephen. *The Unfinished Task.* London: Lutterworth Press, 1957.

Newbigin, J. E. Leslie. *The Household of God.* New York: Friendship Press, 1954.

Nida, Eugene A. *Bible Translating.* New York: American Bible Society, 1947.

————. *God's Word in Man's Language.* New York: Harper & Brothers, 1952.

————. *Customs and Cultures.* New York: Harper & Brothers, 1954.

————. "Principles of Translation As Exemplified by Bible Translating," Reuben A. Brower (ed.), *On Translation.* Cambridge: Harvard University Press, 1958.

————, and W. A. Smalley. *Introducing Animism.* New York: Friendship Press, 1959.

Niebuhr, H. Richard. *Christ and Culture.* New York: Harper & Brothers, 1951.

Niebuhr, Reinhold. *The Nature and Destiny of Man.* New York: Charles Scribner's Sons, 1941–43.

Niles, Daniel T. *Living with the Gospel.* New York: Association Press, 1957.

————. *The Preacher's Task and the Stone of Stumbling.* New York: Harper & Brothers, 1958.

Ogden, C. K., and I. A. Richards. *The Meaning of Meaning.* New York: Harcourt, Brace and Co., 1953.

Oke, C. Clarke. "A Suggestion with Regard to Romans 8:23," *Interpretation,* 11:455–60 (1957).

Otto, Rudolf. *The Idea of the Holy.* New York: Oxford University Press, Second edition, 1957.

Paton, David M. *Christian Missions and the Judgment of God.* London: Student Christian Movement Press, 1953.

Paton, William. *Jesus Christ and the World's Religions.* London: Church Missionary Society, 1916.

Perry, Edmund. *The Gospel in Dispute.* Garden City (N.Y.): Doubleday & Co., Inc., 1958.

Phillips, John Bertram. *The Church under the Cross.* New York: The Macmillan Company, 1956.

————. *Letters to Young Churches.* New York: The Macmillan Company, 1948.

Price, Frank W. *As the Lightning Flashes.* Richmond (Va.): John Knox Press, 1938.

Ranson, Charles Wesley (ed.). *Renewal and Advance: Christian Witness in a Revolutionary World.* London: Edinburgh House Press, 1948.

————. *That the World May Know.* New York: Friendship Press, 1953.

Redfield, Robert. *The Primitive World and Its Transformations.* Ithaca (N.Y.): Cornell University Press, 1953.

Re-Thinking Missions: A Laymen's Inquiry after One Hundred Years. William Ernest Hocking (Chairman). New York: Harper & Brothers, 1932.

Reyburn, Marie F. "Applied Anthropology among the Sierra Quechua of Ecuador." *Practical Anthropology,* 1:15–22 (1953).

Reyburn, William D. "Kaka Kinship, Sex, and Adultery." *Practical Anthropology,* 5:1–21 (1958).

————. "Identification in the Missionary Task." *Practical Anthropology,* 7:1–15, 1960.

————. "Motivations for Christianity: An African Conversation." *Practical Anthropology,* 5:27–32 (1958).

————. "The Spiritual, the Material, and Western Reaction in Africa." *Practical Anthropology,* 6:78–83 (1959).

Richards, I. A. *The Philosophy of Rhetoric.* London: Oxford University Press, 1936.

————. *Interpretation and Teaching.* New York: Harcourt, Brace and Co., 1938.

Riesman, David. *Individualism Reconsidered, and Other Essays.* Glencoe (Ill.): Free Press, 1954.

————, with Nathan Glazer and Reuel Denny. *The Lonely Crowd: A Study of Changing American Character.* New Haven: Yale University Press, 1953.

Rieu, Emile Victor. *The Four Gospels, a New Translation from the Greek.* Baltimore: Penguin Press, 1953.

Ritchie, John. *Indigenous Church Principles in Theory and Practice.* Westwood (N.J.): Fleming H. Revell Co., 1946.

Rowley, Harold Henry. *The Missionary Message of the Old Testament.* London: Carey Press, 1945.

Rycroft, W. Stanley. *Religion and Faith in Latin America.* Philadelphia: The Westminster Press, 1958.

Sapir, Edward. *Language.* New York: Harcourt, Brace and Co., 1939.

Schmidt, Wilhelm. *The Culture Historical Method of Anthropology.* (Trans. by S. A. Sieber.) New York: Fortuny's, 1939.

Schweitzer, Albert. *Christianity and the Religions of the World.* New York: Henry Holt and Co., Inc., 1939; The Macmillan Company, 1951.

Scott, Roland W. (ed.). *Ways of Evangelism: Some Principles and Methods of Evangelism in India.* Mysore: Christian Literature Society of India, 1952.

Seabury, Ruth Isabel. *So Send I You.* Philadelphia: Christian Education Press, 1955.

Seward, Georgene. *Psychotherapy and Culture Conflict.* New York: Ronald Press Co., 1956.

Shafer, Lumen J. *The Christian Mission in Our Day.* New York: Friendship Press, 1944.

Skinner, B. F. *The Behavior of Organisms.* New York: Appleton-Century-Crofts, Inc., 1938.

Smalley, William A. "Proximity or Neighborliness." *Practical Anthropology,* 4:101–104 (1957).

———. "Cultural Implications of an Indigenous Church." *Practical Anthropology,* 5:51–65 (1958).

———. "The World Is Too Much with Us," *Practical Anthropology,* 5:234–36 (1958).

Smith, Edwin W. (ed.). *African Ideas of God.* London: Edinburgh House Press, 1950.

Söderblom, Nathan. *The Living God.* London: Oxford University Press, 1933.

Soper, Edmund Davison. *The Philosophy of the Christian World Mission.* Nashville: Abingdon Press, 1943.

———. *The Biblical Background of the Christian World Mission.* Nashville: Abingdon Press, 1951.

Speer, Robert Elliott. *What Constitutes a Missionary Call?* New York: Association Press, 1918.

———. *The Finality of Jesus.* Westwood (N.J.): Fleming H. Revell Co., 1933.

Spier, Leslie, A. Irving Hallowell, and Stanley Newman (eds.). *Language, Culture, and Personality.* Menasha (Wis.): Sapir Memorial Publication Fund, 1941.

Stewart, James S. *Thine Is the Kingdom.* New York: Charles Scribner's Sons, 1957.

Tax, Sol (ed.). *Acculturation in the Americas.* Chicago: University of Chicago Press, 1952.

Temple, Archbishop William. *Nature, Man and God.* The Gifford Lectures, 1932–1933, 1933–1934. London: Macmillan & Co., 1951.

Thompson, Laura. *Culture in Crisis: A Study of the Hopi Indians.* New York: Harper & Brothers, 1950.

Tillich, Paul. *The Dynamics of Faith.* New York: Harper & Brothers, 1957.

————. *Theology of Culture.* New York: Oxford University Press, 1959.

Toynbee, Arnold. *Christianity among the Religions of the World.* New York: Charles Scribner's Sons, 1957.

Trimingham, J. Spencer. *The Christian Church and Islam in West Africa.* London: Student Christian Movement Press, 1955.

Troeltsch, Ernst. *Die Absolutheit des Christentums und die Religionsgeschichte.* Tübingen: Mohr, 1912.

————. *The Social Teaching of the Christian Churches,* translated by Olive Wyon. New York: The Macmillan Company, 1951.

Tylor, Edward B. *Anthropology.* London: Watts and Co., 1881.

van der Leeuw, G. *Religion in Essence and Manifestation.* London: George Allen and Unwin, 1938.

Vilakasi, A. "A Reserve from Within." *African Studies,* 16:93–101 (1957); reprinted in *Practical Anthropology,* 5:124–38 (1958).

Visser 't Hooft, Willem A. *The Renewal of the Church.* Philadelphia: The Westminster Press, 1957.

Urban, Wilbur M. *Language and Reality: the Philosophy and the Principles of Symbolism.* New York: The Macmillan Company, 1939.

Wallace, Anthony F. C. "Revitalization Movements." *American Anthropologist,* 58:264–81 (1956).

Wallis, Wilson D. *Religion in Primitive Society.* New York: F. S. Crofts and Company, 1939.

Warren, Max A. C. *The Calling of God.* London: Lutterworth Press, 1944.

————. *The Christian Mission.* London: Student Christian Movement Press, 1951.

————. *The Christian Imperative.* New York: Charles Scribner's Sons, 1955.

————. *The Gospel of Victory.* London: Student Christian Movement Press, 1955.

Weber, H. R. *The Communication of the Gospel to Illiterates.* London: Student Christian Movement Press, 1957.

Weymouth, Richard F. *The New Testament in Modern Speech.* London: James Clarke and Co., 1902; Boston: The Pilgrim Press, 1926.

White, Leslie A. *The Science of Culture.* New York: Farrar, Straus and Cudahy, Inc., 1949.

Whitehead, Alfred North. *Symbolism, Its Meaning and Effect.* New York: The Macmillan Company, 1927.

Wiener, Norbert. *The Human Use of Human Beings.* Garden City (N.Y.): Doubleday Anchor Books, 1956.

Yinger, J. Milton. "The Influence of Anthropology on Sociological Theories of Religion," *American Anthropologist*, 60:487–96 (1958).

Zipf, George K. *The Psycho-biology of Language: An Introduction to Dynamic Philology*. Boston: Houghton Mifflin Co., 1935.

Index

Dr. Nida is executive secretary of the American Bible Society in charge of the translations program, and translations research coordinator for the United Bible Societies. Dr. Nida has worked in some 75 different countries with translators producing texts in more than 200 languages. He has written 22 books on translation, linguistics, anthropology, and missions. Books by Dr. Nida published by the William Carey Library include *Customs and Cultures, God's Word in Man's Language,* and *Understanding Latin Americans.*